The First Pacific War

Britain and Russia, 1854–1856

The First Pacific War

Britain and Russia, 1854–1856

John D. Grainger

THE BOYDELL PRESS

© John D. Grainger 2008

All rights reserved. Except as permitted under current legislation no part of this work may be photocopied, stored in a retrieval system, published, performed in public, adapted, broadcast, transmitted, recorded or reproduced in any form or by any means, without the prior permission of the copyright owner

The right of John D. Grainger to be identified as the author of this work has been asserted in accordance with sections 77 and 78 of the Copyright, Designs and Patents act 1988

First published 2008
The Boydell Press, Woodbridge

ISBN 978-1-84383-354-3

The Boydell Press is an imprint of Boydell & Brewer Ltd
PO Box 9, Woodbridge, Suffolk IP12 3DF, UK
and of Boydell & Brewer Inc.
668 Mt Hope Avenue, Rochester, NY 14620, USA
website: www.boydellandbrewer.com

A CIP record for this book is available
from the British Library

This publication is printed on acid-free paper

Printed in Great Britain by
Antony Rowe Ltd, Chippenham, Wiltshire

Contents

Maps	vi
Dates and Names	vii
Preface	ix
Introduction	xiii
1 The Royal Navy in the Pacific	1
2 The Pursuit to Petropavlovsk	27
3 Japan, China, the Amur River	50
4 Petropavlovsk Again	70
5 The Gulf of Tartary	87
6 The Sea of Okhotsk	114
7 The Amur Estuary	138
8 Plans	161
9 The Victims	179
Conclusion	190
Sources and Bibliography	193
Index	199

Maps

1 The lands of the Pacific   2

2 Petropavlovsk   28

3 The Sea of Ohkotsk and the northwestern Pacific   116

4 Eastern Siberia and the Amur River   140

5 'The Riddle of the Mouth of the Amur'   142

Dates and Names

Two calendars were in use among the antagonists in the war of 1854–1856 (three, if the Ottoman Islamic calendar is included). In addition, in the Pacific War the two British squadrons were a day apart, for the future International Date Line, or as the men themselves put it, the Meridian, intervened between their operational areas. This latter circumstance scarcely bothered the British, and it should not bother us.

The solution to this minor problem is to adjust all dates to one system: the Western calendar has been chosen, because the central element of the story is the activities of the Royal Navy. Where necessary the difference in dates will be pointed out; otherwise the adjustments will be made silently.

Where it becomes important is in Russian accounts of these events, which are often careless in using both calendars without pointing out the differences: it can occasionally cause some confusion. Again, adjustments will be made where necessary, and silently, unless it affects matters seriously.

Names are a much more difficult matter. The Chinese have employed two writing systems in the past century, the Russians have had a thoroughgoing revolution and a much less drastic de-revolution, and the Japanese have their own names for the places involved, all of which affect the names given to places at different times; many other places were named by French or British explorers, and re-named by others later; and every local state has its own names for the places. Not to mention the wobbly spelling of Victorian sailors.

Here the solution is to use the common names – thus Sakhalin, not the Japanese Karafuto, or the Victorian Saghalien, and so on – and to remember that this is a book whose central actors are sailors of the Royal Navy, so in general the Western names are used – thus Cape Crillon, rather than Cape Kril'on for the Russians, and De Castries Bay, rather than De Kastri, or simply Castries or Kastri. And I have not been too strict on transliteration from non-Western languages. The goal has been internal consistency, to assist the reader.

Two of the Allied ships had the same name: *Sybille*. To distinguish them I have given the French ship the definite article, *La Sybille*.

Preface

Concentration on the main events of a war can lead to the ignoring of peripheral matters, to the detriment of an understanding of the war as a whole and of other areas and events elsewhere. The 'Crimean' War is one such war. Its very name indicates that events in the Black Sea area have been regarded as central, even all-important. Yet the war was fought elsewhere as well, particularly in the Baltic area, but also in the White Sea and in the Pacific. It is this last area which is my subject here.

As I researched this subject, initially from the point of view of the Royal Navy, it steadily became clearer that the British viewpoint was excessively partial and limited, and that a proper understanding of events in the Pacific at the time needed to take account of the actions of Russians on land more than at sea, and that the Anglo-Russian conflict involved also the Japanese and Chinese in important ways.

Nevertheless, British naval actions were the mainspring of events, for it was in reaction to what the British did that others were moved to act themselves. The war in the Pacific began with the British and French ships looking for a single Russian ship, or perhaps two; in the end, it changed the whole balance of power in the Pacific area, bringing Russia in strength to the coast, damaging China seriously, and alerting both Japan and, above all, the United States to the importance of the region. This was not what the British had intended to happen. But then history is full of ironies.

I will set the scene by taking a look at the role of the Royal Navy in the Pacific before the war began, when its main concern was rivalry with the United States (Chapter 1). The news of the war brought the squadron, under a new commander, Rear Admiral Price, to a less leisurely condition, and combined it with a French squadron. The main task of the ships was to hunt for the Russian ships expected in the area, and assumed to be a menace to Allied shipping. The squadrons, based at

Valparaiso in Chile, had to sail the length of the ocean to find the Russians. Price took the opportunity to call at the Hawaiian kingdom on his way in order to warn off the predatory United States. So far so good, and he was exactly right in sailing to Petropavlovsk, for that was where the ship he was searching for had gone.

The Allied assault on the town was, however, a failure (Chapter 2). This was hardly assisted by Price's suicide just before the attack was to go in. Having failed, the Allies had to withdraw, and this meant sailing all the way to San Francisco, the nearest place which could be the source of supplies. Here was an irony: for the United States was the great uninvolved power in the conflict.

Meanwhile, on the western Pacific side, all the Western naval powers were involved in attempts to persuade Japan to open itself to outsiders. In this, the British and Americans were successful during 1854, at the same time as the war involving three of those powers came closer to Japan (Chapter 3). The brutal treatment of China by those same powers, as a result of the British victory in the Chinese war ten years before, and the more recent British annexation of a slice of Burma were warnings the Japanese had taken to heart. China had descended into an enormous and destructive civil war, and this provided the Russian governor of eastern Siberia, Muravev, with the opportunity to force his way along the Amur River, which was technically under Chinese control, as far as the Pacific, using the excuse that Russian posts on the coast were under threat because of Allied attacks.

The search for a ship had thus expanded to involve all the states of the North Pacific in one way or another, and had shifted the main centre of attention to the Russian coast. The next year (1855), the British insisted on gaining revenge for their defeat at Petropavlovsk (Chapter 4), but the action then shifted to the Amur River estuary. The British Pacific squadron then returned to its Valparaiso base, and the British China squadron became the main instrument of British power in the war. Under Rear-Admiral Stirling it began a search for the Russian posts along the Siberian coast, where the Russian ships (which had left Petropavlovsk before the second attack) might be hidden. This involved a series of explorations in which steamships proved their worth, in the Gulf of Tartary and in the Sea of Okhotsk (Chapters 5 and 6). The ships were found once, but escaped again. The Russian exploitation of the Amur River continued, and at last the British realised that the Russian ships had got away through the sands of the Amur estuary (Chapter 7).

So during the next winter the British prepared to make a much greater effort, which would probably have involved the campaign to destroy the Russian posts on the mainland, and along the Amur River. The Chinese empire was now slowly realising what Muravev was up to, and the British were suggesting an Anglo-Chinese alliance to fight him (Chapter 8).

Then news came of the peace treaty which ended the war. The Royal Navy had by that time found the wreck of the last ship they had been searching for, and had discovered the useful harbour which eventually the Russians made into Vladivostok. The final result was the expansion of Russian territory (though Russia was technically defeated) at the expense of China (which had been neutral), the alerting of the (neutral) United States to the importance of the Pacific area, and the awakening of Japan (another neutral, which had been used by the British as a base) (Chapter 9). None of this had been intended by anyone when the war began. But from then on the Pacific became another area of constant conflict between the great naval powers, a role it retains to this day.

This was a part of the 'Crimean' War which saw hardly any fighting. The only blood that was shed was at Petropavlovsk, and in a brief affray later at De Castries Bay in the Gulf of Tartary (though considerable numbers of Russians died during Muravev's Amur expeditions). Perhaps that is why the conflict has been generally ignored: there is nothing like a battle to attract historians' attention. Yet its consequences were very great, perhaps greater than those in the European theatre, where casualties in the fighting ran into the tens of thousands. The greatest ironies are that the main victim of the fighting was China, and the main beneficiary was the United States, neither of which states were participants in the war.

The war in the Pacific was, to be sure, a relatively minor event, though I suggest its consequences were great. The story here is essentially one concerning the Royal Navy, and it illustrates the difficulties captains and admirals had in operating many thousands of miles from their bases (whether in Europe or in China), in unknown territory, and against an extremely elusive enemy. Despite early mistakes, and in spite of the difficulties, the Navy emerges well from the ordeal.

Introduction

From a European or eastern American viewpoint, the Pacific Ocean is on the other side of the world. From the Pacific, the North Atlantic is a long way off. It can be approached by going west, by way of America, through California or Panama or round Cape Horn, or by going east, by way of Russia and Siberia, or by sea by way of the Indian Ocean. Whichever route is followed, the Pacific is a long distance away, and all the more so in the days of horse- and wind-power. And when you get there it is at the end of the journey. It follows that, depending on the origin of the traveller, the history and geography of the Pacific area are normally viewed through European or American or Russian eyes. Perspective is all, as the term 'Far East' implies. (This is even used by Americans, to whom it is really to the west; note that for Australians it is now the 'Near North'.)

So, just as the approaches were various, the history of the Pacific is also fragmented. This study is an attempt to knit together a series of events during 1854–1856 which concerned many of the people in the Pacific lands, but which were largely perpetrated by extra-Pacifickers. Russians, French, British, Americans, Chinese, Japanese, Hawaiians, Aleuts and Kurile islanders were all involved, but each had their own 'take' on the events. As a result these events have been generally misunderstood, and most accounts, from whatever viewpoint they are written, contain grievous, distorting, even egregious errors. I hope that this account will correct some of these errors, render some justice to some maligned men, and draw attention to some important historical developments.

The great variety of people involved, from British sailors to Chinese mandarins, from Kurile fishermen to French aristocrats, from Russian peasants to American merchants, means that the original source material is scattered in a wide variety of accounts and in many languages. I do not know all the languages involved, which include Russian, Chinese, French and Japanese, as well as English; yet this is less vital than appears, for the central players in these events were always British. It was a British expedition, with French participants added, which was the precipitating cause of the whole sequence, and the others who were involved were largely reacting to what the British did, either actively or unconsciously. Indeed on a longer view it was British explorers and traders who were the root causes of the developments in the lands around the Pacific during the dozen or so years before the naval expedition which is my subject. These developments affected Russians, Chinese, Japanese, Americans, Hawaiians, and others. So once the Royal Navy had been brought on the scene, it is necessary to consider the background to those developments.

As if to emphasise the peripheral nature of the Pacific for the Europeans, it was a war which had broken out in Europe which began these events, though they may seem to have been less sequential than providential, even accidental, in the Pacific. The 'Crimean' War, or, from the British and French points of view, the 'Russian' war, broke out when Britain and France perceived a Russian threat to the integrity of the Ottoman Empire. Because Russia's eastern border lay on the Pacific, and the Royal Navy had two naval squadrons in the Pacific, the war spread into those waters, whether either side wanted it to do so or not. It was in fact the presence of the Royal Navy in Pacific waters which was the cause of fighting in that ocean, but it was Russian imperial ambitions, even the ambition of one man, which compelled the British to fight in the Pacific area.

For there was another set of events, which took place in eastern Siberia, which was also central to this story. The British naval expeditions in the Pacific came into conflict with the Russian advance into the valley of the Amur River: it was a collision of two empire-building states. But other imperialists were also involved: the naval expedition was under French command for a time, and the Russian war was in fact largely the product of the imperial ambitions of that jumped-up dictator, the Emperor Napoleon III; a very interested spectator was the imperialist United States of America, which had recently stolen an empire on the Pacific coast from Mexico, and had added to it another land filched from the Hudson's Bay Company, and had sent naval expeditions into the Pacific for over thirty years explicitly to explore for a way of expanding its empire; the empire of the Manchus in China turned out to be the main victim of the war even though it was not directly involved; the empire of Japan had been compelled, by the United States and Britain, to open a door a little way to the outside world, and this took place in part as a result of the war between Russia and the Western allies; Japan then found itself being used as a cat's paw by both sides. It was not an experience either China or Japan enjoyed.

It is the involvement of all these powers, and many local communities in other parts of the Pacific as well, which makes the events of 1854 to 1856 in the Pacific area important, and the involvement of many of them has been ignored or passed over in earlier accounts. In fact, the war in the Pacific was not a joke, as some have portrayed it, or a matter of bungling incompetence, as others have interpreted it. The war as a whole was a major crisis in world affairs, in which the Pacific played a peripheral but major part; the results for the Pacific as a whole were profound and long-lasting. Here I hope to rectify those historiographical errors by taking the whole of the Pacific events as my subject.

1

The Royal Navy in the Pacific

The only institution in the world in the middle of the nineteenth century which was present in all the oceans and close to all the continents and islands was the Royal Navy. Its presence in the Pacific had been gradually extending since the 1820s, approaching the ocean from several directions. The establishment of a British settlement colony, New South Wales, on the east coast of Australia in 1788 was one stage in the process. Along the coasts of southeast and east Asia the British presence was due to the trading activities of the East India Company, which had traded in Canton for well over a century. The Company's ships were armed, but its officers avoided trouble if possible. Trading posts under British control, either the Company's or otherwise, had extended eastwards: Penang in Malaya in 1786, Singapore in 1819, just as the Company's control of India extended inland at the same time. By acquiring control of Cape Town in 1806, and western Australia in 1839, the British effectively made the Indian Ocean a British lake. However, when the Company lost its monopoly of (British) trade with China and the East in 1833, by a revision of its charter by Parliament, at once things began to change. The opening of the trade brought many more British ships to Chinese waters.[1]

The third approach to the Pacific was by way of the South Atlantic Ocean and round Cape Horn. Here it was the collapse of the monolithic Spanish empire in South America between 1810 and 1825 which enticed the Royal Navy into the Pacific. The great empire was replaced by a series of small, vigorous, quarrelsome states, most of whose governments were none too stable. They were keen to trade, however, and the Navy arrived off the coasts of South America with a variety of tasks

---

[1] M. Greenberg, *British Trade and the Opening of China*, Cambridge 1951; G. S. Graham, *The China Station*, Oxford 1978, introduction.

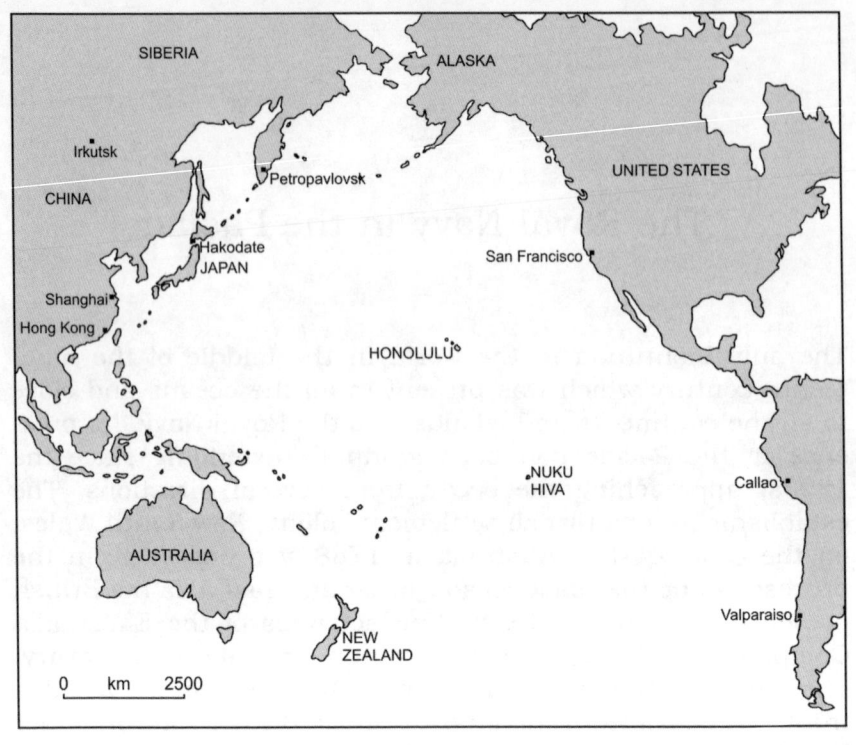

Map 1 The lands of the Pacific

to perform: it had to protect British ships and British subjects, control obstreperous British adventurers, remind locals of the length of Britain's arm, survey the coasts and waters so long closed to them, and, at times, investigate questions of slavery, or the prospect of a canal at the Panamanian isthmus. A squadron had been stationed on the South Atlantic side of the continent from the time of the Napoleonic Wars, using Buenos Aires and Rio de Janeiro as its main bases;[2] a second squadron was then posted on the Pacific side.

Problems and concerns had accumulated in Pacific waters in the early part of the nineteenth century, all of which involved the Navy. In the 1820s the new South American states became independent; from 1833 British traders could operate in China;

---

[2] For a good indication of the tasks of the South Atlantic squadron see G. S. Graham and R. A. Humphreys (eds), *The Navy in South America, 1807–1823*, Navy Records Society 1962.

in the 1820s and 1830s a constant problem was New Zealand; in 1842 France took control of Tahiti; in all these matters the Navy was involved because it was the only local instrument of the British government. The pace of change picked up speed and complexity from 1839 when the 'Opium' War with China began (a better name is simply the First China War). It was the Navy which had conducted that war, using the great Chinese rivers to penetrate the mainland. After three years, by the Treaty of Nanking, the Chinese government was compelled to allow trade at several of its ports, and the island of Hong Kong became British territory.[3]

All of these changes increased the Navy's responsibilities, in part because the Chinese government very much resented having been compelled to succumb, in part because of the increase in the number of British ships which had arrived in Chinese waters since the opening of the trade in 1833, and in part because the Chinese government's defeat had revealed the poor control it maintained over its territory, and piracy began to grow. Meanwhile New Zealand was annexed in 1840, and in 1843 a Royal Navy captain made the Hawaiian kingdom a British protectorate, until he was disavowed by his superior.[4]

This last venture was part of the continuing rivalry, amounting at times to a distinct hostility, between Britain and the United States. Indeed, the arrival of a Royal Naval squadron in the southeast Pacific had been in part the result of the arrival of a small, semi-permanent, United States naval contingent in those very waters. Both squadrons based themselves at Valparaiso in Chile, the first substantial port ships reached after passing Cape Horn, but their ships sailed here and there, showing themselves off as elements of power, mainly along the American coast, but also into the South Pacific as far as Hawaii. And while the US Navy's presence was intermittent, that of the Royal Navy was permanent.

The British interest in the Pacific had also been, until then, intermittent. Sir Francis Drake and fellow pirates had visited the area in pursuit of their personal vendettas with Catholic Spain in the sixteenth century – and in search of loot. Admiral Anson in the 1740s was similarly motivated, and similarly

---

[3] Graham, *China Station*, chs IV–VIII.
[4] R. S. Kuykendall, *The Hawaiian Kingdom*, vol. 1, Honolulu 1938, ch. 13.

seized great wealth in the process. Circumnavigators traversed the ocean several times in the eighteenth century, usually following much the same equatorial track from America to the East Indies. Then came Captain James Cook, whose three tremendous voyages revealed properly for the first time the true dimensions of the ocean, its emptiness, its shores, and the existence of its numberless islands – and that the ocean held resources which could be turned into cash.

The revelation of possible wealth to be acquired in the Pacific brought immediate results. Whales, sea otters, seals and sea cows were hunted almost to extinction within a few decades, and the ships and men who did the work became familiar with the surrounding coasts, and familiar sights to the Pacific peoples in the process. These were the men whose activities, misfortunes and adventures were often to be the concern of the Royal Navy. They paid little attention to formal political boundaries and jurisdictions, and there was plenty of uninhabited or uncontrolled coastline along the Pacific where they could land and hide and work, or lair.[5]

The United States Navy sent the frigate *Macedonian* to establish an official presence in the Pacific in 1819. The British Royal Navy followed, sending a small squadron, at first a detachment from that stationed in the South Atlantic. Both navies had been interested in each other's activities in the southern Pacific during the war between them from 1812 to 1815, when the US frigate *Essex* raided the whale fishery, and British ships hunted the *Essex*. Their interest was partly in the events in South America, and partly in each other's activities. From 1819 onwards, therefore, both had a more or less permanent presence in the southern Pacific. Their use of Valparaiso as their logistical base was logical; this did not make their joint presence comfortable. The *Macedonian* had been a British ship until it was captured in the war of 1812, and then refitted as a US Navy ship; this will have given an added edge to the relationship.[6]

In the 1840s the United States suddenly arrived directly on the Pacific coast. In 1846 Britain and the United States agreed

---

[5] H. I. Kushner, *Conflict on the North-West Coast: American-Russian Rivalry in the Pacific Northwest, 1790–1867*, Westport, CT, 1975.
[6] J. Tertius de Kay, *Chronicles of the Frigate Macedonian, 1809–1922*, New York 1995.

to partition the Oregon/British Columbia territory along the line of the 49th parallel of latitude, despite the generation-long occupation and settlement of the Oregon area by the British Hudson's Bay Company. This was acquired by the United States by its traditional methods: sending large numbers of settlers into the area, blankly denying any previous European interest or control even where it clearly existed, emitting a claim that the area had been originally United States territory, ignoring the interests and wishes of the preceding inhabitants, and drumming up popular demonstrations in favour of war if the United States' demands were not met. The British, who after 1815 were never willing to contemplate another war in North America, succumbed to such pressure, but did manage to hold on to British Columbia, which became a colony.

The same underhand methods were used, with even less excuse, to deprive Mexico of an even larger part of its territory, though, in this case, the Mexicans refused to give in without a fight; the subsequent war lasted two years and caused serious political rifts in the United States. The result of all this diplomatic and military activity was that the Pacific coast south of British Columbia, that is, the later states of Washington, Oregon and California, became United States territory (by 1848). California became a state of the union in 1850. There had been considerable local sentiment, among both former Mexicans and United States citizens, for making it an independent republic; bringing the territory into the union as a new state both blocked that idea and secured the gold which had been discovered there in 1849 for the United States.[7]

The acquisition of California and Oregon by the United States raised in that country the question of a Central American canal. The mass emigration to California from 1849 partly used the Cape Horn passage, and partly went by land across the continent, but a large number of the emigrants sailed to the Panama isthmus, crossed to the Pacific, and sailed north, if they survived the diseases of the land passage. A canal, constructed through Panama or through Nicaragua, would clearly benefit the United States considerably, but, in contrast to the acquisi-

---

[7] H. M. Potter, *The Impending Crisis, 1848–1861*, New York 1976; G. G. van Deusen, *The Jacksonian Era, 1828–1848*, New York 1959; W. R. Brock, *Conflict and Transformation, 1844–1871*, Harmondsworth 1973.

tion of Oregon and California, this was a matter of sea power, not land power.

The British could be intimidated where the issue was control of a large area of continental North America, where any conflict would take place in the United States' own backyard and would no doubt involve an invasion of Canada, but a collision at sea was a different matter altogether. The war of 1812 had been fought in America, not in Britain, even if the occasional frigate had escaped out of United States waters to make easy killings of civilian ships elsewhere. By 1850 the Royal Navy had fleets in every ocean and most of the seas of the world; it had long maintained a substantial squadron in the Caribbean; it had had a squadron of several ships in the Pacific for a generation, and another on the China coast for decades; while the United States could just about maintain a single frigate intermittently at Valparaiso and a couple of ships on and off near China. In terms of sea power the two states simply did not compare, and so when the issue of a canal in Central America arose, Britain was interested as of right, and her views had to be considered.

Discussions ensued, and an agreement was reached, the Clayton-Bulwer Treaty, whereby each state had a veto on any construction of a canal by the other, and incidentally both agreed to refrain from colonising Central America. This was a diplomatic defeat for the United States, whose acquisitive instincts had been directed southwards for some time, and whose interest in the canal was far more acute than was Britain's.[8] It did not actually stop United States attempts at colonising the region, but it did ensure that these attempts were even more unofficial than usual.

Between 1839 and 1850, therefore, the Royal Navy, through its Pacific and China squadrons, actively exerted Britain's power and influence in New Zealand, China, South America, Panama and the Hawaiian Islands; and after the Oregon crisis, a new naval base was developed at Esquimault in British Columbia. This was all in addition to fighting other wars or quasi-wars in the River Plate, Syria and Burma, patrolling constantly to put down the African slave trade, and combating pirates in Chinese and Indonesian waters. And even so, the main power

---

[8] R. W. van Alstyne, 'British Diplomacy and the Clayton-Bulwer Treaty, 1850–1860', *Journal of Modern History* 11, 1939, 149–183.

of the Navy was always concentrated in European waters, in the English Channel and the Mediterranean, for that was where the true competition lay – that is, other major naval powers – even more so than in North America. France had the world's most powerful navy after Britain, and was the potential enemy of choice for every naval man in Britain, a feeling which extended into the ranks of government ministers as well; it was a mind-set fully reciprocated by the French. And this was despite cooperation between the two in wars in South America – the River Plate campaign – and the Mediterranean in the 1840s (and later against Russia and in China).

The Royal Navy squadrons and fleets were usually separated from Admiralty headquarters in London by great distances. It could take many weeks for reports to reach London and instructions to reach the commanders of the squadrons. It was therefore necessary that these commanders be both diplomats and commanders, and it was usually diplomacy which was the more important skill. The slowness of promotion in the post-Napoleonic Navy ensured that most admirals were of a considerable age when they reached that rank.

The command of the Royal Navy's Pacific squadron was a three-year appointment for a rear-admiral. By 1850 the men who had reached their captaincies in the last years of the Napoleonic War were at last reaching the rank of rear-admiral, after long years of often minimal employment in a navy which had inevitably drastically shrunk in the years of peace. With fewer ships and fewer posts they had all had years on half-pay and years of shore appointments, during which they had spent hours scanning the lists of their superiors, hoping for wars in which some would die so that they themselves could further ascend the ladder towards promotion.

The squadron commander appointed in 1850 was Sir Fairfax Moresby, then aged 64, thirty-five years on the captains' list, who had reached the rank of rear-admiral the year before.[9] He was succeeded by Rear-Admiral David Price, appointed on 17 August 1853. He was 63, thirty-eight years a captain, and had been rear-admiral since 1850. He had achieved post rank in 1815, just in time for the ending of the Napoleonic and American Wars, and since then he had had only two appoint-

---

9   W. R. Clowes, *The Royal Navy*, vol. 6, London 1901, 547.

ments, as captain of a ship in the Mediterranean for four years in the 1830s, and as superintendent of the Sheerness dockyard for another four in the 1840s.[10] He was presumed, however, to have the command, diplomatic and seamanly qualities required of a commander-in-chief of a British squadron of ships at a minimum of two months' distance from home.

Price sailed in HMS *President*, a 50-gun frigate which had been launched a quarter of a century before, leaving England on 20 November 1853. Captain Burridge, captain of the *President*, noted in his journal when the ship arrived at Valparaiso that the passage had been something of a record, taking sixty-one days, which he described as 'an unprecedented passage'.[11] The ship arrived on 10 January 1854, and Price and Moresby then spent a fortnight together, discussing the several problems of the Pacific command.

The squadron Price took over consisted of the ship *President*, which was his flagship, the sloops *Trincomalee* (25 guns) and *Amphitrite* (24), the brig *Dido* (18), the store ships *Nereus* and *Naiad*, and the paddle steamer *Virago* (6). Moresby was to sail home in his own flagship, HMS *Portland*, and Price would also have the use of the tender *Cockatrice*. On 1 February Moresby left Valparaiso, having formally resigned his command two days before.[12]

What Moresby said to Price in their meetings is quite unknown, but we can work out something of the issues Price faced from the letters which Price wrote just before Moresby left, and from another series of letters sent after him by the Admiralty after he had sailed from England.[13] On 26 January, Price wrote to the British consuls and other representatives in the several ports in his area of command. This was a formality, informing them of his arrival and of his assumption of authority, but it indicates the geographical range he had to cover: Chile, Peru, New Granada (that is, present-day Colombia), Guatemala, Mexico, the ports along the American coast from Valparaiso to San Francisco, and Samoa and Tahiti in the South Pacific. Moresby

---

[10] Clowes, *Royal Navy*, vol. 6, 548; *Dictionary of National Biography*, David Price.
[11] Burridge's Journal, National Maritime Museum, 94/009.
[12] ADM 50/260, Price Journal. ('ADM' references are in the National Archives (Public Record Office).)
[13] Price's letters are listed in his journal; Admiralty letters in ADM 2/1611 and 1612.

will have explained to him the problems he had been having over Pitcairn Island, whence the 'Magistrate and Councillors' of the island had sent petitions to him. They had been effusive in their insistence on being regarded as British subjects, and had sent a locally-made chest of drawers as a gift for the Queen as a token of their allegiance.[14] This gives an idea of the extent of Price's command: it is 7000 miles (in a straight line) from Valparaiso to both Samoa and San Francisco. And these were not the final limits.

The letters which pursued him concerned the current problems he faced rather than the broad scope of his responsibilities. Other issues were, of course, liable to arise, and did, but the ones which were the subject of the Admiralty letters were those which Moresby will have explicated in their meetings at Valparaiso. Within a day of his sailing from Britain a letter was on its way to him on the subject of a survey to be conducted of the 'Isthmus of Darien' – Panama – by a company called, optimistically, the Atlantic and Pacific Junction Company. Price was ordered to send a ship to San Miguel Bay on the Pacific side, where the survey party appears to have hoped to find a route by way of the Rio Sabana. This was all part of a much bigger investigation, sparked by the demands of the Californian migrants and by some exaggerated and mistaken stories about the ease of the Sabana crossing.

On 10 December – though the letter would take at least two months to reach him – Price was warned that he would need to send a ship with provisions to the Bering Strait. He was to wait until orders arrived, probably in HMS *Diamond*, or by way of a packet boat. The ship's object was to deliver supplies and orders to HMS *Rattlesnake* which was stationed at Port Clarence, in Russian America, on the Bering Strait as a supply and rescue base for the expedition which was searching for the remains of Sir John Franklin's expedition to the North-West Passage. Franklin was, of course, dead several years by this time, but the search for him was fuelled by his wife's indignation and by public criticism of Admiralty incompetence. Here was another aspect of affairs which concerned Price, all the more so when, three weeks later, the Admiralty reported that *Diamond*'s sailing plans had changed, and he was to detach

---

[14] ADM 1/5630; Moresby was very sympathetic, and kept in touch with the children of the Pitcairn islanders after he returned to Britain.

one of his own ships, either *Trincomalee* or *Amphitrite*, for this service. There was no hurry, though, since the ice in the north would not permit access to the base for several months.

A letter of 7 December reported that the Admiralty was pleased with the report by Commander Prevost of the paddle steamer *Virago* on a visit he had made to Vancouver and British Columbia. This was the territory confirmed as British by the agreement of 1846 which had also confirmed Oregon to the United States. It was actually under the paternalistic control of the Hudson's Bay Company, another authority with which Price would have to deal, and the boundary between the company's territory and the Oregon Territory of the United States was not yet firmly decided, so there could well be problems there; it was well to keep a warship in the area, or at least have one visit Victoria Island every so often. However, another letter a few days later contained a rebuke for Prevost. He had apparently taken his ship to Panama, and hearing of the survey being undertaken, had gone to the Gulf of San Miguel and taken a party onshore to conduct a personal investigation. Leaving his ship and undertaking the investigation without orders were the two transgressions he was accused of (though the Admiralty had only a report from the consul at Panama as a basis for this complaint). It did not hinder his career, however, and he reached post rank in April, by which time he had been replaced in *Virago* by Commander Edward Marshall.

It is doubtful that Price would be too concerned about the adventures of Commander Prevost, but two further letters were more important. One reported that the Mexican government had issued a decree concerning the illegal use of the United States flag by vessels in the Pacific. This was a matter Price would need to watch, for there was still plenty of ill-feeling between the United States and Mexico, aggravated by the actions of the United States in 'purchasing' another slice of Mexican territory during 1853 (the 'Gadsden Purchase'); the purchase had been more like extortion, and had outraged Mexican public opinion. It also meant that ships seen flying the United States flag might have to be investigated – a time-consuming process.

The second letter also concerned potential trouble with the United States. The Foreign Office in London became concerned at talk in the United States about the annexation of the Hawaiian kingdom. Ever since Captain Cook's 'discovery' of the Hawaiian Islands – which the British still called the Sandwich Islands

– Britain had felt protective towards that state. One Hawaiian king had journeyed all the way to Britain for a visit, where he died; Captain Lord George Paulet's apparent *coup* in the island in 1843 had been an extreme protective measure and was disavowed when protection was no longer needed; Hawaii was in dispute with France in 1851 over a treaty and received diplomatic assistance from the British ambassador in Paris. So when rumours spread of the possibility of a filibustering expedition from California against the islands, and speeches were made in Congress advocating annexation of the islands, the Foreign Office's reaction was to ask the Admiralty to send a protective ship to Honolulu. The Admiralty did not actually order Price to do so, but it would have been difficult for him to ignore the matter.[15]

This last letter, concerning Hawaii, was sent from London on the day Price arrived at Valparaiso. He had therefore already been ordered, or advised, to send three of his ships on specific missions by the Admiralty – one ship to San Miguel Bay in Panama, *Trincomalee* or *Amphitrite* to the Bering Strait, and another ship to Honolulu. This was before he had even taken the measure of the situation in South America or the South Pacific. And on the day Rear-Admiral Moresby took his leave of Valparaiso in HMS *Portland*, yet another letter was being written and dispatched to Price. This would override all these problems and complicate his life and that of his squadron for the next several years.

Across the ocean, a much larger British squadron than Price commanded was stationed in the ports along the coast of China. The First China War, by which the British broke the Chinese refusal to trade, had succeeded in its object, and five ports between Canton and Woosung (Wosung: the port for Shanghai) had been officially opened, but the defeat of the Chinese forces had also fatally undermined the authority of the Manchu regime. A great rebellion in the interior – the Taiping rebellion – was spreading towards the coast, piracy along the coast, for which Western ships became targets, had greatly increased, and the Manchu government was finding it difficult to respond effectively, at least for the present.

This was a recipe for trouble, of course, and the British ships on the China Station were kept busy hunting pirates,

---

15 ADM 2/1611, 31 June 1854; Kuykendall, *Hawaiian Kingdom*, vol. 1, 411.

and even raiding their camps on land. This was not something the Manchu government approved of, but they could do little to stop it. The rear-admiral in command had a much more complicated task than Moresby and Price in that he confronted also a powerful British Superintendent of Trade. In 1854 this was the newly arrived Sir John Bowring, whose headquarters were at Hong Kong, and who was liable to attempt to give orders to the naval chief. This was not something the Navy could ever accept, and yet at the same time Bowring's wishes could not be ignored. One of the naval commander-in-chief's tasks was to maintain good relations with the Commissioner; this was the more difficult in that they reported separately to different government ministers.[16]

The war against China had ended in 1842, but disturbances had continued ever since – and not simply along the Chinese coast. A second war began in 1851 against the Burmese kingdom, again largely a naval campaign along the great Burmese rivers, the result being a further amputation of Burmese territory. From an Asian point of view, British activity appeared to be infinitely threatening: India conquered, Malaya dominated, China humiliated and reduced to chaos, and now Burma despoiled and sliced up. The progression looked inexorable and deliberate. And next on the list, so it seemed, was Japan.

First, however, the British naval command of the China Station had to be sorted out. Rear-Admiral Collier died in office in October 1849; his successor, Rear-Admiral Charles Austin, was always regarded as a temporary appointee, both by the Admiralty and by himself, and he was quite unwilling to exert himself. He was also even older than Collier, and also died in office, during the Burmese war, in 1852.[17] The next commander-in-chief proved to be a contrast to both of these men, but even more of a disaster.

Rear-Admiral Sir Fleetwood Pellew was another old man, 64 years old on his appointment. He had been a captain since 1808 after a very rapid rise through the ranks (he had been made lieutenant only three years earlier); his father was Admiral Pellew, later Lord Exmouth, one of the most highly regarded

---

[16] A good account of all this is by Graham, *China Station*, ch. 10; *Dictionary of National Biography*, Sir John Bowring.
[17] Graham, *China Station*, 275.

frigate captains of the Napoleonic Wars, and the victor of Algiers in 1816. No doubt having to prove himself all the time against his father's reputation, and at the same time having the full arrogance of his breeding and caste, made for problems; Fleetwood Pellew repeatedly stumbled during his career. The final crash came at Hong Kong.

Pellew took up his command at Rangoon in April 1853, but took six months to reach Hong Kong in his flagship HMS *Winchester*, another 50-gun frigate. When he finally arrived he decided not to permit shore leave for the crew. In some ways he had good reasons: Hong Kong was a notorious trap for sailors, then and later. He also had to consider their health in a difficult climate, and the fact that the disturbed condition of the Chinese coastal areas would likely mean that he had to sail off elsewhere at a moment's notice, to Shanghai particularly, where the Taiping rebels were coming close, or towards Canton.

Yet no commander of a British warship with any sense could expect his crew to accept such a decision with equanimity. The crew had been in Burma, a hostile area, for months, then at sea for six months under a new commander-in-chief who was notorious for his strictness, and now they were to be denied their anticipated relaxation. True, it is likely that most of them would drink themselves into a stupor, or contract a venereal infection, or both, and would end up flat broke, and it would take time for them to shake down again to a sailor's life – no doubt some would desert (a year later HMS *Nankin* lost fourteen men by desertion in Hong Kong), some would be killed – but this was what a British commander must always expect. To try to avoid such troubles by denying the crew their rest and recreation and keeping them on board ship would only create even more troubles.

When Pellew's decision, announced without explanation, became known, forceful complaints were made. Pellew, in paranoid fashion, interpreted this as the prelude to further trouble; he caused the drummer to 'beat to quarters', which in a ship at anchor in a friendly port was nonsense, and it was ignored throughout the ship. Officers were sent below decks to enforce Pellew's orders with naked swords; in the process some men were wounded. That was the end of the 'trouble'; but it was also the end for Pellew. When the report of what happened reached the Admiralty he was ordered home. Yet another commander-in-chief, Rear-Admiral Sir James Stirling, was appointed. Pellew was ordered to Point de Galle in Ceylon, the westernmost point of his command, and Stirling was sent out as quickly as possible.[18]

Stirling came from another naval family. His father had been a captain, his uncle a rear-admiral (though cashiered for accounting 'errors'). The new commander-in-chief was only two years younger than Pellew and had been a rear-admiral only a little over two years, but he was a man of considerable and varied experience. He was made post in 1818, and in the 1820s conducted explorations and surveys along the Australian coast; from 1829 to 1839 he was governor of the new colony of Western Australia. He was a Scot, and this was an unusually tactful appointment, for the new colony was heavily Scottish. Two tours as captain in the Mediterranean followed (1840–1844 and 1847–1850) and preceded his rise to rear-admiral in 1851; his appointment as commander-in-chief of the East India and China Station followed in 1853.[19] This, be it noted, was an employment record which displayed the Admiralty's confidence in him far more than that of Admiral Price who took up his post at Valparaiso at more or less the same time. It implied not only considerable sailorly abilities, but also the tact and diplomacy needed in a colonial governor of a raw new colony.

Stirling learned, as soon as he arrived in early May 1854, that not long before a mixed group of civilians, British sailors and American sailors had attacked and driven back a Chinese Taiping force which had seemed to threaten Shanghai. This had been authorised by the local British consul in Shanghai and had been commanded by Captain George O'Callaghan of HMS *Encounter*, a steam frigate of 14 guns, which was stationed at Shanghai at the time. Stirling showed his quality over and above that of the timid Austin by retrospectively approving the counter-attack, but showed himself equally determined to get his ships and men free of the land so as to deal with the sea-pirates.[20]

The affair at Shanghai had been conducted in cooperation with the American commander of the USS *Plymouth*, a sloop. This working together was fairly unusual at this time, though not unprecedented in Chinese waters, and is mainly a sign

---

[18] Graham, *China Station*, 277–278.
[19] *Dictionary of National Biography*, Sir James Stirling.
[20] Graham, *China Station*, 279–280.

of the fact that the local citizens of both countries felt threatened by the chaos in China. In the meantime another fleet had arrived in the local waters – four American ships, two sailing ships and two steamers of the US Navy – commanded by Commodore Matthew Perry. Perry had called at Edo in Japan, delivered a note demanding that Japan open itself to the outside, and had promised – or threatened – to return for an answer later. He spent the waiting time in and about Hong Kong, and returned to Edo in February 1854. Perry was thus in Chinese waters during the hiatus in command of the British squadron. He collected four more ships for his second visit to Edo, and successfully extracted some minor concessions from the Japanese government, permitting the use by American ships of two ports, Shimoda and Hakodate, and the appointment of an American consul, who was to reside at Shimoda. The basic reason for the Japanese to make these concessions was their appreciation of the condition to which China had been reduced as a result of the effects of the Chinese defeat by Britain a decade earlier. The US Navy had thus taken advantage of the local power of the Royal Navy in gaining its point with Japan.

There were therefore two squadrons of British ships in Pacific waters: one in the far southeast of the ocean with responsibilities which stretched over the islands of that ocean from Samoa to Hawaii, and north along the American coast as far as the Arctic; the other with responsibilities from Africa to Australia and halfway across the Pacific, though, at the time of Stirling's appointment, its main concern was with affairs along the coast of China. Both squadrons had plenty of work to do, especially Stirling's in Chinese waters, where the pirates were constantly active and threatening, but now also in Japan, where Perry's initiative would need to be followed up by a British visit.

Price's command was small, and his instructions meant he had to spread his few ships widely. At that point a new task arrived. Both admirals may well have been warned of potential trouble with Russia before they left Britain – they would have to have been blind and deaf not to notice the steadily increasing tension in the Middle East during 1853 – but they were both warned while on their way to their commands that war was likely.

Price's letter was from the Third Sea Lord, Rear-Admiral Maurice Berkeley, enclosing a copy of a letter from the Foreign

Secretary, the Earl of Clarendon, with his 'views ... in regard to the conduct to be observed by H.M.'s ships in the event of a war occurring between Great Britain and Russia'. But Berkeley insisted that supplies were still to be sent to the Arctic base (which was actually in territory controlled by the Russian-American Company), with HMS *Plover* now named as the ship to which the supplies were to go. No orders seem to have been sent for Commander Richard Collinson in *Plover* to withdraw, but he was to exercise his discretion. Rather more comfortingly, Price was ordered not to send any ships back to Britain while the crisis lasted, and he was to receive the reinforcement of the *Pique*, a 40-gun frigate commanded by Captain Sir Frederick Nicholson Bt, which was sailing from England.[21]

The orders to Stirling concerning the likelihood of war were less urgent, since it was clearly believed in London that little or no fighting against Russia would occur in the Far East. He was ordered on 21 February to avoid calling at Point de Galle, where Pellew had been instructed to hand over command to him, and to sail directly for China as rapidly as possible.[22] But this was clearly going to take some time. He did not actually reach Hong Kong until early in May.[23] By that time war had been declared (on 27 March 1854).

When the news reached them, both Stirling and Price had to begin to take note of any Russian presence in their areas. The Admiralty might have imagined that there would not be much fighting in the Pacific when the warning letters were sent out, but by the time war actually began information had arrived that there were Russian ships in both admirals' seas.

Russia in fact was a Pacific power and had been for nearly two centuries, during which time the area under its control or influence had gradually expanded from Siberia into Alaska. But this power was planted in very thin political and demographic soil. The original rationale for occupation had been, as it had been in much of North America, the acquisition of furs; but the fur animals were now hunted nearly to extinction, particularly the valuable sable. The Russian presence had developed into a generalised trading area, and much of the energy employed was now directed to supplying the ports and

---

[21] ADM 2/1611, 1 February 1854.
[22] ADM 2/1611, 21 February 1854.
[23] ADM 1/5629, 19 May 1854.

inland stations with essentials, in exchange for the minimal fur harvest collected from the local peoples. The Russian Cossacks who led the exploration and exploitation of the huge area of Siberia and the Far East had reached the Pacific coast in the seventeenth century and had left a string of minor posts across eastern Siberia to the Bering Strait, and later explorers had crossed that strait into America. From 1799 all of these posts and ports were under the control of the Russian-American Company.[24]

None of the posts on the Russian coast from the Sea of Okhotsk to the Alaskan panhandle were of any real size. The coasts were hostile to shipping, with many islands and rocks, frequent fogs, and much of the seas were blocked by ice for several months in the year; the posts on the coast were usually difficult to approach, and could only be called ports in the absence of anything better. Many of the local tribes were hostile to the Russian presence, whose basic activity had degenerated in many areas to the extraction of what little surplus the tribespeople produced under the guise of taxation, supplying such essentials as sugar and rye flour in partial exchange.

The main Asian posts/ports were no more than three or four in number. On the Sea of Okhotsk was Okhotsk itself, a minor port which lay at the mouth of a river which was notable for its misbehaviour. For nearly a century attempts to get the post to thrive had been repeatedly thwarted by the river, which had a habit of changing its mouth almost whimsically, or by the sea, whose tides were capable of flooding the whole site with an equal lack of notice. At last in the 1840s a naval governor was given *carte blanche* to relocate the port, and he chose to move 400 kilometres southwest to Aian, a site which had been recommended more than once during the previous century – an indication of the slow decision-making of the various Russian authorities involved. Aian was established by 1850, but Okhotsk still lingered on.

Across the Sea of Okhotsk from these two places was the huge peninsula of Kamchatka, under Russian control for about a century by 1850. Its coasts were rocky and mountainous,

---

[24] For a good outline: Y. Semenov, *Siberia, its Conquest and Development*, trans. J. Foster, London 1965; P. A. Tikhmenov, *The History of the Russian-America Company*, trans. and ed. R. A. Pierce and A. S. Donnelly, Seattle 1978, originally published in 1861–1863.

with capacious bays which looked like good harbours until the lack of inland routes became clear. The main settled area was in fact inland, along the valley of the Kamchatka River, but the production of commercially worthwhile goods had declined since the Russian arrival, again in part due to hostility from the local indigenous people, but mainly because those people had suffered a series of epidemics which had reduced their population drastically, and therefore their economic capacity. There was one serious port in the peninsula, Petropavlovsk on the eastern coast, which was in more or less regular contact with Okhotsk and Aian by sea, and westwards with the posts in Alaska. There were some other, smaller, places here and there, particularly Bolsherets, on the western coast.

The basic problem for the Russians in eastern Siberia was geographical. The rivers they had used as the basic transport routes across Siberia from the west mainly flowed northwards into the Arctic Ocean. Those which reached the Sea of Okhotsk were relatively short, turbulent, barely navigable, and separated from the rest of the Siberian lands by the high mountains in which they had their sources, notably the Dzhundzhur range which ran parallel to the coast for 500 kilometres behind Aian. In order to make Aian worth using, for example, a log road had been built from the Lena River at Iakutsk to the Maia River, a distance of well over 300 kilometres; then the Maia River itself was used for more than 400 kilometres, then another log road was laid across the Dzhundzhur range to reach Aian (another 200 kilometres). It was clearly a route only to be used to transport very valuable goods, or by the financial support of a government subsidy.[25]

Aian was scarcely better as a port than Okhotsk, though as a port it was less subject to erratic behaviour in its harbour. Even so it was closed by ice for more than six months in the year. Furthermore there developed in the 1830s a new factor which had to be considered. A new whaling ground off the south coast of Alaska was found in the 1820s, and this attracted large numbers of whalers from Britain and from the eastern coast of the United States, mainly the New England ports. Hunting for whales spread across the North Pacific into the Sea of Okhotsk

---

[25] See the map in J. R. Gibson, *Feeding the Russian Fur Trade, Provisionment of the Okhotsk Seaboard and the Kamchatka Peninsula, 1679–1856*, Madison, WI, 1969, map 8.

by the 1830s, and the shores of the Russian possessions were soon being used, with or without permission, by the whalers, who landed, gathered fuel, and rendered the whales down to oil and fat and bone. At times – the whole fishery was declining by 1850 – there were many more Americans in the area than Russians.[26]

It was, however, the perceived threat of Britain to the Russian lands which was one of the spurs to a new surge of Russian activity in eastern Siberia. In 1847 a new Governor-General of eastern Siberia was appointed. He was Nikolai Nicolaievich Muravev, a soldier who had made a substantial reputation as a general in fighting in the Caucasus. He was also an enthusiastic imperialist and had already identified Britain as the main threat to the Russian position in the Far East. He further saw control and use of the Amur River as the best means of advancing Russian power in the area. It would, once explored, provide a route connecting Russia's Siberian headquarters at Irkutsk with the sea, at least the possibility of lower transport costs, of imports and exports, or development.

Muravev had spent some time in France, and his wife, only married recently, was French of Russian extraction; possibly he had picked up his anti-British attitude in Paris, though by the 1840s Anglophobia was fairly pervasive in Russian policy circles. In about 1849 or 1850 he explained in a memorandum how the opening of the Chinese ports to British trade – he always said 'English' – had sapped the Russian trade which was conducted by treaty through Kiakhta in the north. He assumed that this was deliberate and was directed in part against Russia, and added that the accession of the new emperor in China, an 18-year-old boy, would allow 'the English ... with their natural entrepreneurial spirit, speed and persistence ... to gain control not only of trade, but also of China's politics'.[27] Thus the gradual extension of British encroachments along the Asian coast was certainly seen by Muravev and others as an eventual threat to the Russian Far Eastern position. By his appointment, Muravev was in a position to do something about it.

---

[26] Kushner, *Conflict on the North-West Coast.*
[27] Translation in B. Dymytryshyn, E. A. P. Crownhart-Vaughan and T. Vaughan, *The Russian American Colonies, 1798–1867*, Oregon Historical Society 1989, 482–484.

In fact it was not Britain which was the real obstacle to Russian expansion in the Far East, but China. In the seventeenth century the Cossack explorers had found the Amur River and had sailed down it, fully realising that it was the real communication link between inland Siberia and the Pacific. But the Manchu Empire, then in its glory days, had insisted, with a large armed force, that the Amur valley was part of its territory. Russia, with little real power in the east, and, in the seventeenth century, a multitude of troubles in Europe, had perforce accepted this, and had even agreed to it in writing, in the presence of a large Manchu army, in a treaty signed at Nerchinsk on the upper Amur in 1689. It was this treaty which had designated Kiakhta, not far south of Lake Baikal, as the one place where trade between the empires could be carried on. Both of these places, Kiakhta and Nerchinsk, were far inland. The Amur route was thereupon closed to Russia.

The exploration and exploitation of eastern Siberia had taken more northerly routes earlier, avoiding the Amur valley. Bering's explorations of the coast had also been in part stimulated by the inaccessibility of the Amur. And it had steadily become clearer that there really was no viable alternative to the Amur route for reaching the Pacific from inland Siberia. The log-roads and tributary rivers route to Aian was hardly satisfactory. Yet China still blocked the Amur route in the 1840s as it had in the seventeenth century.

But times change. By 1850 Russia was stronger, China much weaker. Muravev came east with the personal intention of 'reclaiming' the Amur route for Russia. This was the constant tenor of his language – a claim that Russia had once possessed the Amur route, and was now 'recovering' it. (It is exactly the same tone as was used by the United States President James K. Polk in his claim for Oregon, and even in seizing Mexican land; in the twentieth century it was the language employed by the totalitarian states.) It had not escaped Muravev's attention that China was in a state of collapse, nor that so far as he could discover there had been no attempt to assert any Chinese control in much of the Amur valley for a long time.

Muravev's ideas did not spring pristine and new from his own head. The development of the Russian Far East was a subject which was in the air in the 1840s. In 1845, two years before Muravev's appointment as governor-general, Aian had finally been designated as the port for Kamchatka in place of hapless

Okhotsk. While the explorations and assessments along that coast were going on, attention was also directed further south. In 1846 Ensign Aleksandr Mikhailovich Gavrilov, of the Corps of Naval Navigators, was dispatched on a new investigation of the coast south of Aian. Gavrilov had been involved in a junior capacity in the investigation of Aian, and so was fully aware of conditions in the region. He was dispatched from the Nova Archangelsk (i.e. Sitka) in Alaska in the brig *Konstantin* in April and left Aian on his exploratory mission on 11 July 1846.

Gavrilov was to explore along the Siberian coast south of Aian and the northern part of Sakhalin, and investigate the Shantar Islands between these areas, but his main task, set by the imperial government rather than the Russian-American Company, was to investigate the situation at the mouth of the Amur River. This was a notable geographical puzzle at the time. It was not known if Sakhalin was an island, and the geographical theory most widely accepted was that it was a peninsula attached to the mainland, and that the mouth of the Amur was therefore either north or south of the peninsula. If the river flowed to the south, into the Gulf of Tartary, it would clearly provide a very valuable route from Siberia into the Pacific, avoiding much of the icebound coast – the Gulf is frozen for a shorter period than is the Sea of Okhotsk. It was essential that this endeavour be kept secret, especially from the Chinese, if there were any Chinese authorities present, so Gavrilov pretended to be an American ship – a sign of the ubiquity of such vessels in the area.

In fact he met no authorities at all. He sailed along the north coast of Sakhalin, missing the Amur mouth the first time because of a sea fog, then turned back and sailed into the Amur, reaching about seventy kilometres inland. He enquired about the Chinese presence in the area from the local people, and was told that no Chinese had been seen there in living memory. Next year a trading party travelled south from Aian to make contact with the local inhabitants, called Giliaks, and to explore the area of the Amur mouth in more detail.[28]

Governor-General Muravev became interested as well. He sent Captain-Lieutenant Gennadi Ivanovich Nevelskoi to have a further look. Nevelskoi's ship, the transport *Baikal*, was to go to Petropavlovsk in Kamchatka to deliver supplies, and

---

[28] Tikhmenov, *Russian-America Company*, 273–282.

then to make more investigations towards the Amur. Along the way Nevelskoi met up with Orlov, the leader of the trading party from Aian, and they collaborated, travelling further up the Amur than Gavrilov and between them founding two new settlements: Petrovskoi on the Sea of Okhotsk side of the river mouth, and Nikolaevsk on the shore of the river itself.[29]

This exploration and discovery continued the next year and the year after. No Chinese in authority were ever met, but Manchu merchants were encountered here and there. The locals were eager to acquire manufactured goods, and it turned out that the Russians were intruding into an area which was on the fringes of both Japanese and Chinese trading areas. Neither Chinese nor Japanese merchants actually reached the area, but their goods arrived by way of Manchurian merchants and by exchange among the people of Sakhalin. If the Russians hoped to keep their activities secret they would probably be disappointed: rumour would spread quickly, especially if they were a source of trade goods. Perhaps realising this, Muravev sent a diplomatic note to the Manchu government in February 1851, claiming that foreign navies were active near the river mouth and suggesting a joint Chinese-Russian project to block this. The 'foreign navies' did not exist, of course, but whalers, usually American, were certainly seen in both the Sea of Okhotsk and the Gulf of Tartary. This distortion of the truth is characteristic of the means of persuasion Muravev used.[30]

Muravev wanted to control the river as a means of communication, and as a trade route. Even before Nevelskoi was sent to locate the mouth of the river, Muravev had dispatched an army colonel, Vogarov, on a voyage down the river from inland. He vanished. There was a Manchu post at Aigun on the river, designed expressly to intercept such intrusions. The conclusion was obvious.[31] Muravev made no protest – he should not have sent the man in the first place – but drew his own conclusions on how to proceed. Another expedition, led by Lieutenant-Colonel Akhte, was meanwhile sent to explore the land north of

---

[29] Tikhmenov, *Russian-America Company*, 283–288; Nevelskoi's instructions are translated in *The Russian American Colonies*, vol. 3, 473–478, and are dated 18 November 1848.

[30] R. K. I. Quested, *The Expansion of Russia in East Asia, 1857–1860*, Kuala Lumpur 1968, 37; T. C. Lin, 'The Amur Frontier Question between China and Russia, 1850–1860', *Pacific Historical Review* 3, 1935, 1–27.

[31] Lin, 'Amur Frontier Question', 7.

the river in order to locate the boundary markers supposed to have been placed there by the Manchu government in accordance with the Treaty of Nerchinsk of 1689. Muravev opposed this expedition, since it was shifting the boundary he was after, not finding it. But Akhte took four years, and then found no markers.[32]

Muravev was, in fact, moving cautiously. He may have disliked Akhte's expedition, but he had not pushed forward too vigorously. The Treaty of Nerchinsk had been a major military and diplomatic defeat for Russia, and had successfully excluded Russian explorers and traders from the Amur region ever since. He could not be sure just how vigilant the Chinese government now was in the area. The disappearance of Colonel Vogarov rather suggested that the Chinese guard was still alert; yet the explorers at the mouth of the Amur had found no evidence of a Chinese presence. The defeat of China by the British in the First China War, and the widespread Taiping rebellion did suggest that, even if there was an alert Chinese guard on the Amur, the Chinese government's attention would be directed south rather than north. Nothing had emerged, therefore, to deter Muravev so far.

In the process of exploring the Amur mouth the Russian parties had worked their way along the river upstream for some distance and also south along the coast of the mainland. A bay which had been discovered by the French expedition under La Pérouse nearly a century before, De Castries Bay, was located, and a relatively straightforward route between it and the river by way of a long lake was prospected. The Russians thus knew that Sakhalin was actually an island, and that the strait between it and the mainland was passable, though with difficulty because of the extensive sandbanks.

This was not news which was publicised, though it would have been greeted with some interest in geographical, naval, and even political circles in Europe. It was not, however, a fact wholly unknown in Europe. Forty years before, in 1809, a Japanese explorer, Mamiya Renzo, had worked his way through the strait and up the Amur for some distance – that is, doing the same as Nevelskoi, but from the south. This information was published in Europe by a German doctor in 1851, but no one seems to have noticed, until later. It was one of the complaints

---

[32] Semenov, *Siberia*, 259; Quested, *Expansion of Russia*, 39.

made by British naval commanders in the coming confusions that the strait was assumed not to exist, and yet they were being blamed for not sailing along it.[33]

Admiral Stirling remarked that Findlay's *Directory* with which he had been 'supplied', as he pointedly noted, 'by the Admiralty', and which was dated 1851, stated that 'the evidence tends towards Sakhalin being a peninsula'. A Russian chart sent to him in 1855 'represented a channel from the Sea of Okhotsk but left blank, as if unsurveyed, the southern part of the Gulf of Amur'.[34] The discovery of the channel was therefore being deliberately concealed; Muravev, after all, believed the British were about to seize the area – or at least so he said.

In Europe the news that Commodore Perry and his ships were to go to Japan was widely spread. It was generally assumed that the British would do the same; indeed, had it not been for the problems of Chinese pirates and the Burmese war, it is probable that a British fleet would have attempted Perry's exploit some years earlier. This Muravev knew. With the Russians at the Amur mouth and in northern Sakhalin, it seemed necessary to stake out Russian claims for as much of the potential spoils in the area as possible. Britain had seized territory from China and Burma in the recent past, and now the United States seemed to be about to do the same in Japan, while American whalers were ubiquitous in the northern Pacific. In 1849 Muravev commented that there were 250 American whalers operating in the Sea of Okhotsk, claiming that this was probably an under-estimate.[35] So the imperial government determined to extend its claim throughout Sakhalin, and the Russian-American Company was given the task, or perhaps it is better to say that it was to be done under the cover of the Company. It was hardly the first such organisation to be used as an empire builder.

The plan was to establish two posts, one on the west coast of Sakhalin, and one in the south; the Company, however, did

---

33 J. J. Stephan, 'The Crimean War in the Far East', *Modern Asian Studies* 3, 1969, 257–277, note 37 (on p. 268), quoting a Japanese source.
34 ADM 1/5692, 13 February 1856.
35 Gibson, *Feeding the Russian Fur Trade*, 91; incidentally it is highly probable that some of these whalers knew of the Amur strait, but they did not publicise such information, nobody thought to ask them, and anyway they told such tall stories and outright lies that they would probably not be believed.

not believe that this would be enough and offered to emplace several other smaller posts at various places in between. The first post was established in the south, on Aniwa bay, next to an existing Japanese village – the Russians involved knew full well even before they began this enterprise that Japanese settlers had already occupied much of the south of the island. The post was named Muravevsk and was rapidly fortified in a perfunctory way – it was actually referred to as a redoubt. Another small post was established on the mainland across the Gulf of Tartary, and called Konstantinovsk at Imperatorskaia Gavan ('Emperor's Bay'), about 250 kilometres south of De Castries Bay. The ship which had been used to transport the colonists to Muravevsk, the *Irtysh*, called at Konstantinovsk before setting out for the second projected colony on Sakhalin's west coast, but it got shut in by ice before it could get there. By the time the ship was free to sail again, war had begun.[36]

During 1853 Colonel Akhte, sent to explore the land north of the Amur, reported back. He had taken four years on as thorough an investigation as possible in the extremely rough terrain, and the length of time was explained by the fact that he had found neither Chinese authority nor Chinese boundary markers anywhere.[37] In St Petersburg this seems to have been the final detail which convinced the tsar that the Amur should be claimed – or 'reclaimed', as Muravev put it. The area was clearly under no Chinese control, so despite the provisions of the Treaty of Nerchinsk, the Amur valley had to be regarded as unoccupied, if not unclaimed, land. There was just the problem of the Chinese post on the river at Aigun. The tsar authorised Muravev to send a full-scale expedition down the river as far as the mouth.[38] This would open up the line of communications between the centre of Russian power around Irkutsk and Lake Baikal and the new posts recently established at the Amur estuary, and in Sakhalin.

The Russians knew that the Chinese would object; they knew that they were now involved in some sort of competition with the United States in the whole northern Pacific; they knew that their settlements in Sakhalin were encroaching on

---

[36] Tikhmenov, *Russian-America Company*, 301–304.
[37] Quested, *Expansion of Russia*, 39.
[38] Quested, *Expansion of Russia*, 43; Semenov, *Siberia*, 261–264.

territory already occupied by the Japanese. They imagined – or at least Muravev did – that Britain was keen to seize control of the Amur estuary. And now, during 1853, they picked a quarrel with the Ottoman Empire, one which soon involved both Britain and France as active enemies.

2

The Pursuit to Petropavlovsk

In complete ignorance of Muravev and his ambitions, of Perry and Japan, and with only a general knowledge of events in China, Rear-Admiral Price set about his work in the leisurely way of the peacetime Navy. He had been at Valparaiso for a fortnight before his predecessor Moresby sailed for home, and then he spent a further three weeks in that port before sailing to inspect his area of command. He sent the *Virago* along the South American coast to Arica in southern Peru and then to Callao, the port for the Peruvian capital Lima. A revolution was brewing in Peru, and investigating this took priority.

Price himself, in *President*, and with the store ship *Cockatrice* in attendance, sailed north on 20 February, first to Coquimbo, a voyage of about 300 kilometres, and then to Caldera, a similar distance further north. This place was just south of the Chile–Bolivia border (as it then was), a good place from which to observe the Peruvian problem without getting directly involved. Price may have intended to go further, but at Caldera on 2 March he received mail from Britain. Two of the letters were instructions to send *Virago* to Panama and another ship to carry supplies to *Rattlesnake* and *Plover* in the Bering Strait.[1] There was as yet no clear word about war with Russia.

Price also received mail addressed to Rear-Admiral Moresby, one letter of which was from the British Consul-General in Honolulu, William Miller. Price opened this, since it was clearly an official letter and one relevant to his duties. He did not yet know that there was a letter from the Admiralty on its way warning him to send a ship to watch affairs in Honolulu, but Miller's report was alarming enough for Price to react in that way without these instructions. An apparent attempt at a filibustering coup mounted from California, and aimed at securing

---

[1] ADM 50/260, Price Journal.

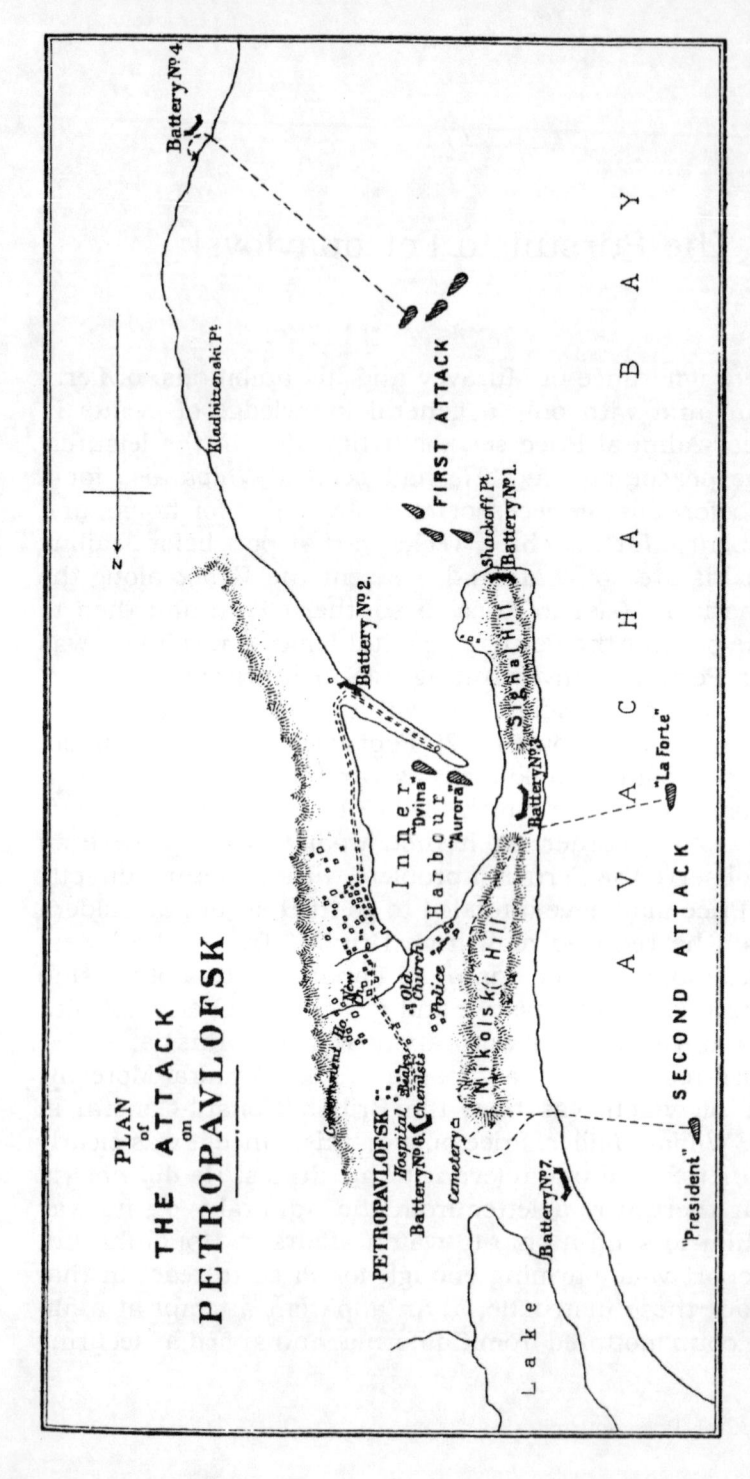

Map 2 Petropavlovsk (from Z. Vladimir (Z. Volpicelli), *Russia on the Pacific*, London 1899, opposite p. 216)

the annexation of the islands to the United States, had failed, but Dr Gerrit Judd, an American who had held several senior ministerial positions under King Kamehameha III, and whose policy had been to maintain the kingdom's independence, had been dismissed as part of the means of pacifying the troubles. Price combined two tasks in one: *Trincomalee* was selected as the ship to be sent with the supplies to the Bering Strait; it could call at Honolulu on the way, thus showing British interest and concern, but it would hardly be able to do anything more.[2]

Miller reported also that 250 whaling ships had been at the port of Honolulu during the summer, but that the likely catch had not been good; most of these ships were American. Also, a new steamship line was about to begin operations between San Francisco and Shanghai, with a regular intermediate stop at Honolulu. The Hawaiian kingdom was clearly being drawn even closer into the American sphere of influence.

Price now turned back, sailing from Caldera on the day after he received the mail, having written and sent his report on Honolulu to the Admiralty. He reached Valparaiso once more on 14 March, where he found the *Nereus*, one of his store ships, the United States frigate *St Laurence*, and the Russian frigate *Diana*. Given the international situation in the Pacific this was an interesting gathering, to say the least. Price was not yet aware that several letters had been sent to him concerning the *Diana*, which the Admiralty was clearly bothered about. The ship had been at Rio de Janeiro, and HMS *Pique* was sent to watch it there. But *Diana* had left before *Pique* had arrived. Meanwhile another Russian frigate, *Aurora*, had been reported at Rio, and seemed to be heading Price's way. There was nothing Price could do, of course, peace still prevailing. The Admiralty, equally, could do no more than warn: 'In the present relations of this country with Russia, all H.M.'s ships should be prepared and on their guard in approaching a ship of war of that nation.'[3]

Price decided that it was necessary to station his force further to the north, at Callao. Not only would he thus be able watch developments in Peru, but he would be several days closer to Britain and therefore would receive news and instruc-

---

2 ADM 1/5630, 3 March 1854; Kuykendall, *Hawaiian Kingdom*, vol. 1, 413–416.
3 ADM 2/1611, 4 and 13 March 1854.

tions all the earlier. (The mail normally now travelled by way of Panama and then by steamer along the western coast of South America.) *Trincomalee* had now been loaded with the supplies for the Arctic base, and it could accompany *President* and the others part of the way, before heading off to call at Honolulu. Then there arrived at Valparaiso the French frigate *La Forte* (60 guns), with Rear-Admiral Febvrier-Despointes on board, together with the *Obligado*, a 12-gun brig. This was yet another preliminary move in the preparations for the Russian war, but Price did not delay his sailing, leaving for the north next day, 21 March.[4]

This time he moved more quickly, reaching Coquimbo on the 25th, and Callao on 8 April. Once again an eclectic collection of ships was present, including *Virago*. Price received more mail, including the Admiralty letter of 1 February warning of imminent war. He issued an instruction to his captains on general conduct to be observed in the event of war. A week later, on the 15th, the Russian frigate *Aurora* arrived at Callao, and Price received news of the departure from Valparaiso of the Russian transport ship, *Kamchatka*, a name he would become all too familiar with later.

Trincomalee was sent off to Honolulu and the Bering Strait on the 18th, carrying instructions on what to do in the event of war. *Trincomalee* was, of course, heading into dangerous waters if war did break out, and Captain William Houstoun surely had anxious conversations with Price on the subject, but the Admiralty instructions were specific, and the supplies for the Arctic ships were clearly important.[5]

Information about the Russian frigates arrived in dribs and drabs, always out of date. While *Aurora* was moored at Callao, Price received the Admiralty letter reporting on *Diana* at Rio; then *Aurora* sailed, and a week later *Pique* arrived, along with letters reporting *Aurora* and *Diana* leaving Rio. Captain Nicholson of *Pique* could report that news anyway, since he had called at Rio on his way. Price now knew that if war had begun he had the task of searching for at least three Russian ships, two of them frigates able to match his own major ship in strength. He was also told of the need to cooperate with the French, and Captain Nicholson was given a copy of the Admi-

---

[4] ADM 50/260, Price Journal, 20 March 1854.
[5] ADM 50/260, Price Journal, 8–18 April 1854.

ralty letters enjoining that cooperation. Nicholson's ship was now the next most powerful to the *President* in the squadron, and he was now Price's second-in-command, having a narrow margin of seniority over Captain Burridge.[6]

Meanwhile a new problem was bothering the Admiralty. Rumours had arrived at New York that 'certain persons at San Francisco' were preparing to fit out ships to act as privateers under licence from the Russian-American Company. Their object, it was thought, would be to intercept the British mail steamers in the Pacific. The rumours had arrived at the Admiralty both from the British vice-consul in New York, and by way of the French ambassador in London, relaying the story from the French Foreign Office. Price was informed, the Pacific Steam Navigation Company was also warned, and enquiries were sent to Washington.[7]

The rumours of American privateering originated in San Francisco itself, in the activities there of the Russian vice-consul Kostromotinov, who was also the local agent for the Russian-American Company. He was concerned that a war with Britain and France would leave the Company's Pacific posts open to Allied attack. His idea was that the activities of a group of privateers would so preoccupy the enemy warships that the Russian settlements would be thereby protected. In fact it was quickly pointed out to him that the Company did not have the right in international law to issue letters of marque for privateers, but the rumour had successfully alarmed everyone involved by that time. It was fully appreciated on all sides that the Company's legal position would not be the first concern if Americans became privateers and attacked British ships.[8]

In fact the Company had moved to protect itself even before the war actually began. Contact was made with the Hudson's Bay Company in London as early as January. The two Companies were neighbours in North America with a long mutual, but vague, boundary, and the Hudson's Bay Company was the Russian Company's best customer, providing supplies which kept the Russian Company's posts alive. The British Company

---

[6] ADM 50/260, Price Journal, 26 April–3 May 1854.
[7] ADM 2/1697, 23 March and 10 April 1854.
[8] ADM 2/1612, 21 and 22 March 1854; F. A. Golden, 'Russian-American Relations during the Crimean War', *American Historical Review* 31, 1925, 462–476.

proved agreeable to discussions – not willing to lose its supply of Alaskan furs – and within a few days both it and the British government had agreed that Alaska – 'Russian America' – should be regarded as neutral territory in the event of war. The Russian government proved harder to convince, scenting a trap. The neutrality was to be reciprocal, and the British clearly limited it to the Russian posts on land; any Russian or Company ships at sea were still to be fair game, a naval blockade of Alaskan ports was not ruled out, and it was not to extend to the Asian possessions of the Company. Maybe it was these limitations which persuaded the Russian government to accept the deal, but even before the tsar indicated his agreement to the British government, on 31 March 1854, letters went out to Price in the Pacific that Alaska was to be treated as a neutral.[9]

At first sight this agreement seems one-sided. British and French control of the Pacific was scarcely disturbed during the war, and the Russian posts in Alaska were clearly vulnerable to Allied attack. Indeed the Russian-American Company itself decided that only Sitka was at all defensible, and that all the other Alaskan posts should not be defended if attacked.[10] But the British knew full well that the United States would hardly ignore any extension of British territory in North America, even under the guise of the Hudson's Bay Company. It was a fixed element in British foreign policy not to go to war with the United States, if it could possibly be avoided. This meant that a threat to British territory on the part of the United States would probably bring a British submission – as had happened in 1846 in the Oregon crisis – unless the threat was one of actual invasion. The United States had already, more than once, indicated its interest in acquiring Alaska, if necessary by purchase.[11] Being pre-empted in this by Britain during a war which was being fought in support of the Ottoman Empire would greatly annoy any United States government, and, being at war already, the British needed to be exceptionally careful to avoid collecting any more enemies.

---

[9] ADM 2/1697, 23 and 24 March 1854; Tikhmenov, *Russian-America Company*, 356; S. R. Okun, *The Russian-America Company*, ed. R. D. Grekov, trans. C. Glasberg, Cambridge, MA, 1951, 235–237.

[10] Okun, *Russian-America Company*, 234–235

[11] E.g. H. M. MacPherson, 'The Interest of William McKendree Gwin in the Purchase of Alaska, 1854–1861', *Pacific Historical Review* 3, 1934, 28–38.

The agreement therefore had advantages for both sides. The Russians did not have to worry about their most vulnerable and distant possessions; the British could go on claiming, and acting as if, the war was for only a limited object, the protection of the Ottoman Empire. This permitted the British to concentrate their naval and military forces in the Black Sea, but it was also predicated on Russian acceptance of that same limitation. If, after being defeated in the Black Sea fighting, Russia refused to make peace, then the limited-war interpretation could swiftly be discarded. This was a matter in which the war in the Pacific would be concerned later.

For the moment, Price was informed, in the same mail-bag which brought the official notification that war had begun, of the neutral status of Alaska. This relieved him of serious worries concerning *Rattlesnake*, *Plover* and *Trincomalee* in the Bering Strait, at least for the present. He was also warned of the story of privateers at San Francisco, and that the *Diana* and *Aurora* had left Rio de Janeiro. But that to him was now old news.

Admirals Price and Febvrier-Despointes concerted their plans, and concluded that their main object had to be to hunt for and dispose of the two Russian frigates which they knew to be at large in the Pacific. On 16 May they sailed from Callao, *President* and *Virago*, *La Forte* and *Obligado*. This little fleet headed first for the Marquesas Islands, French territory, where they collected the French sloop *Artémise* (30 guns). The steam-driven *Virago* had sailed more slowly than the sailing vessels and arrived on 15 June; *Pique* had been left at Callao, but sailed on the 17th directly for Honolulu. The main force remained at Nuku Hiva in the Marquesas until the end of July. By that time the force had been increased by the addition of *Amphitrite* (British, 24 guns) and *Eurydice* (French, 30 guns). Price was agreed to be in command, having an older commission as rear-admiral than Despointes.[12]

The joint fleet sailed for Honolulu, arriving there on 17 July, where *Pique* joined, direct from Callao. Whether *Pique* brought mail is not known, but even so the fleets had been out of touch with their Admiralties now for two months. In fact, of course, there was little either Admiralty could now do or say which would be relevant. It had to be assumed in Europe that the

---

[12] ADM 50/260, Price Journal, 9–15 June 1854.

Pacific squadrons were hunting the Russian frigates, and until reports came in that they had met them, there were no further instructions to send. The British Admiralty did write to approve Price's disposition of *Trincomalee*, and, having received a worry-note from the Governor of Vancouver Island about a Russian frigate said to have been seen at San Francisco, passed this news on. And Pitcairn Island cropped up again. A letter from the British Consul had referred to the prospective removal of Pitcairn's population to Norfolk Island. The Admiralty claimed to know nothing of this, though since Admiral Moresby had arrived in England in April, and always thereafter kept in touch with the Pitcairn Islanders until he died, they should have been up to date on the question. The Admiralty promised to send the information on to Price. The implication of the tone of the letter was that he had better things to do for the present.[13] The islanders were, of course, the descendants of the *Bounty* mutineers.

All this was generally routine stuff, which would not have affected Price's actions had he even received these letters. At Honolulu he and Despointes learned that *Diana* had called there some time before and had sailed on, though her destination was unknown. There appears to have been no news of either *Aurora* or *Kamchatka*. Price took the opportunity of being at Honolulu to give King Kamehameha III an outing on *Virago*, steaming around the harbour and the bay. This was obviously good public relations, and a strong hint to others, American filibusters in particular, that Britain was very concerned to preserve Hawaiian independence.

After leaving Honolulu, Admiral Despointes sent *Artémise* and Price sent *Amphitrite* to San Francisco to check on possible privateers, and to see if any mail had arrived there. Price took the rest of the ships north from Honolulu on 25 July. Of course he had no idea where the Russian ships had gone, other than that they were (probably) somewhere in the Pacific. Logic supposed that they would have gone to a Russian port, or to a neutral port. This second option seemed unlikely, so the Allied squadron sailed due north to make investigation of the likely refuges on Russian territory. The first possibility was Sitka, which the Russians called Nova Archangelsk, whence Gavrilov

---

[13] ADM 2/1698, 16 May 1854; 2/1612, 5 June 1854.

had sailed to explore the Amur; another was Kodiak, on its own island south of the Alaskan mainland; then there was Petropavlovsk in Kamchatka; finally Okhotsk was taken note of. Aian was not mentioned, which suggests that the information the Allies had about Russian posts was well out of date – a supposition which was to be confirmed later. The Alaskan ports, Price had been told, were to be regarded as neutral, and since he headed directly for Petropavlovsk it seems he assumed this would be the first place worth searching.

It is necessary here to make clear that the sources for what took place at Petropavlovsk are by no means unanimous and convincing. We are dependent on less-than-official accounts, though this is not always necessarily a bad thing. Reports were of course written to the Admiralty, but we also have accounts from various other sources. Two descriptive letters were published in *The Times*, written soon after the events, that is, two or three days later. One was by an Irish midshipman on the *President*; the other was translated from a French account published in another newspaper; a third officer sent an account to the *Nautical Magazine*. An account was taken down by Consul-General Miller at Honolulu from an American witness, and another was relayed to the Hamburg consul in Shanghai by the German skipper of a Hamburg barque who had been in Petropavlovsk at the time of the events there. The chaplain of the *President* wrote a letter home, parts of which have been published. There are also Russian accounts, though usually second-hand and produced some time later. None of these is wholly reliable, and in particular we do not have any clear indication from any of the commanders on either side of what they intended, though it is possible to infer a good deal from their actions. Beyond that we have a French account published in the *Revue de Deux Mondes* some years later, written by a participant, Edmond du Hailly, an officer on, probably, *La Forte*. Like the Irish midshipman, he was not privy to command decisions.[14]

---

[14] Official accounts are in ADM 1/5631 and were published by R O'Byrne in *O'Byrne's Naval Annual of 1855*, London 1855 (reprinted 1969); *The Times*, October 1854; 'The Attack on Petropaulovski', *Nautical Magazine*, 1855, 50–54; ADM 1/5661 (from Shanghai and Honolulu); Z. Vladimir, *Russia on the Pacific*, London 1899, 214–224; E. Du Hailly, 'Une Campagne dans l'Ocean Pacifique', *Revue de Deux Mondes*, 1858 (in two parts); M. Lewis,

It is here that the question of dates becomes a little awkward. The joint fleet had passed what would later be called the International Date Line on its voyage north from Honolulu, and consequently it was now theoretically on a different date: for the fleet the arrival took place on 28 August; in Petropavlovsk it was a day later. Indeed it was even a completely different date, for in the town they were still using the old Russian Julian calendar, which was twelve days behind the Gregorian dating used by the Allies: for the Russians the Allied attack was on 17 August. It is also to be noted that Admiral Price had now moved outside his command area; the China and East Indies command of Rear-Admiral Stirling stretched as far as longitude 170° west, which put Kamchatka in the China command area. If he thought of it – or even was aware of it – Price had the excuse of having followed the enemy, in more or less hot pursuit.

Virago had been something of a liability on the voyage from South America. She was slow, with only a limited supply of coal, and had had to be towed part of the way. Now the ship came into her own. The little steamer went into the bay and inspected the town's defences. The Russians claimed she was flying the American flag, but Captain Westergaard told the Hamburg consul at Shanghai that he could not make out what flag was being flown. Not that the Russians were in any doubt as to the nationality and purpose of the ship, possibly the first steamer to reach Petropavlovsk, no matter what flag it flew. *Virago* stayed about three miles offshore, sounding and inspecting the defences. Price himself was on board.

What he saw was fairly daunting. Petropavlovsk was a town on a bay inside a wider bay. The greater bay, Avatcha Bay, was roughly semicircular, with indentations. One of these was Petropavlovsk harbour. It was protected from the open sea by a long narrow ridge, lying north–south and parallel to the mainland; a lake lay behind the town, almost a resumption of the harbour. The town lay on the lowland connecting the ridge and the mainland. The bay behind the ridge formed the harbour, and was divided into an inner and outer harbour by a sandspit, which left only a narrow entrance into the inner harbour. The

---

'Eye-witness at Petropavlovski, 1854', *Mariner's Mirror* 39, 1963, 265–272. The interpretation of events in these accounts is usually greatly different from that I adopt here.

protecting seaward ridge was formed of two hills, Nikolski Hill, close by the town, and Signal Hill on the seaward end, the two being connected by a saddle.

Its situation made the harbour pleasantly safe from storms, and it tended to be visited by any explorer or traveller in the area: Bering, Cook and La Pérouse had all been there. In 1847 S. S. Hill, a British traveller (viewed with some suspicion by the Russians, who thought he was a spy), who had visited Muravev in Irkutsk and had been at Okhotsk, called it a lonely little seat of power in a vast country. While he was there, HMS *Herald* called, a survey ship which was searching for evidence of Franklin's fate. The place, as Hill noted, was surrounded by hills, some of them active volcanoes, covered by forests of birches and limes, virtually undisturbed by the axe. He also found an Englishman, a former bricklayer and sailor who appeared to have settled there.[15]

General Muravev had visited the town in 1849 and had made grandiose plans to fortify it, intending it to be the main Russian naval base in the Pacific, but, appreciating the impossibility of his great idea, for the moment, he contented himself by pointing out the best places for siting batteries for defence. His eye was good, and the batteries proved to be well placed.[16] The Governor of Kamchatka was Rear-Admiral Vasili Zavoiko, who began his career as an army officer and had switched over to the navy, a move which was possible in the Russian system. He proved to be sensible and determined.

One battery was placed on the very end of Signal Hill, at Sharkoff Point, and another small one of only three guns faced it across Avatcha Bay. If an attacker got past these two, a third more powerful one was sited on the sandspit, just where it joined the mainland. These three between them dominated the approach through the outer harbour. Two further batteries were placed at two points along the seaward ridge, one below a saddle joining Signal Hill to Nikolski Hill, the other north of Nikolski Hill where there was an area of lowland, between the hill and a freshwater lake. This was clearly a particularly vulnerable spot, for there was a track leading from that place into the town; another battery was placed behind Nikolski Hill

---

[15] S. S. Hill, *Travels in Siberia*, London 1854.
[16] Vladimir, *Russia on the Pacific*, 214–216, 223.

at the approach to the town itself. All these were of no use, however, if the assault came through the bay.

This was all of interest, of course, but would not normally have concerned the British and French, who were not particularly interested in attacking minor Russian posts, but *Virago*'s reconnaissance also revealed that the frigate *Aurora* was in the harbour. The ship was placed behind the sandspit, which provided some shelter, in such a way that her guns could fire over it towards the outer harbour. Beside *Aurora* was *Dvina*, a transport ship armed with a few guns, placed to do the same. Some of the guns from both ships had been landed to reinforce the batteries, but in effect the ships formed two more batteries firing into the outer harbour. And during the summer, Muravev, who saw Petropavlovsk as his first line of defence, sent several hundred men to reinforce the town.[17]

An attack on a fortified town was not what had been intended when Price had set out in search of *Diana* and *Aurora*, though it was always likely that this would be the outcome, given the substantial lead the Russian ships had gained in the pursuit, and the unwillingness of the Russian navy to stand and fight the Royal Navy in the open sea. Price now had two choices: he could blockade the town or he could attack it. The first was hardly practicable. It was already the end of August; within a month any blockading vessel – and the ship had to be close by for the blockade to be both legal and effective – would be driven off its station. Ice would close the harbour and soon after the blockaders would be frozen out, and the blockaded ships in. The Allied squadron was thousands of miles from supplies. Therefore, to deal with *Aurora*, Price had to attack the town's defences.

He and Despointes discussed the matter. Neither wrote down what they intended at that meeting, but the plan was obvious, and was put into effect later. The batteries around the outer harbour were to be bombarded into silence, and then the Allies were to enter the inner harbour to attack the ships, or perhaps to bombard them into ruin from the outer harbour. This discussion took place on the morning of the 30th. At 1 p.m., Admiral Price, in his cabin on *President*, shot himself.

---

[17] Muravev's concerns are detailed in a memorandum for the Grand Duke Constantine (the tsar's brother), translated in *The Russian American Colonies*, 492–499.

He used a pistol, and aimed at his heart. He was not pronounced dead until some time later, at 4.30 p.m. Suicide is the only possible verdict, for this was a man familiar with weapons, and he would not have been careless with them. This was not a verdict to the liking of the Royal Navy, and various alternative theories were floated, but suicide is the only one which is convincing. The only close evidence is that of the chaplain of *President*, the Rev. Thomas Holme, who wrote to his wife about it. He went to the Admiral's cabin directly after he was shot, and Price said, 'Oh, Mr Holme, I have committed a fearful crime. Will God forgive me?' He had aimed at his heart, but had in fact taken the bullet in his lungs. Holme describes a truly morbid scene, with Price lamenting his crime, Holme reading and praying to him, and various officers, including Febvrier-Despointes, popping in to see how he was getting on.

The reason for his action is a more difficult thing to decide, and since he apparently left no explanation, we are in the dark. He had finished writing his official journal not long beforehand, and it gives no hint that he was other than normal in his state of mind. Holme says he was much affected by the death of a seaman in a fall a few days earlier, and they had then 'thought much of death and judgment'. This was not the best mood for a man about to lead his men into battle. Holme says that Price 'could not bear the thought of taking so many noble and gallant fellows into action ... whom some fault of his might bring to destruction'. Holme, in short, believed that Price had lost his nerve.

The obvious explanation is that he felt inadequate in the face of the coming action. It had certainly been a long time since he had seen action, in the war of 1812 against the United States. He had had a very active time between 1805 and 1815, three times wounded, twice taken prisoner. Maybe the prospect of fighting again depressed him, but if so he should never have accepted the command. One element in his decision must have been the long years of non-employment, of living on half-pay, which was a clear indication of the Admiralty's concept of his abilities, and he must have known that. Possibly he had felt that the search for the Russian ships had taken a long time. He had certainly not hurried, but there is no sign that he had deliberately delayed. He had to accommodate the squadron to the speed of the slowest ship, *Virago*, and he had to exercise tact in cooperating with the French. He cannot be convicted of being laggard in travelling the whole length of the Pacific, and he had found one of the Russian ships at the first Russian place he had investigated.

His conduct of his command had until that point been sensible and cautious. Holme says he had been 'very weak and vacillating in everything he did', but there is no sign of this in the evidence he left behind. He had done the tasks set him; he had taken sensible initiatives. He had investigated the Peruvian situation without getting involved; he had looked in at Honolulu to show the flag on his own initiative, just as he was expected to do; he had contacted the French squadron and had worked well with the French admiral; the possible threat of American privateers had been countered by a sensible measure; he had tracked down one of the Russian ships. Nothing he had undertaken had been badly done.

And yet he had killed himself. The only reasonable explanation is apprehension at the prospect of attacking Petropavlovsk, fear of failure, and a squeamishness resulting from a long absence from action. Failure was, of course, a real prospect, as the result showed, but his plan was the only one which gave any chance of success in the relatively brief period of time available to him. It was a reasonable plan in the circumstances, one which promised to give the Allies access to the harbour and to the ships they had been chasing, with relatively few casualties. Certainly the only alternatives – a blockade or a landing – were either impossible or impossibly costly.

The Admiral's slow death stopped any action during that day. Command of the whole force devolved to Rear-Admiral Despointes, but command of the British squadron now fell to Captain Nicholson of *Pique*. In consultation with Nicholson, the admiral decided that Price's original plan should be implemented next day. The death of Price does not seem to have otherwise affected the British. One of his officers considered that he was 'a healthy old man', but none expressed any affection for him – and he had been in the command for nine months by that time.

The next morning was calm. *Virago* again proved her worth. With *La Forte* and *Pique* lashed to either side, and *President* in tow behind, she pulled the whole Allied force into the outer harbour. The three ships were placed in line to tackle the Sharkoff battery on the end of the peninsula (so-called from the name of its commander), and the small three-gun battery to the south. Then the strong battery on the sandspit was shelled. This last had ten heavy guns and was clearly the most formidable, but the other two had to be dealt with first because of their enfilading fire.

It was normal for the Russians to count the number of guns on either side and to contrast them. Often this is thoroughly misleading – a case will appear later – but here the calculation is justified. The three ships had between them about 140 guns; the Sharkoff battery had five and the small battery across the harbour three. The difference is partly made up by the greater size and steadiness of the guns on the land, and the protection they had from the battery construction, but the ships were undoubtedly stronger.

The Sharkoff battery was tackled first. The three big ships were anchored in line, and opened fire; some fire was also directed at the small battery. Meanwhile *Virago* took on board marines and seamen from the bigger ships, both French and British, and landed them to eliminate the small battery. This had been under the command of Midshipman Popov, who pulled his gunners out of the battery when it came under attack, and retired up the nearby hill. The main difficulty the marines had was in getting through the dense undergrowth. The guns were spiked, either by Popov himself before he pulled out, or by the landing party – or perhaps by both – and the landing party then returned to *Virago*. In the meantime *Virago* had been rather battered by the fire of the guns of the great battery on the sandspit. When the landing party withdrew, Popov and his men returned, though their guns were useless.

The pounding of the Sharkoff battery had reduced it to impotence in the meantime. It was not well fortified and was backed by the rocky hillside of Signal Hill. Any rounds which missed the battery itself hit the hillside, bringing splinters and rocks down into the battery. The Allies also thought that other rounds which missed both the battery and the hillside ended up hitting the town or the ships, causing, so it was assumed, further damage.

This all took up the morning, by which time both outer batteries had been silenced. A breeze developed in the afternoon, and the three Allied ships were able to move further into the bay, to tackle the big battery on the sandspit at closer range. The guns on the Russian ships were also fired, now that they bore on the attackers, but an afternoon's bombardment silenced the battery, though the troops did not leave it, and a Russian sentinel had paced back and forth all afternoon, to the admiration of the Allied sailors. By the end of the day – it would be dark by soon after 5 p.m. – the Allies could assume that three of the enemy batteries had been silenced, if not wholly destroyed.

The three Allied ships withdrew for the night, *Virago* towing *La Forte*, the two British ships kedging out on their anchors. Casualties on both sides had been light, the Russians losing six men killed and thirteen wounded, the French one man killed and six wounded when *La Forte* was hit, the British none at all (though Chaplain Holme claims that there were up to a dozen dead and wounded on *President* – the fact that he was wrong about this rather makes one wonder if his account of Price's death was more imaginative than accurate). The expenditure of powder and shot and shell had been enormous: *La Forte* had fired over 800 rounds, the British ships fewer. Such a rate of firing could not be continued for much longer. The Russians were not much better off, but they had used fewer guns.

Next day, a party landed to bury Price, at a spot called Tarenski Harbour, or Bay, some distance from the town, across Avatcha Bay. He was buried without military honours 'under a small birch tree upon which we cut his initials and the date of his death'. The Russians meanwhile busily repaired their batteries, so that the Sharkoff battery and the sandspit battery were both back in fighting condition by the time the Allies had decided what to do, though they cannot have been as well made as before the bombardment began. The burial party had picked up two or three American sailors, deserters from whalers, who could give them some information about the town's defences. A small Russian sloop had also been captured, with nine sailors on board. The new information thus gained caused the existing plan to be abandoned.

Despointes and Nicholson discussed what to do. Possibly with a view to later enquiries, both conducted part of the discussion by letter, and summarised their conversations in writing later, Despointes in French, Nicholson in English; these letters are preserved in the Admiralty files.[18] After the first attack, and

---

[18] ADM 1/5631, and in *O'Byrne's Naval Annual*.

after the funeral, Admiral Despointes set out his objections to repeating the same tactics as before. He claimed there were two reasons for the Allies' presence in Petropavlovsk: to protect their commerce in the form of British and French whalers, and to make an attack on land posts. They had, he said, achieved the first aim (presumably by blocking up *Aurora* – he makes no mention of *Diana* at this point), but the second had proved very expensive. And he was not keen to try again, because the port was too well defended, by '*50 pièces de canon de gros calibre*'. Two frigates were not suitable vessels for such work.

It is worth commenting on Despointes' assertions, something Nicholson did not challenge. Price's mission was to find and eliminate the two Russian frigates he had been told had come to the Pacific; Despointes may have had other, variant, instructions, but the elimination of *Aurora* was surely part of them. Price, and therefore Nicholson, certainly did not have instructions to make attacks on land posts, though to eliminate *Aurora* and *Dvina* some sort of attack on Petropavlovsk was required. Despointes in other words was arguing for an extension of Price's/Nicholson's instructions. Nicholson showed himself not unwilling to accept this.

Nicholson replied to Despointes' letter the next day, after discussing the issue with Despointes in person. He rehearsed Despointes' summary, restated it in his own words, and then agreed with it, adding that it was necessary to keep the squadron in fighting trim in case other Russian warships turned up. But he then said that it should be possible to 'attempt the capture of the frigate ensconced in the harbour', by a landing. The ship could then be destroyed by turning the guns of the captured batteries onto it. He was evidently thinking of the sandspit battery, which was the only one whose guns could be brought to bear on the frigate without moving them a good distance and over hills. It might be that the guns would be spiked by the enemy; even so, half of the frigate's guns were on shore; her capture would not be too difficult, if a force of sailors and marines could occupy the sandspit. Nicholson said that the three British captains under his authority were also in favour of this idea.

It is evident that it was from the British side that the idea of a landing to destroy *Aurora* and *Dvina* came, perhaps from Nicholson himself. This in turn may well have been Price's eventual intention after the suppression of the outer batteries, but put off because the bombardment took longer than anticipated. Price had certainly included a small landing force to eliminate the small battery from the beginning, and it seems unlikely that the Russian ships could have been taken or destroyed without a landing. But it seems that Despointes, despite his earlier insistence that attacking land posts was included in his remit, now demurred.

Despointes' reply to this is not preserved, but Nicholson again summarised the admiral's arguments in his letter later the same day (2 September). Despointes had said, it seems, that he felt they ought to cruise to search for *Diana* 'and the corvette and brig accompanying her'. (This was correct information, but this was the first time anyone in the squadron had mentioned the other ships.) Nicholson bowed to his authority as commander-in-chief, though with no enthusiasm. This attitude, perhaps expressed with the superciliousness of a captain in the Royal Navy who was also a baronet, clearly got through to Despointes, who wrote asking a set of questions regarding the proposed landing, thereby indicating his partial agreement to undertake it. Nicholson quoted them in his reply on 3 September, in which he argued that the costs of the landing would certainly be worth the results. The batteries could be destroyed, he said, and the ships must thereupon be taken as a result; important prisoners would be taken, and the town's defences destroyed. Further, the Allied attack was necessary to avoid the 'loss of our good name', which would occur without making a second attempt.

Nicholson, no doubt, was keen to gain a reputation by commanding in such an action, but he was also concerned not to simply sail away after a single attempt. Despointes in his first letter said that he had discussed his ideas with his own captains, and with Captain Burridge of *President* and Commander Marshall of *Virago*. By the end of the correspondence these two captains had been brought round to Nicholson's view, at least so Nicholson said. We can only guess at what arguments Nicholson had used, but the 'loss of our good name', together with the prospect of gaining a reputation, may well have been those which worked with his colleagues, as they clearly did with him. And the Royal Navy did not believe it was acceptable to be beaten.

The two batteries on the seaward peninsula, at the saddle between the hills and at the northern end of Nikolski Hill, were known about, being visible from the sea. It was now learned, apparently from the American deserters, that there was a road of sorts leading into the town behind the northern battery (which the British referred to as Round Fort), and that another battery was in place to defend the town along that road, near the town itself. The total garrison of the town was estimated to be fairly small, and no doubt the casualties from the bombardment had been exaggerated in Allied minds. The new plan was to bombard the two seaward batteries, then land as large a force as could be gathered, sailors and marines, for an assault on the town by land along the 'road'.

This plan was arrived at after several long discussions between Admiral Despointes and the two senior French and British captains, Captain Nicholson and Captain de la Grandière of *La Forte*. It bore all the hallmarks of a compromise. There would be an equal number of French and British forces landed – 350 of each – and *President* would fire at one battery while *La Forte* tackled the other; when the batteries were silenced the landing would be made.

The attack took place on 4 September, four days after the original seaborne assault. At first all went well. The landing party was put on board *Virago*, which was lashed to *La Forte* and pulled *President* and, on the other side, pulled along the boats for the landing party, which were thereby protected by the larger ships from shots from the shore. *President* was dropped off opposite the saddle battery, and *La Forte* was pulled along to the Round Fort. Both batteries were rapidly silenced, the ships firing from no more than 600 yards. The numbers in the landing party were so great that the British ships at least were left seriously undermanned; *Pique* had only a skeleton crew, after as many men as possible were put on board *President* to make up the gun crews for the bombardment.

With the silencing of the Round Fort battery, the landing party was put on shore under the command of Captains Burridge and de la Grandière. So far all had gone to plan, such as it was, but that had been because the sailors were acting as sailors in warships. Now they were out of their element and things began to go wrong. The Russians, well warned that an attack was pending by the ships' movements and the bombardments, adopted the same tactics as Midshipman Popov – they left the shattered batteries and occupied the hills. As the Allies landed, they were fired on from the hill above by men who were invisible in the dense brush. It would seem that the plan had not been explained to the men, so, instead of marching around the northern end of the hill and then along the road, some of them moved up the hill to get at those who were firing at them.

Climbing the steep slope, and being fired on, and operating out of control, the sailors and marines were soon beaten. They reached the top of the hill, but still the Russians were hiding in the brush, and their fire was now so close and so intense that the British and French were driven back, over a precipice. The rest of the landing party had actually begun to move along on the lower land, as intended, attacking the town from the direction which had been planned, but were there bombarded by the battery near the town firing grape-shot. The Allied forces, in short, had divided and were defeated in detail. Both Allied groups now retired, or rather fled. Many of the men on the hills fell over the precipice and rolled down to the beach accompanied by rocks and boulders and loose earth, acquiring broken limbs in the process. Re-embarkation was successfully accomplished. The attempted harassment of this process by the Russian troops was blocked by a party of a hundred men who occupied the ruined battery and covered the evacuation.

Casualties in this attack were considerable. The Allies lost over fifty men killed or missing, and three times that in wounded, several of whom died during the next days. The Russians lost about half that, though they over-estimated the Allied casualties at 300. The landing party, 700 strong, had in fact been defeated by a Russian force which was less than half their number, but one which was better commanded and which fought more sensibly in the conditions.

The dead were buried next day, beside Admiral Price, who thus at least found some company, though rank and nationality remained distinct: one officer had his own grave, and the British and French sailors and marines a mass grave each. There seems to have been no real discussion of what to do next; withdrawal was the only option left. Another landing was not possible in the face of the local forces and after such casualties, and it seems that a return to the original bombardment plan was never considered. The Royal Navy did, however, gain a consolation prize as the squadrons left Avatcha Bay. Two Russian ships came in sight, a schooner and a three-masted merchant ship. The *Virago* took the schooner, called *Anadis*, which proved to be a Russian government vessel. *President* chased the merchant ship, *Sitka*, for four hours. She proved to be a Hamburg-built supply ship of the Russian-American Company, carrying supplies to Petropavlovsk, mainly gunpowder and flour, and some civilian passengers. The schooner was burnt; extravagant ideas about prize money stirred among the crew.

That was effectively the end of this campaign. It was impossible to get at *Aurora*. It was assumed that she had been badly damaged by the bombardment, but there is no evidence for this. It was now impossible to take the town. Damage and casualties were assumed, wrongly. The shortage of ammunition prevented a further attack, and the squadrons were now short of many supplies and had many wounded to care for. Winter was approaching and the ice would soon begin to form. The two squadrons separated: the British were to go to Vancouver Island for the winter, the French to San Francisco. Admiral Despointes was now ill, and died in March the next year. If it was intended to go on with the hunt for the Russian ships, or to make another attempt on Petropavlovsk to gain revenge, at least there would be commanders-in-chief next year who knew what to expect.

The basic problem had been that the aims of the expedition had always been unclear. Price and Despointes assumed that they had to search for *Diana* and *Aurora* to prevent them disrupting trade in the Pacific by commerce raiding. Despointes seems to have had instructions to attack Russian posts on land; the British had been told that Russian Alaska was neutral territory. (The Russians did not bother to suggest an agreement as to neutrality with the French government, assuming rightly that the British agreement would act as a restraint also on the French.) But there was no sign that commerce raiding was what the Russian ships would engage in. When *Aurora* was located it was assumed that it was necessary to sink or disable her, but it must have been clear that, having reached a friendly port, the ship was simply staying there; transferring many of her guns to the shore batteries made that clear.

Once it was decided to attack, there was a fatal dithering over how to do it. Price's plan evidently was a bombardment to deal with the defending batteries around the outer harbour. The obvious next move would be to reach the sandspit, seize a beachhead there, and then attack the ships. This was, it seems, what Nicholson, who would by then have had access to Price's papers, originally proposed to Despointes. There was no point in attacking the town, for it was the ships alone which were the Allies' problem. It may not even have been necessary to seize a beachhead, for most of *Aurora* was reachable from ships in the outer harbour, and many of its guns had been landed, as Nicholson pointed out in one of his letters. If the big sandspit battery could be dominated – as it had been in the first bombardment – the ships in the harbour could then have been so badly damaged by bombardment from the ships as to be rendered useless, at least until next year.

This might have worked, though some casualties were unavoidable as the ships moved closer in. But Price killed himself, possibly after contemplating the casualties his men might suffer, and Despointes, once persuaded to make a landing, evidently felt that a different method of attack was requisite. The discussions on this – perhaps 'disputes' would be a better term – took so long that the Russians were ready when the new attack came. It seems probable that the Russian defenders had been shaken by the relative ease with which their main batteries had been destroyed and reduced to silence. A swift follow-up attack was clearly what should have been attempted. Instead several days were occupied in burying Price, seeking information, discussing what to do, and making a new plan.

This new plan involved using marines and seamen, used to fighting on board ship, to climb steep, forested hills under fire, without preparation, and without the troops understanding what was intended. The difficulties of the terrain had been clear in the landing which had dealt with the small three-gun Popov battery on the first day of the fighting: the men had had more trouble getting through the brush than in attacking the battery; it was surely clear that the larger landing party would have the same problem.

Above all, the men were being sent in pursuit of the wrong objective. The only purpose in conducting a land attack was to capture the town, but this was not what the squadrons were there for. To attack by land was to attack the Russians at their strongest point: they had soldiers whose *métier* had been to fight in just this sort of landscape, and they acquitted themselves very well in the face of the Allies' greater numbers. In retrospect it seems clear that the worst service Price ever did was to shoot himself and leave Despointes and Nicholson in command, and Despointes' plan – presuming it was his – was very bad.[19]

Not only that, it was also badly executed. This began with the command system: two naval captains in charge meant a divided command. As soon as they landed, it seems clear that the sailors and marines largely dissolved into a rabble. The charge up the hill was pointless and produced wholesale disorganisation so that any officers who tried to exercise command – none seem to have done so – could not do so because the men had scattered. The only group who tried to attack the town along the road, as intended, were stopped as soon as they came within range of the grapeshot of the town battery, partly because they were fewer in number than had been intended, and partly because they could hear the fighting continuing on the hill to their right, and behind them. A year and a half later, the First Lord of the Admiralty, who had by then had time to read the papers, commented to Price's successor that the land attack had been 'badly managed. How far it was Burridge's fault I cannot say, but from the account I heard of it not only was the attack wrongly made but badly executed.'[20] It was a fair summary.

All together the attack was a failure due to bad planning, minimal reconnaissance, and incompetent command. It deserved to be defeated, just as the earlier bombardment, had the plan been carried through, deserved to succeed. One of the most notable results, however, is that Price and Despointes both died and escaped blame, and so, even more remarkably, did Nicholson. Captain Burridge was the one who appears to have been most severely criticised.

---

[19] The Russian account in Vladimir, *Russia on the Pacific*, 216–224, indicates a second attack by a landing party from *La Forte* at the saddle battery, but this did not take place.

[20] BL Add. Mss 49565, 1 April 1856. ('BL' references are in the British Library.)

3

Japan, China, the Amur River

Commodore Matthew Perry's voyage to Japan had been well publicised, deliberately so. This gave time for the Japanese to be informed, by way of the Dutch factory at Nagasaki, so that the government in Edo might prepare itself. At the same time it also alerted European states to the prospect of the United States gaining a particular advantage in Japan. This had not happened in China, where the opening brought about by the British victory in the war of 1839–1842 had been rapidly followed by the extension of the same privileges to several other Western states. But Japan was known to have an effective government in full control of its territory, so that an agreement with one foreign power might well lead to the exclusion of all the rest. The best way to ensure that the United States did not monopolise Japanese attention was therefore for other powers to go there as well.

The British certainly intended to do so, and had been discussing a visit for several years, but their forces in Chinese waters – and it had to be an armed visitation – were fully occupied, not merely with the Chinese pirates and the Burmese war, but with the rapid changes in command which the China Station underwent – from Collier to Austin to Pellew to Stirling in three years. France had naval forces in the East which could be sent to Japan. Russia, a close neighbour of Japan's to the north, which had had occasional dealings with that country for a couple of centuries, sent a full expedition from Europe, on the Perry model.

The limitations on Russian power in the area were, however, considerable. The expedition, headed by the Vice-Admiral Efim Vasilevich Putiatin, sailed from Kronstadt in October 1852 with one frigate, the *Pallas*.[1] Putiatin first went to Britain where he

---

[1] G. A. Lensen, *Russia's Japan Expedition, 1852–1855*, Gainesville, FL,

purchased an iron-hulled screw schooner, the *Fearless*, and renamed it *Vostok* ('East'). He also bought four 68-lb guns for the *Pallas* and a supply of new carbines. When *Pallas* arrived at Portsmouth, the ship required repair – the Russian Admiralty had not allocated a new ship to the expedition – and Putiatin decided not to risk the Cape Horn route, as had been planned, but to go by way of the less stormy Cape of Good Hope. Two other Russian ships had been told to join him at Hawai'i, the corvette *Olivutza*, and the Russian-American Company transport *Kniaz Menshikov*; he sent word to them of the change in plan, and appointed a new rendezvous at the Bonin Islands south of Japan. Also *Pallas* and *Vostok,* using as they did different propulsion systems, sailed separately.

Putiatin's experience with *Pallas* led him to request a replacement, and from Singapore in June 1853 he asked for the new frigate *Diana*. By way of Hong Kong, where he joined up again with *Vostok*, he reached the Bonin Islands early in August. The other two ships had already arrived, but the squadron had been unable to buy supplies at the islands, which had all been bought up by Perry not long before. This was in a way good news, for it meant that Perry's work in Japan was clearly not yet complete. Putiatin took his squadron north and entered Nagasaki harbour on 22 August 1853.

The pattern of his contacts with the Japanese authorities resembled Perry's: the Japanese policy was 'one of peace and procrastination'. Putiatin's dealings with Japanese officials were long-winded, repetitive, and without any immediate result. He spent three months on this frustrating task, and then sailed off to Shanghai. In the meantime he had learnt that the crisis with the Ottoman Empire was now involving Britain and France, and it looked steadily more serious with every message he received. At Shanghai he heard that *Diana* was on the way to join him, coming round Cape Horn. He sent orders, which were to await her at Hawai'i, that she should go to De Castries Bay in the Gulf of Tartary, well out of the way, and a place it was unlikely any enemies would think of as a Russian base. Early in January (1854) he was back again in Nagasaki harbour.

1955, and *The Russian Push Towards Japan: Russo-Japanese Relations, 1697–1875*, Princeton, NJ, 1959, are the main sources for the account here of the Russian expedition.

Another month passed. Perry's tactic of confronting the Japanese Shogunate in Edo Bay was more productive than Putiatin's of using Nagasaki, which was a long way from Edo; the distance could be used as a delaying tactic by a government intent on procrastination. Consequently, although Putiatin spent longer in Japan than Perry, it was Perry who got the first treaty, opening two small and distant ports – Shimoda on the end of its peninsula south of Edo, and Hakodate in Hokkaido – to minor contacts.

Putiatin took his squadron to sea again early in February, going first south to the Ryukyu Islands, while *Vostok*, which he used as the means of contact with outside events while he was held in Nagasaki, joined him from Shanghai. By this time it was known that war between Russia and the Ottoman Empire had begun, and that France and Britain were increasingly threatening. Putiatin went on further to the south, to Manila in the Spanish Philippines. A French naval steamer, the *Colbert*, was in the harbour, and the Spanish authorities were distinctly unwelcoming of the Russian presence. Spanish-Russian relations were in a bad state at the time because of the Russian attitude to the Spanish queen. The recent marriage of the Emperor Napoleon III to a Spanish woman put these neighbours on friendly terms. *Colbert* would be certain to report the Russians' presence. These factors persuaded the Russians to leave Manila once more on 11 March.

The *Olivutza* was sent to Petropavlovsk; the other three ships then returned yet again to Nagasaki, but only for a week. Perhaps Putiatin knew that the Japanese were still negotiating with Perry, and that until the negotiations were concluded, no other country would be able to make any progress. Meanwhile, by his repeated visits, he was able to keep on reminding the Japanese of his presence and of his wishes, without being too assertive.

He took his ships north this time, surveying the east coast of Korea, and making fleeting contact with the reclusive Korean government, which was even less welcoming, if that were possible, than Japan's. By this time, early in May, the wider war had been going on in Europe for two months. The news reached Hong Kong in May, but it seems that Putiatin had it only a very little later, probably through Shanghai and *Vostok*. He certainly received new orders by way of *Vostok*, which he met again on the coast of Sakhalin. He was to go to De Castries

Bay, in the Gulf of Tartary, and place himself under the orders of Governor-General Muravev. He did so, but had to wait there for Muravev's arrival; the two men met there at last on 4 July.

Muravev had refused to allow the news of war with Britain and France to deflect him from his primary purpose in the East, which was to open up the Amur route from inland Siberia to the Pacific. After all, the outbreak of war with Britain fitted in perfectly with his belief that Britain aimed to establish control of the Amur by seizing control of the estuary; all the more urgent, therefore, was it to seize control first for Russia. On 14 May 1854, as the message that war had begun was reaching Stirling in Hong Kong and Price in Callao, and as Admiral Putiatin was surveying the coast of Korea, Muravev set out on his grand adventure.

His earlier preparations had all led up to this expedition. He had sent a one-man expedition along the river, and the man had disappeared. He had sent exploring expeditions around the Sea of Okhotsk, which had established posts on Sakhalin, on the mainland opposite, and at the mouth of the Amur and along the lower course of that river. Now he organised a grand expedition which was to link up these several coastal posts with the main centre of Russian authority in the east, at Irkutsk on Lake Baikal. He intended to take a substantial force along the Amur River all the way to the river's mouth, a distance of about 3000 kilometres.

This risked conflict with China. Desultory negotiations between Russia and China at several places over several years on the topic of trade had made a little progress. It was clear that China was very reluctant to agree to any changes. There were also discordant, even contradictory, voices on the subject within the Russian government, some of whom were not anxious to tangle with the Chinese.[2] In the result, the dominant voice was Muravev's, in favour of expansion, but only because he was present on the border in person. He did not have the full support of the central government in St Petersburg, but he understood clearly that a forward move on the Chinese frontier, in the context of a war with Britain, would gain imperial approval, at least if it was successful. And with the central government distracted by its war in Europe, this was the best

---

2 Semenov, *Siberia*, 260–269; Quested, *Expansion of Russia*, 31–32, 45–46.

moment for a headstrong ambitious governor in eastern Siberia to launch out on his own.

For Muravev's eyes were fixed on Britain as his enemy, not just in the Turkish war, but as the one power which he thought was intent on seizing control of the mouth of the Amur. He was convinced of Britain's greed and enmity, and the new war convinced Muravev that it was necessary to reach and secure control of the Amur mouth before the British forestalled him. Beyond that, the minor posts which had been set up by his agents in the last few years in Sakhalin and on the mainland were now very vulnerable to the dominant sea power in the region. The area of danger and action was clearly the Pacific coast; he would conduct the river expedition himself.

The Amur expedition therefore had to be substantial. Muravev thought he might be fighting the British when he reached the Pacific, and the only way to get past the Chinese fortified town on the river at Aigun was by having with him such overwhelming numbers and power as to convince the Chinese commander in the fort that attempting to stop him would be pointless. On 14 May, amid great ceremony, a speech by Muravev, and blessings by a local priest, the convoy set sail from Nerchinsk on the Shilka River, a major tributary of the Amur. This was the obvious place to begin, but it was also full of symbolism: it was the place where the treaty of 1689 was agreed, between a small Russian party and a Chinese negotiating team backed by large forces; and Muravev made sure that the icon of the Virgin from Albazin, a town which had been founded and then abandoned to the Chinese after 1689, was present with the priests. More ceremonies occurred at Ust-Strielka, where the Shilka joins the Amur, and at the site of Albazin itself. The whole expedition was given a powerful religious-nationalistic air by its commander.

The expedition consisted of about a thousand soldiers, including a line battalion of about 800 men, a group of Cossacks, and a division of mountain artillery, and was carried on a fleet of seventy-five barges and rafts led by the small armed steamer *Argun*. It was the size of the force Muravev commanded which convinced the Chinese commander at Aigun that he could not prevent the passage. But Muravev also gave him a way out. He had informed the commander and the provincial governor that he was coming, and how many troops he would bring with him. This information had also been sent on to Peking, but so late that no reply had been received, and too late for instructions to reach Aigun from Peking. This Muravev no doubt knew would happen. So the fort commander at Aigun was trapped: he did not know if he should try to stop the expedition or not; and he could see that he was militarily quite unable to stop it anyway. He could be pretty sure that whatever he did he would be in the wrong.

He, like the Japanese government, procrastinated – just as his own government was also procrastinating. He spoke of the impossibility of navigating the river, which was dangerous, so he said, but his bluff was called. Above all, he could see that the sheer size and strength of Muravev's force was such that if it came to a fight he would certainly lose, while to make a fight of it would involve his emperor in yet another war while rebellion growled in the south. Then there was the little steamer, pumping out smoke, clanking and groaning, a vessel the like of which neither he nor his people had ever seen before. It was all too much. The commander let the expedition through, passing the problem up the bureaucratic ladder for someone else to deal with.

Muravev had sent a note to Peking late in April about his expedition, but it did not reach its destination until July; by that time a report had come from the governor of Kirin, Chingshun, about the actual expedition. He was passing on the report made by the Deputy Commander of Aigun, Husunpu, who had had the task of actually interviewing Muravev. This message reached Peking late in June, long after the Russian expedition had reached its destination. (The Deputy Commander claimed that there were 2000 men involved; this is the only time the Russians told the truth about their numbers, and yet the commander decided there were twice as many; either he could not estimate numbers accurately, or he exaggerated to excuse his failure to prevent the expedition.) The Xianfeng emperor took note, refused to believe Muravev's excuse of needing to confront the British, but added, 'it seems unworthy to put difficulties in their way'. The commander at Aigun was ordered to improve his defences; this would not be enough to prevent any further expeditions; he was not sent any more troops. He cannot have been sorry to see that the Russians would be attacking the British – the defeat by the latter in the First China War cut deep.

While the Chinese government was slowly informing itself

of the Amur expedition, the expedition itself had sailed on. Despite under-estimating the distance to be travelled by more than 500 kilometres, the post at Mariinsk was reached on 14 June. There had, of course, been problems along the way – shipwrecks, unknown hazards, rocks, and so on – but the accomplishment of the voyage shows that Muravev had been correct in his assumption that the river could become a useful highway to the sea. He also noted, with satisfaction, that since Aigun there had been no sign at all of any Chinese authority anywhere along the river. Wherever he met groups of the natives, he found them willing, so he claimed, to become the subjects of the tsar, though whether they understood what that meant is less than clear.

Mariinsk was chosen as his temporary headquarters. It was 300 kilometres upstream from the mouth of the Amur, on the shore of Lake Kizi, a wide lake which emptied into the Amur from the east, and whose eastern end was within less than fifty kilometres of the sea at De Castries Bay. Muravev made the journey himself, along a route cut through the forest. He found the steamer *Vostok* at the bay and used it to sail south to Imperatorskaia Gavan where he met Admiral Putiatin. Then he sailed in *Vostok* north, through the strait separating Sakhalin and the mainland, to Petrovskoi, north of the estuary. The ship was sent on to Aian, and Muravev went by land to Nikolaevsk.[3]

On meeting Putiatin, Muravev found that the Admiral had collected the small Russian detachment from Muravevsk on Aniwa Bay in the south of Sakhalin, and had brought the men to Imperatorskaia Gavan, on the grounds that such a small outpost was needlessly exposed in wartime. Now Muravev had to decide on his own policy with regard to these small posts. Nevelskoi at Nikolaevsk had wanted to spread his men out all over the area, including Sakhalin, to try to force the British to declare a blockade, and so implicitly acknowledge Russian sovereignty. Muravev, however, decided that it was more important to be strong in the most important places. Small groups could be mopped up all too easily, as Putiatin saw, possibly leaving no Russians in the area at all, which might be decisive when it came to negotiating peace.

---

[3] Vladimir, *Russia on the Pacific*, 210–211.

Mariinsk was the key position. It was well up the river and yet within relatively easy reach of both Nikolaevsk, near the estuary, and De Castries Bay; but when Muravev arrived he found it was held by only eight men – not that there were many Russians in the whole area until Muravev's expedition arrived. Nikolaevsk was the place at which the entrance to the river must be guarded; it had only thirty men. There were twenty-five at Petrovskoi, on the shore of the Sea of Okhotsk, north of the estuary, and ten each at De Castries Bay and Imperatorskaia Gavan. On the other hand, Muravev had brought his reinforcements, and he now had considerable naval forces as well. *Pallas*, though in poor condition, was at Imperatorskaia Gavan, and the steamship *Vostok* had demonstrated its usefulness repeatedly both to Putiatin and Muravev – it had successfully got through from De Castries Bay to Nikolaevsk, despite grounding several times. Muravev also had three transports, *Irtysh*, *Dvina* and *Baikal*, with six, ten and four guns respectively, and two company ships, *Nikolai* and *Kniaz Menshikov*, unarmed. *Diana* arrived at De Castries Bay soon afterwards in accordance with the orders sent her by Putiatin. Most of these ships were armed, the two frigates with forty guns or more each.[4] (And the *Aurora* was soon to arrive at Petropavlovsk, though Muravev probably knew nothing of it until later.) With his thousand men Muravev now also had the seagoing ships with which to move them wherever he wished in his area.

Muravev chose to hold Mariinsk with the Cossacks and 200 of his soldiers, who were to work to expand the forest path towards De Castries Bay into a passable road. The mountain guns were also held at Mariinsk, whence they could be moved by water to other places. Two hundred more men were sent to Nikolaevsk. He was therefore establishing a firm grip on the river mouth with substantial forces – substantial, that is, for the area. The rest of his soldiers, 400 men, were sent to reinforce Admiral Zavoiko's forces at Petropavlovsk in the *Dvina* transport, where they were present in time to drive off the Allies' attack at the beginning of September. The men collected from Sakhalin were sent on to Alaska. They were employees of the Company, which had in effect now lost control of the Okhotsk

---

[4] T. W. Atkinson, *Travels in the Regions of the Upper and Lower Amoor and the Russian Acquisitions on the Confines of India and China*, London 1860, 120–122.

area of operations: they would be better employed where the Company still operated.[5]

The movements of the Russian ships under Admiral Putiatin were watched with some attention by British officials in the East, in so far as they could be discovered. The problem was that once having pinpointed them in one location, these same officials then made guesses as to where they thought the squadron would go next. At Manila, the British Consul, J. W. Farrer, saw the Russian squadron on its visit in March, and at once wrote to Vice-Admiral Pellew reporting their numbers, names and strengths (being slightly wrong in all cases). He then wrote that 'on the night of the 11th [they] left for Kamschatka, or for Batavia, as it is thought'. Since these two places were in diametrically opposite directions this looks very like deliberate Russian misinformation.[6]

Farrer also, in the same letter, reported Putiatin as claiming that Commodore Perry 'had taken possession of' the Ryukyu Islands in the name of the United States. There was certainly some dispute between Perry and the local authorities there. The Ryukyus were in the control of Japanese officials working for one of the lords in the southern island of Kyushu, who was only partly under the control of the Shogunate in Edo. No doubt Putiatin was interested in any dispute between Japanese officials and the American expedition. It may well be that he had exaggerated the problem – the United States certainly did not 'take possession of' the Ryukyus. This looks as though Putiatin was carefully sowing seeds of confusion on top of his deceptions. If the British were investigating Batavia and the Ryukyus, and perhaps Kamchatka, he could go elsewhere with relative impunity.

Pellew, who had been dismissed by the time Farrer's letter reached him, and was waiting at Point de Galle in Ceylon to be relieved by Stirling, sent it on to the Admiralty. He added a covering letter which added a further layer to the misinformation, reporting that he had spoken to a Spanish officer who had been at Manila, a colonel, who had told him that *Pallas* had been damaged and that Putiatin was looking for a neutral port in which to stay while making repairs.[7] This was also partly

---

[5] Vladimir, *Russia on the Pacific*, 211–212.
[6] ADM 1/5629, 15 March 1854.
[7] ADM 1/5629, 15 April 1854.

true, for *Pallas* had been aground twice during its voyage, rot had been found in its timbers, and Putiatin had asked for *Diana* as a replacement, but he was not searching for a port in which to make repairs. The story had its effect, however. Apart from China, where the British were ubiquitous along the coast, the nearest neutral port with facilities for repairing a ship such as *Pallas* was either Batavia or Surabaya in Dutch Java. This therefore reinforced Farrer's conjectures. Pellew added his incendiary opinions on the Ryukyus and the United States as well. If this had all started with Putiatin's talk in Manila – and he by that time was sailing north along the coast of Korea – it was well done.

This was the sort of information Stirling received when he took command in Chinese waters in May, at more or less the same time that the news arrived that Russia and Britain were at war. By that time it is likely that rather more firm information had arrived that the Russian ships had been at Nagasaki in April – the Dutch there busily informed on everyone to everyone – but had then quickly left. The purpose of Putiatin's expedition was as well known as that of Perry, and it was likely that he would not move far from Japan until his mission was accomplished. But within a month the Hong Kong Superintendent of Trade, Sir John Bowring, passed on further information, this time concerning the Russian activities on the Amur. His letter is dated 14 June, and he refers to the Russian wish for free navigation along the river. His authority was a French steamer captain at Nanking, who claimed that a treaty had been agreed ceding all the territory north of the river to Russia.[8] This was not the case, but, of course, it is a sign that the Russian demands on China were becoming known, and this naturally directed British attention towards the Amur.

The British had not shown any interest in the Amur area before, Muravev's fantasies about British ambitions for the area notwithstanding, so it was in fact Muravev's own voyage down the river which stimulated that interest, and it had come by way of the captain of a French ship at Nanking, who had heard of it in conversation. Bowring reported from another source, the vice-consul at Ningpo, who had been told by the Catholic Archbishop of Chekiang (a Frenchman), who had been at Manila

---

8 ADM 1/5629, 14 June 1854.

when Putiatin arrived and had spoken with him, that Putiatin was well aware that war was imminent; he would therefore be on his guard. This is the sort of intelligence everyone had to work with during the next several months, second-, third- and fourth-hand rumours, conjectures, distortions and misinformation.

No doubt other, even less credible, items of information came to Stirling as he settled into his new command and struggled to dominate the Chinese pirates who threatened to strangle European trade on the China Sea. Meanwhile Admirals Price and Despointes chased the Russian ships the length of the Pacific and suffered death and defeat at the hands of Admiral Zavoiko and Muravev's reinforcements at Petropavlovsk in September; and Governor-General Muravev fortified the entrance to the Amur River in June and July. The news of the repulse of the Allies from Kamchatka permitted Muravev to release Putiatin to continue his mission to Japan. *Diana* had arrived; *Pallas*, on its last legs, was now virtually abandoned at Imperatorskaia Gavan, crewed by a caretaker group of just ten men. On 15 October, Putiatin in *Diana* sailed again for Japan.[9]

By this time Rear-Admiral Stirling had freed himself from local cares in China sufficiently to make his own visit to Japan. He would have known of Putiatin's several visits, and in fact he went to Nagasaki, the same port used by Putiatin, not by accident. It was, of course, the one place in Japan with a permanent foreign presence, the Dutch post at Deshima Island, but Perry had gone to Edo Bay, with success; Stirling could have done the same. Perhaps he felt it would be less threatening to go to Nagasaki, but the prospect of finding or meeting the Russian squadron there was surely an added inducement.

His concern, Stirling said later, was mainly to ensure that Japan was not being used by the Russians as a base from which to sail to harass British shipping; a second concern was to do just that himself. He wished to have some Japanese ports made available for his own ships to acquire supplies of food and water, and fuel if possible. The negotiations were bedevilled by translation difficulties, and by the failure of the Japanese negotiators to understand what he wanted, which was the fairly abstract concept of benevolent neutrality, an idea confined to European usage. But Stirling eventually got his treaty: he could

---

[9] Lensen, *Russia's Japan Expedition*.

use the ports of Nagasaki and Hakodate. The first was the site of the Dutch factory, and so fairly used to foreign vessels; the other was in the northern island of Hokkaido, one of the ports also conceded to the United States' use, and well away from Edo, so the foreigners would be out of sight.[10]

The contrasting concessions to the British and the United States negotiators reflect the differing purposes of Stirling and Perry. The latter was trying to open up Japan to foreign, specifically US, trade; the former was concerned more with the immediate problem of the Russian war. For Stirling, Hakodate, the closest Japanese port to the Russian territories, was to be his advanced base. When the text of the treaty was examined in London it was deemed unsatisfactory precisely because it ignored most commercial issues, and Stirling was told to try again.

The treaty was signed at Nagasaki on 14 October, the day before Putiatin and *Diana* left De Castries Bay to return to Japan. This time, instead of going to Nagasaki, which would be to advertise his presence, he went to Shimoda.[11] This was the other port opened to United States use by the treaty negotiated by Commodore Perry, and was much closer to Edo than was Nagasaki. Even so, the negotiations still went slowly and he and the Russians in *Diana* were still there two months later. This was not a hardship, of course, since there were no Russian ports available by this time; all their Pacific ports were iced up from October. In effect the war in the Pacific was now suspended for the winter; nothing could be done until the ice released its grip in the north, when the Russian ships could be released, or the Allies' ships could reach them. The winter was thus the time for planning for the next year.

The news of Price's and Despointes' disaster at Petropavlovsk reached the Admiralty in November. Price was still being referred to as in command in the Pacific on the 20th; by the 25th his successor had been appointed.[12] It was in exactly that period that news of the defeat was sent on to London by Sir John Bowring, to the Foreign Office. He based his report on the

---

10 W. G. Beazley, *Great Britain and the Opening of Japan,* London 1951, 113–144; Stirling's report of his activities and negotiations is at ADM 1/5629, 26 October 1854.
11 Lensen, *Russia's Japan Expedition.*
12 ADM 2/1699, 28 November 1854; BL Add. Mss 79612, 25 November 1854.

interview of Captain Westergaard by the British Consul Rutherford Alcock at Shanghai, and he was to some degree uncertain, referring to 'some disasters' at Petropavlovsk.[13] The Admiralty's information had clearly travelled by way of the United States, and no one in Captain Nicholson's command had thought to send the news directly to China.

Yet it was the China Station which was to be most closely concerned with Russian events from now on. The Admiralty finally put the various elements together early in December and wrote to Stirling on the 4th, reporting the appointment of the new Pacific commander-in-chief to replace Price. He was to be reinforced by two of Stirling's ships, for the purpose of dealing with Petropavlovsk – though the word 'revenge' was not actually used. The extent of Russian activity at the mouth of the Amur, rumours of which had arrived, was also to be investigated, and this was to be Stirling's own task.[14] It was also realised all round that there was no need to hurry. The seas around Kamchatka and in the Sea of Okhotsk as far south as the mouth of the Amur would be closed by ice until April or May. It gave the British several months to get ready.

The new commander-in-chief of the Pacific station was Rear-Admiral Henry William Bruce, a scion of a Scottish gentry family (like Stirling). He was, like Price, in his sixties; he had reached post rank six years later than Price, however, in 1821, and had received his flag two years before his appointment to the Pacific. He had had the usual breaks in his service, but at least he had seen action recently, as Commodore of the anti-slavery patrol off West Africa, where his vigour had been notable. His orders are dated 28 November, but he had been contacted soon after Price's death became known in the Admiralty, and his appointment was dated from the 25th. It will have taken a day or two to draw up his orders; the Admiralty had in fact acted very quickly.

The Admiralty had been able to exercise close direction over affairs in the Black Sea and the Baltic during the recent fighting.[15] Indeed the development of the telegraph and railways and steamers had made it possible to do so in Euro-

---

[13] ADM 1/5661, 22 November 1854.
[14] ADM 2/1697, 4 December 1854.
[15] A. D. Lambert, *The Crimean War: British Grand Strategy 1853–56*, Manchester 1990.

pean waters for a decade already. This was not possible in the Pacific, though there was already talk in the United States of a Pacific cable, and one American promoter was soon pushing the idea of a telegraph line through Siberia and Alaska into Canada and the western United States. So Bruce, like Price and Stirling, would have to exercise his initiative within the context and limits set by his orders. This, however, did not stop the Admiralty from giving detailed instructions in a rather verbose manner.

In essence the instructions were to collect and supply the squadron, join with the French, and attack the Russian ships in Petropavlovsk. Bruce was expressly forbidden to land an attacking force. 'The destruction of the batteries and of the town is of secondary importance', he was told, but Price and his colleagues had seen right away that the batteries at least had to be destroyed if the ships were to be reached. Bruce was to receive reinforcements, two ships detailed from the China Station by Admiral Stirling, and HMS *Monarch*, a line of battle ship of 84 guns, which was to be sent out as his flagship, though he was not to wait for her arrival if the rest of the ships were assembled. When she arrived she would be the most powerful warship between the American coast and Africa. In fact sending *Monarch* was not just a part of the Russian war; her presence was as much designed to impress the United States. US foreign policy tended only to respect immediate power. The issues of the Hawaiian kingdom, Vancouver Island and the Panamanian isthmus were all involved, and now William Walker, an American adventurer, was operating in Nicaragua, another potential canal route. The effects of the war in the Pacific were not confined to Russia and its immediate enemies.[16]

The United States, under President Franklin Pierce, was still in an expansionist mood. Commodore Perry's intervention in Japan was part of this, and the filibustering of Walker in Nicaragua was another example. Pierce had expressed the prevailing American political attitude to the European war to E. A. Stehl, the new Russian chargé d'affaires in Washington, in March 1854: if the United States was compelled to become involved, 'one may say with certainty ... that we will not take the side of the enemies of Russia'. This convoluted formulation

---

[16] ADM 2/1697, 28 November 1854.

was hardly encouraging to Russia, but it makes it clear that, to the United States, it was Britain which was the immediate menace. This was one of the factors in the British government's acceptance of the idea of Alaskan neutrality.

The US press had made a good deal of the Allied defeat at Petropavlovsk, and so gaining revenge for that was necessary, since the destruction of Russian naval strength in the Pacific would be a deterrent to US actions: hence also the presence of *Monarch*. Bruce was thus as concerned with the policy of the United States as with the war with Russia, and his orders to, in effect, retire to patrol the American coast after dealing with Petropavlovsk were in part designed to avoid aggravating Anglo-American relations, but also to maintain a strong Royal Navy presence in full view of the United States. By concentrating naval activity in the western Pacific, the British assumed, rightly, that the possibility of US involvement in the war was much reduced.[17]

Bruce reached Valparaiso, travelling by way of New York and Panama, on 6 February, a journey from Britain of about six weeks. He left Valparaiso with *President* and *Rattlesnake* (no longer part of the Arctic adventure) on 26 February, leaving *Obligado* at Valparaiso. *Pique* and the store ship *Nereus* had already been ordered to Honolulu and on to the rendezvous which had been appointed for the meeting with the two ships he was being loaned from the China squadron. Bruce was operating at a much greater energy level than Price had been – but then this was wartime and Price had been appointed in peacetime.

Bruce had met much the same set of problems at Valparaiso as had confronted Price a year before. He had to write letters to all the governments and British consuls, from Chile to Vancouver Island and from Panama to Raiatea and Honolulu, announcing his appointment. The Chilean government had 'appropriated' two anchors from *Nereus*, and he had to arrange for them to be paid for, though no doubt he would rather have had the anchors back. Peru was still in upheaval and the present government refused permission for a survey to be made of the guano deposits in the Chincha Islands, duties

---

[17] V. N. Ponomarev, 'Russian Policy and the United States during the Crimean War', in H. Ragsdale (ed.), *Imperial Russian Foreign Policy*, Cambridge, MA, 1993, 13–192.

on which provided the government with a very large slice of its revenue. The proposed survey was more to discover what conditions on the islands were like for the Chinese workers than to gain information about the guano itself. A murder in Valparaiso also concerned Bruce.[18]

There was also a letter awaiting him from the consul at Honolulu. This may have included details of the fighting at Petropavlovsk, for Consul-General Miller had been diligent in enquiring of visiting ships' captains as to what had happened. But the main problem was that King Kamehameha III had died on 15 December. His nephew and heir, Alexander Liholiho, was proclaimed king within an hour throughout the city, and he took his oath to maintain the Constitution a month later. It was nevertheless, as in all monarchies, a nervous time. The new king took the throne name Kamehameha IV and quickly reappointed the former ministers; continuity of a sort was thereby guaranteed. Nevertheless Miller asked again that a Royal Navy ship be sent to provide an indication of support for the new king.[19]

The instructions with which Bruce had been provided before he set out for his command were supplemented by later letters which he received when he called at Callao on 6 March. One letter reminded him that the Russian-American Company's territories in America were to be regarded as neutral, but 'this neutrality only extends to operations on land, and that the ports and coasts of the Russian Possessions in question will be liable to a naval blockade'. He had been instructed to investigate Sitka in Alaska, the Russian-American Company's headquarters, if the ships at Petropavlovsk had already left, and had been instructed not to indulge in landings, so this was a not-too-subtle reminder of these aspects of his orders. The prohibition on landings was further driven home by another letter, which commented on Nicholson's report, which had apparently only reached London after Bruce's departure. Nicholson's zeal and gallantry were appreciated, but the landings he had ordered were to be taken as an object lesson in what to avoid.

A third Admiralty letter implied a change in Bruce's tasks. On 20 January he was ordered to return the China ships to

---

[18] ADM 50/308, Bruce Journal, 6 February–6 March 1855.
[19] ADM 50/308, Bruce Journal, 6 February 1855; Kuykendall, *Hawaiian Kingdom*, vol. 1, 427–428, and vol. 2, 33–39.

Stirling as soon as his work at Petropavlovsk was completed, and in addition he was to send *Pique* across to Stirling. In his original instructions there was added a vague paragraph that 'every effort should be made to sweep both shores of the Northern Pacific to destroy the enemy's ships, and to harass and injure the Russian settlements to the utmost'. But now he was to give up control of three of the ships, *Pique*, a 40-gun frigate, and the steamers *Encounter* and *Barracouta* (Stirling's ships) which were the most useful of his vessels for such work. The implication was that Stirling would be doing the harassing and injuring in the western Pacific, while Bruce retired, as he eventually did, to the traditional area of his command on the eastern, American, coast, and the islands of the southern Pacific.[20]

Bruce, with *President* and *Rattlesnake*, reached Callao on 6 March, where he was joined by the *Naiad* store ship and the French frigate *Alceste*. He found that the French Admiral Febvrier-Despointes was dead or dying, and that his temporary replacement was Captain Le Guillon Penacros of *Alceste*, but that a new admiral, Fourichon, was on his way from France. He was momentarily distracted at Callao by a report on the activities of the United States survey party at Darien which had bothered Price the year before. And the guano issue revived, in the form of a report on the appalling conditions being endured by the Chinese indentured labourers who were digging the guano on the Chincha Islands. This, of course, explained Peruvian reluctance to permit the requested survey. Bruce's vigour in his command of the slavery patrol argued a strong anti-slavery conviction on his part; the conditions of the Chinese labourers were as close to slavery as could be found without using that name. But Bruce could not wait; these problems would have to be put aside, however reluctantly; on 10 March, after only four days' stay, he sailed for Honolulu.[21]

In the meantime the Admiralty was also writing to Stirling, the letters going to the Pacific the other way around (i.e. eastwards by way of Suez rather than westwards by way of Panama). Stirling was ordered to send the two steamships to Bruce, the paddle steamer *Barracouta* (6 guns), and the screw

---

[20] ADM 2/1697, 28 November and 4 December 1854, and 20 January 1855; 2/1702, 6 December 1854.
[21] ADM 50/308, Bruce Journal, 6–10 March 1855.

steamer *Encounter* (14 guns). *Encounter*'s captain was George O'Callaghan, who had commanded the sortie from Shanghai which had dispersed the threatening Taiping insurgents, an aggressive attitude which would eventually be useful in the North Pacific. *Barracouta* was commanded by Commander F. H. Stirling, the son of the rear-admiral. The ships were given a rendezvous in the North Pacific and sent off to await Bruce's arrival with his own ships. The rendezvous, set by the Admiralty since the two admirals could not communicate with each other directly, was 50°N and 160°E, 300 kilometres south of Petropavlovsk, in a thoroughly stormy area of ocean.[22]

Stirling also brought up *Sybille* from the Indian Ocean squadron. *Sybille* was another 40-gun frigate, the flagship of Commodore Charles Elliot, a man whose rank would permit him to be detached into independent work. Stirling was also informed that the Admiralty had news of the presence of two Russian frigates at the mouth of the Amur: it was assumed that Stirling was already after these ships, and if not, he should get about it at once.[23] A month later, on 20 January, they had news also of the fortification of the Amur estuary, the supposed annexation of Manchuria, 'and the military possession of the valley of the Amur'. This was an exaggerated report of Muravev's actions, partly from a report in a Californian newspaper. Stirling was to see to the 'distressing and annoying' of that settlement, and to destroy the fortifications. And yet another ship, the *Nankin*, another 50-gun frigate, would be sent to join him from Britain, while the *Pique* would also come from the Pacific squadron after Petropavlovsk had been dealt with.[24]

While Stirling's resources were thus being increased, and his tasks widened, one aspect of the whole situation in the East was simplified. On 23 December, at Shimoda in Japan an earthquake caused a *tsunami* which wrecked the Russian frigate *Diana*. (Shimoda city itself was also badly damaged.) The Russian crew largely survived and at once set to work on repairs. The guns were taken out and stored in a warehouse under Japanese guard. The ship was judged more or less seaworthy on January 17, and a prize offered by the Japanese government produced a crowd of local Japanese ships

---

[22] ADM 2/1697, 28 November 1854.
[23] ADM 2/1697, 4 December 1854.
[24] ADM 2/1702, 20 January 1854.

and sailors who were able to tow her towards the sea. But the weather changed; the Japanese sailors anticipated the change (from the formation of a cloud on Mount Fuji, so it was said) and abandoned the tow. A storm blew in, and this time the ship was sunk.[25]

No doubt dismayed, but undaunted, the Russians got permission from the Japanese authorities to build a new ship. This they did at Heda, a sea port further along the peninsula from Shimoda, where their methods of construction very much interested the local Japanese boatbuilders. The ship, called *Heda* in honour of the place where they were working, would not be big enough to carry all the men off at once, so they began looking for alternatives. One of these ventures is described by the bandmaster of the USS *Powhatan*, one of Perry's ships, in a letter which is preserved in the Admiralty archives, having been acquired somehow by Stirling. This vessel came to Shimoda late in January, after *Diana* had been sunk, and the American sailors made contact with the Russians. A French whaler arrived. It was called, rather provocatively, *Napoleon III*. The Russians plotted to seize this whaler, and sent for their fellows from Heda to assist. But some English and French sailors who were serving in *Powhatan* learned of their plans and wrote to the French captain of the whaler to warn him. When the Russians arrived from Heda to seize the whaler, it had gone.[26]

Despite this abuse of Japanese hospitality (which in fact the Japanese may never have actually heard about), Admiral Putiatin secured his treaty in February. It was in fact a version of what had become the more or less standard treaty, virtually the same as those given to Perry and Stirling, though it agreed to open three ports to the Russians – Shimoda, Nagasaki and Hakodate – whereas Britain and the United States were allowed only two. This was carefully kept from the latter for as long as possible.[27]

None of these treaties was regarded by the merchants of those countries as in any way satisfactory, since trade was scarcely mentioned in any of them, but, as Stirling and Perry both noted, they were a beginning, and it was unlikely that anything more could have been included without the Japanese

---

[25] Lensen, *Russia's Japan Expedition*.
[26] ADM 1/5657, 10 March 1855.
[27] Lensen, *Russia's Japan Expedition*.

refusing altogether to make a treaty. The Japanese, on the other hand, regarded the treaties as a maximum, not a minimum. Judging to a nicety the relative strengths of the naval powers in their region, they refused point-blank to conclude a treaty with France. Anyway, for the present there were no Russian ships at sea likely to require supplies in Japan, because of the war, and the British admiral had gained what he needed – in effect, the use of a forward naval base in north Japan at Hakodate, from which he could campaign into Russian waters in order to deal with the Russian frigates and the fortifications at the mouth of the Amur. It was a clear abuse of Japanese neutrality, given that there was a war on when Stirling gained his treaty. Valparaiso and San Francisco could be used by the Allies because they had been normal naval bases in times of peace. Stirling was trading on the ignorance of European wartime etiquette which he had understood when gaining his treaty. And he continued to do so.

4

Petropavlovsk Again

The Allies' activities in the Pacific during 1854 had been marginal and accidental, with no visible effects on the wider war. The presence of the Russian frigates, which led to the discovery of one of them at Petropavlovsk, had been inadvertent, and the hunt for them had been in large measure an improvisation. The ship the Admiralty had been watching was *Diana*, but the one which Price discovered was *Aurora*; he had gone to Petropavlovsk because he seems to have heard in Honolulu that that was where one of the ships he was searching for had gone. All this was quite unplanned.

No serious planning had been undertaken for a war in the North Pacific by anyone, and the neutralisation of Alaska was a sign that neither side had seriously thought that the war would penetrate to that ocean. It was the coincidental presence in the ocean of Admiral Putiatin's naval expedition to Japan – which had set out in response to the news of the American expedition – which in turn triggered Allied activity. It was General Muravev's personal ambitions and his seizure of the Amur route which insisted on the war expanding and continuing in the Pacific. And it was Muravev's mistaken assumption that Britain was interested in controlling the Amur estuary which brought him within range of Allied sea power.

And yet if there was ever an instance of a European crisis driving events all around the world this was one such case. Between October and April or May the North Pacific Ocean froze, and so did the Amur River. In the winter of 1854–1855 the European participants rethought their strategies and made their plans for the Pacific. Mid-May was the target for new ventures on all sides. During the winter Muravev returned to St Petersburg to shore up his political support; Admirals Bruce and Fourichon were dispatched from London and Paris to take command of their Pacific squadrons; orders from London and

Paris moved ships and men into position; ministers in Europe searched for information, on the positions of ships, on the treaties they had agreed to, on the situation on the Amur and in Petropavlovsk, and on the enemy's plans. And neutrals sought to take advantage of the warring countries' preoccupations. Far from being a 'Crimean' war, or even a 'Russian' war, this was a conflict of interest and concern to the whole world. And 1855 was the crucial year.

The death of King Kamehameha III of Hawai'i in December 1854 was one of a whole series of deaths and displacements which took place during that winter. Admiral Price was, of course, already dead, and Bruce had been appointed his successor. Admiral Despointes died in March 1855, by which time his successor Fourichon was already on his way to take his place. In February the British government under the Earl of Aberdeen progressively collapsed, to be replaced by an unsteady coalition under Viscount Palmerston. The French and British army commanders in the Crimea both died. And in March Tsar Nicholas I also died. The British and Russian governmental changes in particular altered the character of the war. The new British government had to be more belligerent than its predecessor in order to gain public and Parliamentary support; the new tsar, Alexander II of Russia, on the other hand, was much less keen on the war than his father had been.

Admiral Bruce's instructions were to deal with Petropavlovsk and then to leave the war in Siberia to the China squadron. Admiral Stirling collected information during the winter about the Russian victory at Petropavlovsk, about Muravev on the Amur, and about troops being sent from Sakhalin to Petropavlovsk. Just back from his negotiations at Nagasaki, Stirling also noted that the Japanese authorities had seemed apprehensive about what the Russians were doing; the Japanese had, he said, sent agents to find out what the position was in Sakhalin.

Stirling added all this together in a report to the Admiralty on 15 March 1855. He listed the Russian naval resources in the East as three heavy frigates, three corvettes, two armed transports, and a small steamer. Assuming that these ships were all collected together into a fleet, he assumed that Petropavlovsk would be their rendezvous and base. There were reports of various ships visiting or being seen near Petropavlovsk after the Allied expedition had left, and these reports were taken as signs that he was correct in his assumptions. Stirling then went on to speculate on what the purpose could be of such a concentration of naval strength, and where that fleet might go. He was, that is, dealing in capabilities, as men in intelligence do, working out what the Russians were able to do, and then basing his own dispositions and actions on that, but – and here was the cause of his error – he was doing so from the point of view of a trained Royal Navy admiral. As more information came in, his conclusions would necessarily be modified, but it was only by going out and operating on his theory that more information could be acquired.

It was possible that the Russian ships might all just stay in port, of course, though he thought that would be unlikely, given the ice-bound coast, for the ships and crews would deteriorate badly in the winter. So Stirling argued that the Russian squadron must sail, and that the obvious area for its activity was the 'southern latitudes'. He concluded his speculations with a most unpleasant thought: 'If they put to sea and keep together, their force will be much superior to any that I have here, or can maintain on either of the two subordinate stations in the Straits [of Malacca and Sunda] and in Australia.'[1]

No doubt Stirling gradually discovered that his speculative projections were wrong. And no doubt also several of his assumptions were mistaken. He paid no attention to the purpose for which Putiatin had come to the East, assuming he would ultimately become an active belligerent; he showed no comprehension of the work Muravev had done and was doing in the Amur valley, though he knew something of it; he ignored altogether the potential force available in the British Pacific squadron, and therefore the likely disruption of any Russian plans based on Petropavlovsk; he ignored the sheer size of the Pacific in imagining a Russian sortie from Petropavlovsk to Australia; but above all he was using his own reactions and training as a British naval officer to imagine what a Russian naval officer would do. But this was not necessarily the best approach. The Russian naval tradition did not encourage long-range raids and great confrontations.

In London, distance apparently lent perspective, and the information available to the government about what was going on in eastern Siberia was rather better than any Stirling

[1] ADM 1/5657, 10 March 1855.

collected. The news of the repulse at Petropavlovsk was known there in early December, but it was the news of the establishment of Russian power at the mouth of the Amur which was taken most seriously. The Second Secretary at the Admiralty, Captain William Hamilton, had already written to Stirling on 20 January, that the Admiralty 'consider it highly desirable that any fortifications which the enemy may have erected at the mouth of the River Amoor should be destroyed'.[2]

This reaction seems on the surface to confirm Muravev's concern that the British were interested in securing the Amur estuary. In fact, of course, it was purely a result of his own move into that area. The British interest was less in gaining control themselves, and more in preventing Russia establishing its power there. This is not something which would necessarily involve seizing the territory for British possession. That the letter came from the Admiralty is clue enough: the British fear was that Russia was intent on establishing a naval base. So each side was concerned to prevent the other from gaining control of the area, but each was operating under different compulsions. The result of the strange competition was quite unpredictable – Muravev was operating at a distance of 3000 kilometres along a river which was unnavigable for eight months in the year, and the British were operating by sea at the very extreme range of their naval capabilities, and were constantly distracted by events in China, Japan and America, not to mention the main seats of the war in Europe. Each side had a dire need to gain accurate information about the other.

The two British squadrons in the Pacific therefore were enjoined to cooperate in dealing with Petropavlovsk, an operation which was inevitably to be under Bruce's command, for it was the Pacific squadron's defeat which had to be reversed. Then, under Stirling, there was to be a campaign against the Russians in the Amur area, if that was where they were, and if they could be discovered. Already there was a contradiction built into the situation, for the Amur settlement was seen clearly as the most dangerous and significant Russian move in the area, yet, because of the events of the previous year, Petropavlovsk was to be dealt with first. And at a deeper level, there was still another contradiction. Both Bruce and Stirling were enjoined to avoid a land campaign. A new First Lord of the Admiralty, Sir

---

2   ADM 2/1697, 20 January 1854.

Charles Wood, had taken office in February and began writing to his admirals overseas soon after. It was the custom for First Lords to run two parallel series of letters with commanders-in-chief of overseas stations: the public letters came from the Admiralty; the 'private' letters from the First Lord personally. This was helpful when the First Lord was a man like Wood, whose letters generally amplify the official letters; in a man like Sir James Graham, his predecessor, who used the private letter system to run his own strategy, it could paralyse an admiral's decision-making capability. First Lords also liked to receive 'private' letters from overseas admirals, in which background and unofficial information and comments could be passed on, including comments on colleagues, naval and diplomatic. Both Bruce and Stirling received this treatment. Wood wrote to Stirling on 9 March. He confirmed the instructions he had been given already under Sir James Graham's preceding administration, and emphasised the 'importance of nipping in the bud if possible any elements of a naval force on the part of Russia', an instruction which was somewhat expanded later in the same letter: 'Do all you can to destroy any incipient naval establishment, but I need hardly caution you against any attempt on land, where you are not very sure of your ground. The affair at Petropavlovsk is a bad warning.'[3] This is an accurate indication of British concerns, and of the limits within which the British admirals were working.

This was the nub of the matter. The lesson drawn from the failed attack on Petropavlovsk was that ships and sailors should avoid such landings. There does not seem to have been any serious investigation into why the landing failed, or what was being attempted; Sir Charles Wood was still vague about it a year later. It was simply taken that operations on land were the army's business, and the navy should avoid them. It was not an attitude which would much assist Stirling in his coming campaign.

The Admiralty's instructions were the root cause of the strangeness of the campaign of 1855. The contradictions involved were less of a problem, but the wrong priorities were assigned and this did cause difficulties. To forbid an admiral to make a landing on a hostile shore and then to order him to find and destroy the enemy naval base was nonsensical. Both

---

[3] BL Add. Mss 49562, 9 March 1855.

admirals effectively ignored the order to make no landings, and certainly Stirling did not press it on his subordinates in any way which could be construed as an order.

The real problem was that the Admiralty was determined to gain revenge for the defeat at Petropavlovsk, whereas by January it had become clear that the main problem in the region was the developing Russian strength in the Amur estuary. That this was understood at the Admiralty is clear from the letter sent to Stirling on 20 January. So to concentrate first on Petropavlovsk was to tackle the least important matter in preference to the most important. Bruce, using two of Stirling's ships, would obviously take several months to deal with Petropavlovsk, if only because of the huge distances involved; only then would Stirling receive *Encounter* and *Barracouta* back, with *Pique* added, and so be able to get on with searching for the reputed Russian base. He was, to be sure, receiving help from the ships sent up from the Indian Ocean, but this only allowed him to form a single force, whereas at least two were required. The correct strategic approach would have been to ignore Petropavlovsk for a time, and pin down the Russians at the Amur first. As it happened, Muravev was cooperating in this, by his own plans.

The initial move, therefore, belonged to Bruce and the Pacific squadron, to gain revenge at Petropavlovsk. However, he could only act when he had achieved the rendezvous with the two ships to be loaned him by Stirling. *Encounter* and *Barracouta* were given their orders to sail and left Shanghai on 25 March. They had a long sail, and were not to use their coal on the voyage so that they would have full reserves of fuel when the rendezvous was made. This would ensure they had power enough to operate when they reached Petropavlovsk and later in the Sea of Okhotsk. The rendezvous was set, by the Admiralty, for 23 April. The ships' logs indicate that they arrived early, on 13 April.[4] The ships they were to meet were not there. (The dating is again awkward – for Bruce it was the 12th.)

Bruce had sailed from Callao on 10 March, but had only reached Honolulu, where he was to meet his other ships and replenish with water and stores – and to show the British flag as support for the new king – on 10 April. He had not delayed anywhere since reaching Valparaiso, and it is difficult to see

---

4   ADM 53/5961, log of *Encounter*, 13 April 1855.

how he could have moved much quicker. He had left Valparaiso two days before his orders insisted, he had spent only four days at Callao, and for a man who did not dawdle in port, the voyages were no doubt accomplished as speedily as possible. But it was in the nature of sea voyages in the sailing ship era that they should take longer than intended, that a group of ships which set out on the same day for the same destination should arrive at very different times; it was quite impossible to keep appointments.

Bruce sailed after a stay at Honolulu of only eight days, during which *Brisk* arrived and then *Alceste*. *Brisk*, a small steamer, had come from Britain; Bruce had left orders for her at Valparaiso. *Alceste* had left Callao at the same time as Bruce in *President*, but had taken seven days longer on the voyage. The ship therefore had just one day in harbour, and no doubt it was the arrival of these two ships which triggered his departure. *Brisk*, it seems, had been delayed at the Falkland Islands by the governor, but still reached Honolulu in time to join the squadron; it did not delay the onward voyage.[5] Bruce was, again, moving as fast as possible. He had said in Callao, in a letter to the Admiralty, that he would not delay if the French did not arrive, but he does not seem to have operated on that notion in Honolulu, and once Captain Le Guillon Penacros in *Alceste* did arrive and joined the squadron, Bruce had no choice but to coordinate movements with him. He was still missing both *Monarch* and *Amphitrite*, but would not wait for them.

The timing had already gone awry, not by sloth, but simply by the need to cover great distances and by the naval equivalent of Clausewitz's friction of war. When the British squadron left Honolulu, *Encounter* and *Barracouta* had been at the rendezvous for four days. They had been spotted by the Russians in Petropavlovsk almost as soon as they arrived, and the Russians were obviously expecting to be attacked.[6] Bruce's squadron became scattered on the voyage north and the ships arrived at the rendezvous one at a time. This time *Alceste* arrived first, on 12 May, then *Brisk*, with news of the approach of *President*

---

[5] ADM 50/308, Bruce Journal, 10–18 April 1855; BL Add. Mss 47555, [2 June 1855].
[6] Vladimir, *Russia on the Pacific*, 230.

and *Dido*. Then a storm blew up and scattered the incipient gathering.[7]

It was another week before the squadron was more or less together again. Bruce himself did not get into the bay of Avatcha until the 20th, partly because of fog, but then 'six of the ships being together, I trusted to the prompt appearance of the seventh, and accordingly proceeded to the port'. He sent *Barracouta*, under steam, into the bay to reconnoitre the harbour, just as the *Virago* had done the year before for Price. This time the report was both encouraging and disappointing – Petropavlovsk was deserted. The Russians had gone.

There was now no reason to hurry. The *Barracouta* towed *President* into Petropavlovsk harbour next day. There were no ships in the harbour, and in the town, when Bruce and his people landed, there were only three men, all Americans. One of them greeted him, no doubt with a grin, by saying, 'I guess ye're rather late, Admiral.'[8]

Gossip among the crew of the *Obligado*, which was not present, was later repeated by a French officer, Lieutenant Rosencourt, to a Californian reporter and his report was repeated in a New York newspaper, and then in *The Times*.[9] One of the Americans was said to be originally French, a naturalised US citizen. The three men are said to have placed United States flags over their houses and shops, and insouciantly claimed that, since the place was deserted by the Russians, it was now theirs. One can imagine Bruce's grim appreciation of the jest. The story must have come to the men of the *Obligado* from the men of the *Alceste*, and this long chain of evidence renders the story rather suspect. It does, however, have a ring of authenticity about it. Certainly it was normal for Americans in the Pacific to adopt an attitude of impertinent defiance towards Britain – their government at home took much the same stance.

It turned out, when the Americans could be brought to a state in which they spoke sensibly, that the Russians had evacuated the town as soon as *Encounter* and *Barracouta* were spotted nearby, back in April. The ships in the harbour, the

---

[7] ADM 53/5961, log of *Encounter*, 13 April–12 May 1855; J. M. Tronson, *A Voyage to Japan, Kamschatka, Siberia, Tartary ... in HMS Barracouta*, London 1859, 86–95.
[8] Tronson, *Voyage*, 96.
[9] *The Times*, 10 September 1855; also in ADM 1/5665.

frigate *Aurora* and the *Dvina*, and at least two merchant ships, were loaded with soldiers, officials, their families, and others who wished to leave, and had slipped out to sea while one of the dense fogs of the area hid them from the British ships – which were anyway at the rendezvous several hundred kilometres away. The feat of 'escape' was not particularly noteworthy. This had taken place on 17 April, three days after the *Encounter* and *Barracouta* had arrived. The Russians had to cut a way through the ice for the ships to get out.

The evacuation was undertaken by the orders of the Russian government, so the Americans said. In fact the orders had come from Governor-General Muravev, by this time back at Irkutsk, and he presumably discussed the matter with the ministers and the tsar during his winter visit to St Petersburg. Consul-General Miller at Honolulu interviewed George Cushing, the supercargo on an American ship which visited Petropavlovsk after the British had left, and he reported his findings to the Foreign Office. This story is in certain details confirmed by Bruce's reports, and by the report from a San Francisco newspaper.[10] Bruce made contact with the temporary governor of Kamchatka before he left, and Captain Houstoun of *Trincomalee* – the comings and goings of the British ships will be considered later – was left at Petropavlovsk by Bruce when the rest of the squadron sailed, and he continued that contact. The governor was Captain Martinov, an aide-de-camp to Muravev who had been sent all the way from St Petersburg overland. He left the capital early in December, reached Irkutsk late in that month and went on right away to Okhotsk which he reached late in January. Then he travelled – 'in sledges drawn by dogs', says Miller – to reach Petropavlovsk on 2 March (old Russian calendar – 14 March by the Western reckoning).

Houstoun and *Trincomalee* were left by Bruce to try to effect a prisoner exchange. But the fact that he did so indicates that, besides the evacuation which had taken place by sea, he knew that many of the inhabitants, together with some of the soldiers, had simply moved some way inland, understanding full well that the British would never move far from their ships. Houstoun reported that the local Russian military strength after the evacuation was 230 Cossacks and 120 marines. At least some

---

[10] ADM 1/5677, 5 December 1855; 1/5656, 17 July 1855; *The Times*, 12 September 1855.

of these – probably most – were the original garrison of the town, though others were among the men whom Muravev had sent across in *Dvina* the previous summer.

The people at Petropavlovsk had expected to be attacked, just as Muravev had also expected it. The British were thus perpetrating the cardinal military mistake of doing what the enemy expected. Bruce noted that a lot of work had gone into rebuilding and extending the batteries. He counted nine batteries which could have contained fifty-four guns, which was two more batteries than the year before. He seems to have been quite impressed. They 'had been constructed with much skill and labour, by means of fascines strongly bound together, 25 feet thick, staked and filled with earth, and some of them ditched around, with covered ways leading from one to the other, and trees planted in the rear'.

What he saw, in fact, were empty batteries, for the guns had been removed and buried, and the people had left. Bruce explored the town to make sure that the evacuation had been complete. The account by the French officer Edmund du Hailly remarks on the *'tristesse'* he felt in the deserted town, with streets empty and silent, and music still open on the piano in the governor's house. An English account mentions the many dogs which had been left behind, which begged for biscuit. Bruce decided that the absence of resistance to his 'conquest' permitted him to avoid destroying the whole town. His ships explored the bay and others nearby, and found only a single ship, 'a fine Russian whaler called the *Aian*', in a nearby bay. It was destroyed, being apparently Russian government property, which was deemed to be a legitimate target. Bruce does not mention further destruction in his report, but the story told by the French lieutenant of the *Obligado* claims that the barracks, arsenal, storehouses, 'and all government buildings' were burned or blown up. Elsewhere it is said that Bruce was angry when this happened; one would suppose it was the result of unauthorised looting.[11]

While this was going on, the rest of the Allied squadron straggled in. Bruce had entered the harbour with only six ships, his flagship *President*, the French frigate *Alceste*, the brig *Dido*, and the three steam vessels, *Brisk*, *Encounter* and *Barracouta*.

---

[11] Du Hailly, 'Une Campagne'; Tronson, *Voyage*, 94–100.

Of these only *President* (50 guns) and *Alceste* (50 guns) were of any real strength, and it seems unlikely that, in the face of the batteries described by Bruce, and in view of the prohibition laid on him against landing, the Allies would have made much impression on the town. One may imagine that Bruce was very thankful he did not have to attack.

On the 21st, the day after he took the whole squadron into the harbour, *Pique* arrived, having met *Encounter* outside the harbour, where it appears to have been placed on patrol.[12] Bruce spent another three weeks in the place, partly to explore, partly no doubt hoping some Russian ships might turn up, as *Sitka* and *Anadis* had the year before. He was also waiting for the rest of his ships, and trying to make contact with the Russian commander. He knew that two sailors at least had been captured by the Russians the year before, and also that *Obligado* had three Russian prisoners on board. He hoped to effect an exchange, but to do so he had to enter into negotiations, and he had to have *Obligado* present. One of the Americans he had found in the town agreed to travel inland to find Martinov. It turned out that he, and the wife of the governor, Madame Zavoika, who was heavily pregnant, had only gone about twenty kilometres away, to a village called Avatcha. The whaler the British had found and destroyed had been intended to take Madame Zavoika, their children, and their servants away, but her pregnancy was too advanced, and then the British arrived.

This search and discovery all took time. Bruce meanwhile attended to a difficult matter after *Pique* arrived. A marine, George Anderson, on board that ship had committed some offence. A court martial convicted him and sentenced him to death. On the 7th a contingent from each of the British ships rowed over to *Dido* to witness the execution.[13] No doubt this was most unsettling to everyone. Bruce will have been anxious to get away, or at least to achieve something more comforting to erase the memory. On 9 June he moved the squadron out of the harbour, and on the 11th he seems to have decided to give up waiting for the rest of the ships, having waited long enough. He sailed, having decided that it was his duty to chase *Aurora* and *Dvina*, and having worked out that they had gone

[12] ADM 50/308, Bruce Journal, 30–31 May 1855.
[13] ADM 50/308, Bruce Journal, 5–7 June 1855.

to the Amur estuary. But then, as he was leaving, *Amphitrite* turned up and, with her, more news, in particular that there was already a squadron of Allied ships active in the Sea of Okhotsk, which could deal with the fleeing Russian ships without Bruce's help. *Amphitrite* had been used by Bruce, as by Price, in sailing between San Francisco, Vancouver Island, Honolulu, and wherever he was; one of Captain Frederick's tasks was to collect mail, and this was the source of Bruce's new information. This news relieved Bruce of the need to sail westwards with his whole squadron, and he could now wait again.[14]

He turned back into Petropavlovsk harbour. On the same day the French corvette *Eurydice* arrived, and could tell him that the French admiral was close behind. But by now, with firm information on which to operate, Bruce began to disperse his squadron. On the 13th, *La Forte*, carrying Admiral Fourichon, arrived (he was described in the Californian newspaper as an energetic man of 45 years, and so twenty years younger than any of the British admirals). He could explain that *Obligado* was close behind, also coming from Honolulu. So Bruce again had to wait, for the Russian prisoners were on that ship. She turned up at last on the 18th, by which time the exchange of prisoners had been arranged.

Bruce received a British sailor from *Pique*, and a French sailor from *La Forte*. Since *Obligado* only arrived next day, Bruce was apparently able to persuade Captain Martinov of his good faith in the matter; no doubt Admiral Fourichon could add his promises as well, and then *Obligado*'s arrival sealed the issue.

Bruce does not mention it, but elsewhere it is noted that Pierre Langlois, the French sailor, had lost an arm in the fighting. The British sailor, William Garland, found that his ship had once again sailed without him, and he asked to be assigned to *Brisk*, which was agreed. The recovery of these men may have helped to offset the unpleasantness of Anderson's execution, but the best thing for everyone would be to get away from Petropavlovsk.[15]

Just as the ships had arrived at irregular intervals, so they departed at various times and to a variety of places. *Encounter* was the first to leave, on 12 June (according to *Encounter*'s

---

[14] ADM 50/308, Bruce Journal, 11 June 1855.
[15] ADM 1/5656, 15 June and 17 July 1855; Tronson, *Voyage*.

dating – it was on the 13th for the Pacific squadron. Tronson, on *Barracouta*, had commented on the date difference; there was no attempt to harmonise between the two groups, and he found it odd that they were on an ordinary working day on *Barracouta*, while the Pacific squadron ships were having Sunday religious services. *Pique* and *Amphitrite*, when they went west to join the China squadron, adjusted that dating, but not for some time: *Pique* did so finally on 16 July, noting in the log, 'changed days to that of the China squadron', by skipping a day.[16]

Encounter was sent to report to Stirling at Hakodate in northern Japan, on the assumption that he and his squadron would call there. Next day, the 15th, the other ships destined to join the China squadron, *Barracouta* and *Pique*, were sent off, this time to the Sea of Okhotsk and the Amur estuary. The *Amphitrite*'s mails had reported that it was Stirling's intention to cruise there, so Bruce was covering both possibilities by sending these ships to the Amur, and *Encounter* to Hakodate.

Amphitrite, normally used for detached duties, was also sent to the Amur. The reason for sending the ship to Stirling may well have been to send on mail which had arrived for him. One letter Bruce opened on the 13th was from the Admiralty reporting that the new Hawaiian king had accepted the joint assistance of Britain, France and the United States in support of his throne. This suggested that there was trouble in that region; Bruce will have felt some impatience to investigate, now that his role in the war was apparently over. And indeed the treaty was never ratified.[17]

Admiral Fourichon sailed off in *La Forte*, taking *Obligado* with him, on the 19th, heading for San Francisco. He had sent *Alceste* away the day before, and the day after, the 20th, Bruce finally got away in *President*, with *Brisk* and *Dido* in company. *Trincomalee* was to remain at Petropavlovsk in order to collect the released prisoners. Captain Houstoun's job was presumably no more than that, but his contacts with Captain Martinov resulted in his giving a pass for Madame Zavoika and her children and servants to travel to join her husband. No doubt he

---

[16] ADM 53/6189, log of *Pique*, 16 July 1855.
[17] ADM 50/308, Bruce Journal, 13 June 1855; Kuykendall, *Hawaiian Kingdom*, vol. 2, 40–42, 199.

discovered, if it was not already known, that Admiral Zavoiko had gone to the Amur with *Aurora*.

The new baby was now born, and on 1 September the American merchant ship, *Behring*, arrived, carrying goods which her company had been regularly supplying to Petropavlovsk for a dozen years. It was on this ship that the young American supercargo, George Cushing, was sailing. He found that the population was still away, and the town was inhabited only by 'some Cossacks and trappers under the command of a lieutenant'. Martinov had left by land – no pass for him – as soon as the snow was thick and firm enough for travel, and presumably as soon as the British had vanished. Cushing was persuaded without difficulty to provide a passage for Madame Zavoika and her nine children to the Amur – where, of course, he could expect to sell his cargo, and gain information.[18]

The town was therefore once again under Russian control by the beginning of September, but only in the persons of relatively few troops. No doubt the inhabitants would return to the shelter of their homes for the winter. As the *New York Herald* commented, this seemed to be the policy 'on which the Russians have always acted – of retiring into the interior, and avoiding a decisive engagement'.[19] This is, of course, a popular misconception of Russian strategy: abandoning houses and cities is scarcely a worthwhile policy when standing and fighting would work instead. It would seem that the original attack in 1854 had been more frightening to the Russians than the British imagined, and they had no wish to experience another bombardment and attack, which they no doubt expected would be by a larger force and conducted with much more determination. (They were not to know that Bruce had been forbidden to stage a landing.) But there was also the policy of Muravev to be taken into account. He had always considered the Amur valley and the estuary to be the decisive points, and everything had to be subordinated to the defence of those places; hence the removal of the troops from the town in April. This had left Petropavlovsk with little more than 300 trained troops for its defence, not even enough to man the many batteries, even if they were trained artillerymen; in the face of the expected odds, withdrawal became the sensible option.

---

[18] ADM 1/5677, 5 December 1855.
[19] Cutting in the Admiralty files: ADM 1/5665.

Admiral Bruce, having accomplished his main task, which was to see to the removal of the Russian ships from Petropavlovsk, and being assured that they would now be dealt with by the China squadron, returned eastwards to his station. He had sent three ships to join the China squadron, and had added a fourth, *Amphitrite*, temporarily. His ally Admiral Fourichon had taken two of the French ships to San Francisco, where two Russian ships, including *Kamchatka*, remained. Bruce had also to check on the situation in Russian America, so his first move was to take his squadron east to Sitka. There, on 13 July, he was joined by Fourichon. A joint squadron, consisting of *President*, *La Forte*, *Alceste*, *Eurydice*, *Dido* and *Brisk*, patrolled outside the town. For the first time during the 1855 campaign, this force was half British and half French; at Petropavlovsk it had been very predominantly British. Four days later *Monarch* and *Trincomalee* arrived, the former having gone first to Petropavlovsk. Bruce shifted his flag to the battleship.[20]

The Russian settlements in Alaska were, of course, neutral as between Britain and Russia in the war, though this was not their status towards France. It was assumed that since France was Britain's ally, the French would abide by the neutrality agreement, though the French were not in fact bound to do so. The British had made it clear from the start that the neutrality applied only to the land; the ports could be blockaded and any ships attacked, as had been carefully explained in emphatic terms to Bruce by the Admiralty.[21] The status of any ships actually in the harbours was unclear, and Bruce and Fourichon were hunting for the Russian warships. Bruce's visit to Sitka was thus partly a reconnaissance, simply to check on the place, but also partly to ensure that no warships were present. If, for example, *Aurora* was found in the harbour, he would almost certainly have attacked it, perhaps after a negotiation with the Company authorities. It would be as great a threat, perhaps more so, if it was based at Sitka as it had been at Petropavlovsk.

The one steamer with the squadron, *Brisk*, was sent along the channel through the islands to find out the situation, with Bruce on board. His interest was solely in the possible presence

---

[20] ADM 50/308, Bruce Journal, 13–17 July 1855.
[21] ADM 2/1697, 5 December 1854.

of naval ships, and on receiving an assurance that there were none, and no doubt seeing round the harbour for himself, he left. For the Russians at Sitka, neutrality may well have been their salvation. They had already survived a serious attack by the local Kolosh tribesmen earlier in the year, in which several Russians were killed, and their fort assaulted.[22] Had the fort been bombarded by the Allies, the Kolosh would no doubt have joined in with relish. It would have been the end of the settlement, at least temporarily.

The British agreement to Alaska's neutrality had been a response to the known attitude of the United States, which was very sensitive on the issue of the area's future. There had already been suggestions that Alaska be purchased from the Russian Company, but a continuation of the status quo would be almost as acceptable. The one change the United States would oppose was Alaska's acquisition by Britain. Russian America was in fact being sheltered by the United States, since Britain could not risk an extension of the war into Canada – for that would be the first United States target. In effect the neutrality agreement over Alaska was the main element which prevented the Russian war becoming a truly world war, and now that Petropavlovsk had been avenged, and it was clear that Sitka was not being used as a military or naval base, the Pacific squadron could resume its peacetime role. Any threat felt by the United States faded.

Sitka was the only place the Company had been prepared to defend. Had its posts been open to attack, the coast could have been swept clear of the Russian presence; the capture of Sitka by the Allies would have been the capture of Russian America. At that point, only Petropavlovsk, undefendable, and the small Russian presence in Kamchatka would have been left to the Russians east of the Amur estuary.

Bruce had done his job. He sailed south, calling at Vancouver Island, where he discovered that there was an incipient crisis brewing with the United States over possession of an island between Vancouver Island and the coast of the Oregon Territory. The presence of *Monarch* no doubt assisted in calming the situation, and this problem became his main preoccupation for the next year or so. The end of the Russian war, early

---

[22] ADM 50/308, Bruce Journal, 13 July 1855; Tikhmenov, *Russian-America Company*, 352–353.

in 1856, meant that the United States' threats became less effective, since the Royal Navy could devote its full attention to the American coast. *Monarch* could overawe the much slighter United States power in the area. But for a time Bruce had to visit Vancouver Island regularly and station a ship there more or less permanently. Then there was the problem of Hawaii, the question of Pitcairn Island which revived once more, the issue of the Chinese slaves digging for Peruvian guano, the Isthmus of Darien and the American survey party, and the American filibusters in Nicaragua. He had enough to keep him and his ships occupied and all of it concerned the United States. There had been plenty of combustible material affecting Anglo-American relations without the added complication of Alaska. Bruce's squadron was as much involved in the war by not fighting as it had been at Petropavlovsk.

5

The Gulf of Tartary

Rear-Admiral Stirling had been deprived of his two main steamships, *Encounter* and *Barracouta*, by orders of the Admiralty in March 1855, and did not receive them back until late June, though he then also received another ship, *Pique*. He was also joined by two more ships, the French *Constantine* (30 guns), and *La Sybille* (40 guns), giving him a suddenly considerably larger force. He also had a complex problem before him.

There was not much Stirling could do in regard to the major part of the problem, which was to find out what was going on at the mouth of the Amur, and if possible stop it, until the ice broke up in late April or in May. He knew of the wreck of the *Diana* at Shimoda by early April at the latest, because he referred to it in instructions to his captains, but he also knew that the crew were still alive and active, and so they had to be watched for. He knew that Admiral Putiatin had succeeded in making a treaty with the Japanese government, and he very much wanted to know what was in it, both for his own purposes and for his government's. His own concern in concluding a treaty had been to ensure that Japan did not favour Russia in the war; he could assume that the Russians had the same concern and priority in reverse; the terms were therefore of interest, particularly in regard to the ports which the Russians might use. He was told, by Lobscheid, a Prussian missionary who had been in Japan acting as an interpreter at Shimoda, that the treaty was one 'of peace and alliance', and that it included a settlement of boundary disputes.[1] This certainly sounded ominous, though he knew enough of local conditions to maintain a certain scepticism. It was clearly Stirling's duty to check this information, and to see if the terms of

---

[1] ADM 1/5657, 3 April 1855.

his own treaty were operative, for it had not yet been tested. So Japan was part of his problem.

The issue of the Amur was more awkward but more to the taste of a sailor, perhaps. He knew that the Russians were busy at the estuary, and he had an approximate idea where that was, but he did not know how to approach it, nor did he know what other posts or garrisons or settlements the Russians had in the general area between Japan and Kamchatka, or where the Russian ships were. *Diana* he knew was accounted for; the rest might be anywhere. Geographically, the matter of the Amur had to be approached from two directions, from the north by way of the Sea of Okhotsk and from the south through the Gulf of Tartary. This necessarily involved dividing his forces, for to reach the Sea of Okhotsk his ships would need to sail east of the long island of Sakhalin. The base port of Hakodate which he had induced the Japanese to allocate to British use – though that is not how they would have put it – was the best which Stirling could have acquired in the circumstances. He did not know if there was a passage between Sakhalin and the mainland, and in fact the British went on for most of the year believing that no passage existed, as European geographical theory of the time and the latest information at his disposal insisted. That was something the Russians did know by now, and had made use of, and it was one of their main advantages. (It was known in Japan, in a restricted way, but Stirling does not seem to have been able to ask about it, even if the knowledge had penetrated into the official circles he dealt with.)

There was also the possibility that the Russians had the use of a harbour in Sakhalin or on one of the Kurile Islands. He knew from the Japanese that the Russians had been active in Sakhalin a couple of years before. The Japanese will have known this from the reports they had received from the people of the village next to Muravevsk, established in 1853. Those people had rapidly left as soon as the Russians arrived, but had then drifted back. The Russian post had been fortified to some extent. How much Stirling had heard about this is not known, but he had to assume that the place still existed. And if a Russian post at the southern end of the island had been established, he had also to assume that there might well be others along the island's long coasts. This was something else to check.

The Kuriles was another issue he had to investigate. The

Kuriles are a long chain of islands, thirty-six in number and with a lot of uninhabited rocks around and amongst them, stretching from the northeast corner of the Japanese island of Hokkaido to Cape Lopatha, the southern tip of Kamchatka, a distance of over 1200 kilometres. Four of the islands at the southern end of the chain are of some size, as are two or three at the northern end, and the whole chain was inhabited by Ainu, a people related to the inhabitants of both Hokkaido and Sakhalin.

The islands had been explored by several European voyagers, including William Broughton of Britain fifty years before, and were laid claim to by the Russians. The southern islands of Kunashira and Iturup had been colonised by Japanese settlers during the eighteenth century, and there is also much earlier evidence for Japanese interest in the islands as far as Kamchatka, going back to the eleventh century. It is this clash of interests which has largely fuelled Kurile history for the last two centuries. Control of the whole chain by one power clearly confers also control of the whole Sea of Okhotsk and the approaches to the coast of 'Tartary', the name given at the time to the later Russian province south of the Amur.[2] The boundary agreement Stirling had heard about from Lobscheid referred in part to the Kuriles, and had allocated the southern islands to Japan. These were the ones already colonised by Japanese settlers from Hokkaido. The rest were assigned to Russia, whose Russian-American Company had been active amongst them. The boundary lay between the islands of Iturup and Urup. Probably Stirling knew little of these islands, other than that they were there, but he had to assume that there could be harbours in them where Russian ships might be based. This was another possibility which had to be checked out.

Another aspect of this complex of problems which Stirling had to consider was the whereabouts of the Russian warships which he had thought not long before might form a squadron to scour the Pacific. He knew *Diana* was wrecked, and that *Aurora* and another ship were blocked in the harbour at Petropavlovsk for the winter. He did not know where the others were, precisely how many there were, and what their plans were – though he

---

[2] J. J. Stephan, *The Kuril Islands, Russo-Japanese Encounter in the Pacific*, Oxford 1974.

had to assume that, being ships, they would sail somewhere, and being warships, that they were dangerous. Therefore these ships had to be searched for. He could hope that Admiral Bruce would account for those at Petropavlovsk, and the return of the two ships of his he had loaned to Bruce would tell him the result there. Fortunately the geographical investigations he had to make in the waters between Japan and Kamchatka covered all the places where these ships were likely to be, so the search for the Russian ships could be combined with the investigation of the Amur estuary he had been instructed to undertake.

This therefore was the large problem Stirling had tackle. It in effect reduced itself to two parts: an investigation into the Gulf of Tartary, particularly the Sakhalin coast, and a cruise in the Sea of Okhotsk to investigate the Russian coastal posts, most of which were known. In allocating ships to tasks he had also to consider the relative power of the two opposing squadrons. It was still possible for the two remaining Russian frigates to combine against him, though their invisibility did suggest that this was unlikely – but it was yet another factor to be kept in mind. The Admiralty would not be at all pleased to learn of the loss of any of its precious ships. He had also to bear in mind that Rear-Admiral Bruce might need help at Petropavlovsk. And, of course, there was always the problem of the Chinese pirates, and the need to protect the trade along the Chinese coast from Shanghai southward.

Some of his ships were therefore left at Hong Kong and Shanghai on trade protection duties, but he took his main force north. His main base for the search would be Hakodate, assuming the local authorities there had been told of their fate by the Japanese government. He gave orders on 6 April 1855 to Commodore the Hon. Charles Elliot, captain of HMS *Sybille*, to lead a small squadron to Hakodate, consisting of his own ship, *Hornet* and *Bittern*, the former a new screw schooner with 17 guns, the latter an elderly brig with 12 guns. *Sybille* herself was a 40-gun frigate.[3] Elliot therefore had a substantial force, including one of the ever useful steamers, and enough guns to face any likely Russian force – the destruction of *Diana* had made a lot of difference.

Elliot was to gather intelligence at Hakodate on what was going on in Sakhalin and the Kuriles, and then to investigate

---

[3] ADM 1/5657, 6 April 1855.

the southern and western coasts of Sakhalin, searching for Russian bases, settlements, and ships in the Gulf of Tartary. This cruise was to last only until the end of May, by which time Elliot was to be back at Hakodate. He was to tell the local authorities in Hakodate that the treaty agreed the year before, by which the town was to be available for British ships to call at and replenish their stores, had been ratified. By the time he got there, Stirling assumed that this would be the case. Elliot's visit was thus to be a test of the efficiency of the Japanese government in imposing the new regime on the port city.

A week later, on 13 April, Stirling gave orders to Captain Sir William Hoste, Bt, of HMS *Spartan*, to investigate the Kurile Islands, 'from Itouroup (the southernmost Kurile Island) to Cape Lopatha' (the southern cape of Kamchatka). He was to sail outside Japan (that is, to the east), and to disguise his ship by painting her black so that she seemed to be an innocent merchant ship. He was to look for the fugitive Russians from the *Diana*, who might be heading for Petropavlovsk, intercept any ships, Russian or neutral, which might be carrying contraband of war, and gather intelligence on the Russian posts and settlements in the islands. He also was to time his voyage so as to be back at Hakodate by 31 May.[4]

Stirling sent *Saracen*, a 'surveying schooner', whose Master was J. Richard, to Hakodate on 14 April. His course was to take him past the coasts of Formosa and Japan where he was to survey the positions of 'any of the headlands you deem desirable', but his main task was to make a detailed survey of the port of Hakodate itself, and the coasts nearby. He was otherwise to await Stirling's own arrival.[5]

Having distributed orders and ships, Stirling himself set out on 16 April in *Winchester*, together with the French frigate *La Sybille*, for Nagasaki. There he would meet, he hoped, the French Admiral Guérin in the small frigate *Constantine* (30 guns), with the steamship *Colbert* (which had been at Manila when Putiatin had visited the year before). This junction was achieved, though another French ship, the frigate *Jeanne d'Arc*, had run aground at Shanghai and was sent back to Europe for repairs. Further problems soon reduced the French efforts even more. *La Sybille* was hit by an outbreak of scurvy; *Colbert*

---

[4] ADM 1/5657, 13 April 1855.
[5] ADM 1/5657, 4 April 1855.

sailed from Nagasaki only to hit a rock off the Japanese coast. And everything took a long time.[6]

Stirling had gone to Nagasaki in part to continue the negotiation of the terms of entry for British ships to Japanese ports which he had accomplished the year before. He was interested in learning the terms of the treaty with Russia, but he also wanted to expand the terms he himself had agreed to the year before, though he had not yet heard that they were regarded as unsatisfactory in London. The demands he now made were quickly rejected by the Japanese negotiators. Stirling did not have authority from home to enter into new negotiations, and did not press the matter.[7] He sailed from Nagasaki – he had brought his ships into the inner harbour as a negotiating ploy – on 19 May. He was to be at Hakodate by the 31st, to receive the reports of Elliot and Hoste. He will have hoped that he would by that time have received *Encounter*, *Barracouta* and *Pique* from Admiral Bruce, though he did not know that it was only as he sailed from Nagasaki that the rendezvous with Bruce's squadron had been made, a month later than the Admiralty had intended.

He left with the French, but *Colbert* struck a rock on the 21st. Commandant de Montravel, captain of *Constantine*, was thus constrained to return to Nagasaki with the injured vessel to negotiate with the Japanese there in order for the damaged ship to be repaired. So only *La Sybille* sailed with Stirling, its crew increasingly unwell. He and his depleted squadron reached Hakodate on the 29th, finding there two of his smaller ships, *Saracen*, the survey ship which was surveying the nearby Japanese coast, and the paddle steamer *Tartar*. Stirling wished to investigate the situation at Hakodate by interviewing the local *bugyo* or governor, but he did not have time on this visit. He probably knew he would not, since he had appointed the 31st as the rendezvous for Elliot and Hoste, but during the night after his arrival, *Bittern* sailed in with news from Elliot which changed his plans.[8]

Bittern brought a report from Elliot on the progress of his voyage and search until 19 May – the day Stirling left Nagasaki – and a second report of the 23rd reporting that he had found a

---

[6] Du Hailly, 'Une Campagne', part 2, 176–177.
[7] Beazley, *Great Britain and the Opening of Japan*, 133–135.
[8] ADM 1/5657, 2 July 1855.

group of Russian warships and asking for Stirling's presence.[9] Stirling, with his squadron and the French *La Sybille* and *Constantine* (which had caught him up by this time), immediately sailed to assist, positioning himself in La Pérouse Strait, between Hokkaido to the south, and Sakhalin to the north, and so blocking the way from the Kurile Islands from the east, and the route out of the Gulf of Tartary. The strait is about fifty kilometres wide, and is bisected by the eloquently named Danger Rocks: it is therefore relatively easy to patrol. As Stirling left Hakodate, *Spartan* came in, and was brought along as well. The ships Stirling had with him were certainly numerous and strong enough to block the strait.

No report appears to survive from Captain Hoste, but Stirling later refers to *Spartan* having completed her duties in a satisfactory manner, though an inspection of Spartan's log shows that Hoste, beset by unwelcoming weather, had managed to sail only as far as the island of Urup, which is the next along after Iturup; the great majority of the islands were therefore ignored, which scarcely qualifies as an inspection of the whole chain.[10] It would seem, from later events, that he suggested that Urup might be worth further investigation.

Stirling's information was now much clearer. Bruce was supposedly in, near, or in control of, Petropavlovsk. The Kuriles, if not clear of the enemy, were certainly inhospitable. Elliot had located a group of Russian ships in the Gulf of Tartary, according to his reports. So now the admiral was in a position, when he heard the latest from Elliot, to block up and eliminate this Russian force. It must have seemed that he had located the main Russian naval force in the Pacific and that he was about to destroy them all.

Elliot's squadron had consisted of just three ships. With them he had to investigate a sea-gulf whose mouth, from Cape Crillon at the southern end of Sakhalin, to the coast of the mainland, is 230 kilometres wide, and which is 700 kilometres long from Cape Crillon to Cape Lazarov. Beyond Cape Lazarov, by the theory accepted by most European geographers and Admiralties, was the root of the peninsula which was Sakhalin. This was a huge coastline to investigate with just three ships, only one of which was independently powered, in an area subject to

---

[9] ADM 1/5657, 19 and 23 May 1855.
[10] ADM 53/5881, log of *Spartan*, 17–31 May 1855.

dense sea fogs, and the search was to be accomplished in a very short time. Elliot, in other words, could not linger anywhere, but he needed to check every bay and visible habitation. He concentrated on the coast of Sakhalin, presumably because it was closest to Hakodate, his point of origin.

Elliot had reached Hakodate on 28 April, after a voyage from Hong Kong of just three weeks. He reported that he was 'well-received' by the local authorities, and that the town was now directly under central government administration instead of that of the local lord of Matsmai, 'the governor with two hundred officials having arrived' from Edo; this was the *bugyo* whom Stirling had hoped to interview. This was information that Stirling would be pleased to have; it meant that the city was being prepared for the presence of foreign ships, and that it was unlikely that there would be too much obstruction from the officials. He also thought that he would be more likely to be able to adjust matters to his liking by dealing directly with the governor and his officials, who would be more sensitive to the wider implications. Elliot noted that there were relatively few regulations in the port, the most irksome being that which insisted that supplies had to be bought through the authorities. He got both water and firewood, but not fresh meat – which the British still did not understand was not a major item in the Japanese diet.

Elliot met the governor, who put on a stately show; Elliot's aristocratic origins led him to appreciate his 'great politeness and good breeding'. He passed on the message about the exchange of ratifications which was to take place at Nagasaki, but otherwise only 'the ordinary exchanges and civilities' took place.

On the voyage from Hong Kong, Elliot had repeatedly met American ships – a surveying vessel, USS *Vincennes*, near the Ryukyu Islands, and numerous whalers in the Sea of Japan. Now at Hakodate on 2 May, another American ship appeared, hesitated before turning into the harbour, and then turned away when its crew saw the British ships. *Hornet* and *Bittern* were sent in chase, but they were hampered by the current, while their quarry was favoured by the westerly wind, so that it got away with ease. This became significant later.

More information was acquired in discussing visiting ships with the Japanese authorities. Elliot's main purpose in calling at Hakodate, apart from acquiring supplies and testing the system, was to gather information from the Japanese about the Russian position to the north. He got little, and gained the clear impression that it was official policy to withhold information. He and Stirling had no cause of complaint on this score, for it was Stirling who had introduced the Japanese to the concept of benevolent neutrality, which meant not favouring either side, and therefore not providing information which would assist either side. But he did find out that an American ship had called at the port earlier, sheltering from the weather – Hakodate was a permitted port for American ships as well as British – and that it had on board something over a hundred Russians, part of the crew of *Diana*. The ship passed through the Straits of Sangar (between Hokkaido and the main island of Honshu to the south) from east to west. Given that *Diana* had been wrecked at Shimoda, this implied that the American brig was taking the Russians to the Amur by way of the Gulf of Tartary or by way of the Sea of Okhotsk. This had happened in mid-April, the ship sailing west from Hakodate on the 18th.

The Japanese had clearly made considerable enquiries about the ship and its passengers, and Elliot was told that there were also about 500 Russians still at Shimoda. The news of this ship helped him, and later Stirling, since its direction implied that it was the Amur which was the centre of Russian concern, and that therefore they could largely ignore the southern parts of the Gulf of Tartary, both the mainland coast and the Sakhalin coast. By the time Elliot had gathered this information, he had only three weeks left for his main task.

He sailed again on 7 May, reaching La Pérouse Strait on the 12th; the Straits of Sangar, between Hokkaido and Honshu, could be very difficult, and five days was a reasonable passage. Elliot had intended to examine the Gulf of Aniwa, the southern part of Sakhalin, where Muravevsk had been briefly established, but after only a short time a favourable breeze persuaded him to leave it for later. Had he explored the bay he would have found that the Russians' abandonment of that post only confirmed his earlier deduction that they had concentrated at the Amur. He sailed into the Gulf of Tartary, and 'ran a considerable distance up the west coast of Saghalien during the night. According to the map of the Island the whole of the west coast is studded with settlements ... [but we] found it to be nearly destitute of inhabitants' – though how thorough his investigation could be in the night is doubtful. Note that he refers to Sakhalin as an 'island'. The Admiralty description of the west coast, published in 1919, is that 'harbours are very bad', so there was little opportunity for detailed investigation; at the same time the lack of harbours would suggest few Russian settlements, and there was nowhere for the ships he was looking for to hide.

The weather held him in the area of 50°N for a few days and he looked more closely at the Sakhalin coast in that area by sending exploratory parties ashore. None of them could communicate with the native Sakhalinians except by signs, but Elliot did work out that they were conveying that a 'three-masted ship had passed up the Gulf six days before', that is, on the 11th. This could not have been the American brig, which was two-masted, which had been at Hakodate a month before, but it could have been the ship which evaded *Hornet* and *Bittern* at Hakodate. So he was now looking for at least two ships. At 'Salmon Cove', Commander Vansittart, his second-in-command in *Sybille*, went ashore and communicated to some degree successfully with a local man. By drawing in the sand this man described 'the Channel with the Amur, which from signs and drawings he represented to be shoal and sand'. He also indicated that De Castries Bay was the place where the ships were, or were likely, to be found. (This 'Salmon Cove' is presumably not the place of that name in the Gulf of Aniwa, but another somewhere on the west coast of Sakhalin.)

This was precise and accurate information, but Elliot remained sceptical about all of it. Next day he went north to Jonquière Bay, which had been the site of another brief Russian post, called Alexandrovsk, and was to become the main centre on the island when the nearby coal deposits were proved workable. Elliot certainly attempted again to communicate with the people he found there, without much success, and he did not notice the remains of the Russian settlement. He did note, on the other hand and as was to be expected, that it was a particularly good anchorage.

He was now in a rather awkward situation. The prevailing wind in the summer in the Gulf of Tartary is southerly. He had been caught in one storm already, and on the 19th another blew up from the south, which persuaded him to put back into Jonquière Bay soon after setting out. The Gulf, as he knew, even if he had not been across to the western (mainland) coast, was steadily narrowing towards the north, and he was in danger of being trapped by the southerlies on a lee shore. Even if there was a channel ('if there is one', he remarked), it was, according to the diagrammatic Sakhalinian, shallow and shoal and sandy. He did not want to be driven anywhere near such an area. But the suggestion that there was a strait to the north had to be investigated, both for the possibility of a channel and to find the reputed ships. It was a time for caution.

Elliot finished his preliminary report on the 19th, and next day he took the squadron across the Gulf to the west coast to look into De Castries Bay, which was the most likely place for the Russian ships to be, and which had been indicated as the ships' base by the Sakhalinian. After that he intended to investigate the head of the Gulf to see if there really was a channel through to the Amur. The three ships of his squadron crossed the Gulf in the morning and then turned north. *Bittern*, the small brig, was inshore of the larger frigate *Sybille*, and *Hornet* was going slowly to conserve her fuel. *Bittern* opened De Castries Bay, looked in, and saw a group of Russian ships.

This was what Elliot had been looking for, but what he saw was rather more than he had been expecting, and required a closer examination. *Hornet* got steam up and went in to discover the conditions of the bay. Commander Forsyth cautiously sounded into the bay 'to the entrance to the inner anchorage'. It was clearly possible to sail that far, for the largest Russian ships which he could see were of *Sybille*'s size and more, but the area was wholly unknown to the British, and Elliot could not afford to have his main ship go aground in such a place. When *Hornet* came out, he and Vansittart went on board for a personal reconnaissance of the whole bay and the positions of the Russian ships.

There were five ships. One was a frigate of about 44 guns, and so equivalent to *Sybille*; there were two corvettes of about 20 guns each; a heavier ship which Elliot thought might be another corvette, or maybe a store ship; one which was definitely a store ship; and a topsail schooner; he thought he saw a steamer also, 'going up a creek out of sight'. Elliot was not quite correct – one of his 'corvettes' was a transport, and there was no steamer present – but given the circumstances precise identification was scarcely possible.

He tested the Russian force. *Hornet* fired two guns in the Russians' direction. The nearest corvette – not the frigate – replied with one gun. *Hornet*'s shots did not reach the Russians by some distance, which Elliot estimated to be about 3000 yards; the Russian reply, however, reached to within a quarter of a mile of *Hornet*. Elliot was able to make out that the Russians were moored in a line head to stern, with springs on their cables to allow the ships to swing at their anchors and so fire broadsides in several directions. This was at the end of an uncharted bay which he could see (it was about low water) had in it several dangerous shoals and rocks and a barely understood entrance. If he took his squadron in, he would also be approaching under fire, as that Russian shot had shown. He withdrew to think it over.

What Elliot and his squadron had found was the refugee squadron from Petropavlovsk. When it had became clear, on 17 April, by the sighting of *Encounter* and *Barracouta* at their rendezvous, that the British had returned and would therefore attack it again, Admiral Zavoiko, the Governor of Kamchatka, decided that his evacuation had to happen at once. He had received orders to do so a month before, ever since Captain Martinov had arrived overland from Governor-General Muravev at Irkutsk, and ultimately from St Petersburg. Zavoiko must have hoped he would have until the ice melted to sail away, but the appearance of *Encounter* and *Barracouta* outside the town on 14 April persuaded him that the Allies might well attack soon, and that he must leave at once.

He had the *Aurora* frigate, the armed transport *Dvina*, the corvette *Olivutza* (the ship sent from Manila by Admiral Putiatin; it arrived after the Allied squadron had withdrawn in 1854, and had stayed over the winter), and two smaller transports of the Russian-American Company, *Baikal* and *Irtysh*, plus a small vessel which is variously called a boat or a schooner. Onto these ships he crowded the troops who had been sent to assist him by Muravev the year before, plus officials and others; the rest of the population, including his own wife and children, remained behind, moving to inland villages where they will have assumed they were safe from the British. Ice still blocked the harbour; a way was cut through it and, shielded by fog and by the fact that the two British ships were well out of sight at their rendezvous 300 kilometres away, the convoy sailed.

The ships were overloaded, carrying supplies and stores as well as almost 800 people. It is said that only sixteen of *Aurora*'s guns could be used, because of the crowding and the deck cargo. Nevertheless, between them the ships were a substantial force – along with *Aurora*'s 44 guns, even if all of them could not immediately be used, *Olivutza* and *Dvina* had 20 or so each, and the two transports 6.

The voyage went slowly, first along the Kamchatka coast and then along the chain of the Kuriles. They did not know where the Allied ships were other than that some were clearly headed for Petropavlovsk and that others were based in China. The ice still blocked most of the Sea of Okhotsk, so they had to travel from island to island along the Kuriles, on the western side, since there was more likelihood of meeting enemies to the east, and so technically they were in the Sea of Okhotsk. The distance was perhaps 1500 kilometres to the southern part of Sakhalin; even so the journey took a month. Presumably this was at least in part deliberate. The main danger point was La Pérouse Strait, to reach which the convoy would need to pass north of Hokkaido, probably keeping clear of the coast, even out of sight, and then would have to approach the strait with great caution. It was an obvious place which any enemy who expected them would patrol. No doubt the small ship, the boat or schooner, could be used as a scout. A period of waiting somewhere on the coast of Aniwa Bay to see if the strait was clear would be especially nerve-racking. They would seem to have been passing through La Pérouse Strait while Elliot was at Hakodate, and had preceded him, as the Sakhalinian reported, north along the Sakhalin coast, about six days in advance of the British force.

The passage of the Russian convoy therefore took from 17 April, when the ships left Petropavlovsk, to the middle of May, for they were in De Castries Bay before Elliot found them on the 20th. They must have missed being seen by *Spartan* by only a small margin, for Hoste took his ship along the southernmost Kurile Islands during May, returning to La Pérouse Strait on the 30th. As it happens, there was also an American survey ship investigating the Kuriles at the same time.[11] None of these three national groups saw any of the others: it is a mark of the sheer size of the area involved.

The Russian convoy turned north into the Gulf of Tartary, but avoided the Sakhalin coast and crossed directly to the

---

11 K. J. Bertrand, 'Geographical Exploration by the United States', in H. R. Friis (ed.), *The Pacific Basin: A History of its Geographical Exploration*, New York 1967.

mainland. *Aurora* reached Imperatorskaia Gavan on 17 May, *Olivutza* the next day. *Dvina* and *Irtysh*, sailing separately, went straight to De Castries Bay in the north. At Imperatorskaia Gavan, Zavoiko found the frigate *Pallas*, which had been abandoned by Putiatin the year before as too rotten to sail any further. Its caretaker crew of ten men was still there. *Olivutza*'s skipper had a story, from men on an American whaler he had met, that an Allied fleet had left Honolulu for San Francisco in January. This may well have been an invented story, for it is based on no known Allied movements (unless it was *Amphitrite*, which had certainly been at Honolulu in January), but it provoked anxious discussion among the Russian commanders. After a council, Zavoiko took *Aurora* and *Olivutza* from Imperatorskaia Gavan to De Castries Bay, which they reached on 13 May.[12] (Ten days later, Bruce discovered that Petropavlovsk was deserted; the day before, Elliot was in La Pérouse Strait.)

The Russian ships were now within reach of contact with their posts on the Amur at Mariinsk and Nikolaevsk, and De Castries Bay was, of course, a Russian post itself. Colonel Nevelskoi himself came to see Zavoiko. He could tell him, if the admiral did not already know, that it was possible, with care and slowly, and with shallow draught ships only, to get through to the Amur by the sand-strewn waters to the north, but that the way would not be open until the ice broke up about the end of May, another two weeks or so. There was nothing Zavoiko and his people could do but wait.

By going across first to Imperatorskaia Gavan, Zavoiko had successfully, though inadvertently, avoided contact with Elliot and his squadron in the Gulf, though the three-masted ship which had been spotted from Sakhalin six days before Elliot's passage was no doubt *Aurora* moving up from Imperatorskaia Gavan to De Castries Bay. As Elliot was exploring along the east coast, *Aurora* and *Olivutza* were moored across the Gulf. But Elliot was bound to find more substantial traces of them soon. *Irtysh* and *Dvina* had sailed straight through to De Castries Bay, and this was a bay known to navigators from La Pérouse's voyage. If Zavoiko had not decided to move *Aurora* and *Olivutza* northwards, these two small ships would have been taken by Elliot on the 20th or 21st – he would not have

---

[12] Vladimir, *Russia on the Pacific*, 231–232.

hesitated to tackle them as he did when faced by the five ships ready and waiting for him.

Elliot, having contemplated the bay and challenged the Russians, pulled away in the evening, and moved in again the next day. There had been no movement by the Russian ships, which implied to Elliot that they were determined to stay where they were, knowing that Elliot's squadron was not strong enough to deal with them, and being unwilling themselves to take the offensive. Once again, he was obviously thinking as a trained Royal Navy captain, with a tradition and expectation of aggression. He was not able to think himself into the position of the Russian commander whose priority had been to bring refugees and stores to safety. But to take his ships into an unknown bay in the face of a more powerful enemy was not a move even the most aggressive captain would recommend. Sending for assistance (and incidentally passing the responsibility to a more senior officer) was the correct procedure.

Russian and other accounts are gleeful at this situation, regarding it as equivalent to the timorous Russian kitten tweaking the British lion's tail. They point out that the Russian ships were heavily loaded, that less than half of *Aurora*'s guns could be served because of the crowded decks, and they count the number of guns of the two forces to show that the Royal Navy ran away from an inferior force.[13] But this is to contrast two different forces at different times. *Aurora* may well have been overloaded when the ship left Petropavlovsk in April, but at De Castries Bay she had used up much of the stores she was loaded with. At the prospect of being attacked, the squadron certainly put ashore superfluous personnel and cargo, some of which was found by the British later. We are surely not expected to believe that Zavoiko had been anchored in the bay for several days, had put springs on his cables, and had carefully arrayed his ships for defence, and yet had still kept his refugees on board, and had failed to ensure that his guns could be fired.

The master of *Hornet*, when he wrote up his log, included the comment that one of the ships, 'apparently a store ship', was carrying a Russian merchant ensign, and he commented that

---

[13] Vladimir, *Russia on the Pacific*; this interpretation is adopted, without investigation, by Western historians of Russia, such as D. W. Mitchell, *The History of Russia and Soviet Sea Power*, London 1974.

he 'observed a large number of men being sent on board the latter ship', that is, the merchant. This was at the time when *Hornet* was in the outer bay and exchanging shots with the Russian ships. Zavoiko was thus moving his surplus people onto a ship he did not expect would have to fight. The Russian ships were fully ready to fight.[14] All the ships were now cleared for action. They could certainly service all their guns by this time.

If it is therefore a matter of two squadrons of unencumbered warships facing each other, the number of guns becomes relevant. Here we have a difficulty in that while the number of British guns is known and constant, the count of the number of guns on the Russian ships varies with the account one reads, as does their size and quality. The number of guns on *Dvina* in particular varies wildly, from six to twenty-four. Some had certainly been landed at Petropavlovsk to furnish the land batteries, but the evacuation of that place had been in train for a month before the ships left. There were no guns in the batteries when Bruce inspected them; it follows, as is to have been expected, that the ships' guns had been returned to their ships. *Dvina* was again fully equipped. Nevertheless, tabulating the two forces' guns gives the following results:

British		**Russian**	
Sybille	40	*Aurora*	44
Hornet	17	*Olivutza*	16 to 22
Bittern	12	*Dvina*	6 to 24
		Baikal	6
		Irtysh	6

This gives Elliot's force 69 guns, a generally accepted figure, while Zavoiko's had between 78 and 102 guns. Nor will it do to claim that the transports had only 'light' guns; this may be true, but the fight would have taken place at fairly close quarters inside the fairly constricted bay. Even light guns can throw a ball a thousand yards, and kill, and some at least of the Russian guns had a long enough range to threaten *Hornet* at 3000 yards.

If the Russian accounts are uncertain as to the strength of their own forces, how much more so must Elliot have been.

[14] ADM 53/6292, log of *Hornet*, 20 May 1955.

And even in the accounts which reduce Russian gun power to its slightest, the two forces were about equal. Given the unknown waters, and the availability of reinforcements, Elliot was quite correct in waiting. He did not turn away because he had been frightened off by an inferior force. After all, he believed the Russians were trapped, with no way out.

The criticism of his conduct on the British side assumes that British naval captains will attack where possible. Elliot is implicitly accused of cowardice – Stirling's later rather extravagant endorsement of his conduct implies that he knew such thoughts would occur. All involved, from the Admiralty to Stirling and Elliot, knew also that he would be criticised by the British newspapers, operating from a firm base of invincible ignorance, and in the knowledge that an attack on officialdom, especially an unfounded one, sells newspapers.[15] Next year, the First Lord had to console Admiral Bruce in the face of similar newspaper attacks, telling him to ignore them, which, he claimed, was what the politicians did. But Royal Navy officers were not politicians; they needed protection by the politicians. They also needed protection *from* the politicians at times. If Elliot had attacked a superior force he would undoubtedly have been criticised for it, and if it turned out that the ships really were still loaded with refugees, that criticism would be doubled – and Russian propaganda would join in. There was nothing he could do in the circumstances which would evade adverse accusations. Waiting for reinforcements and passing the buck was as good a tactic as any, both politically and militarily.

It is also worth quoting the account of a Royal Engineer officer, Captain Whittingham, who was travelling on *Sibylle* at his own request. He describes the Russian ships as:

> protected by ... a rocky shoal and, a few hundred yards behind it, so placed as to fire on the outer harbour without much obstruction ... the Russian frigate was moved with springs on her cables and broadside to the impenetrable-looking passage ... Behind it [at] the other passage, which alone seemed available, a long corvette mounting 18 or 20 guns, was moved with springs on her cables and her broadside being on the channel.[16]

[15] BL Add. Mss 49565, 1 April 1856.
[16] P. B. Whittingham, *Notes on the Late Expedition against the Russian Settlements in Eastern Siberia*, London 1956, 88–89.

Elliot worked out which these ships were. They were, he decided, the ships from Petropavlovsk, which had been evacuated. They had run up to the head of the Gulf of Tartary either to get through the strait, if it existed, or to hide until the British ships, with the opening of the Sea of Okhotsk, moved away north; they would then sail out to attack, he thought, the China trade. Once again, he was thinking as a Royal Navy captain; the Russian admirals and captains never showed anything like that sort of initiative.

He also worked out that the frigate was the *Aurora*. He knew that *Diana* was sunk, and, for some unstated reasons, he decided it was not *Pallas*. One reason was, of course, that he had decided that the squadron was from Petropavlovsk, and therefore the frigate had to be *Aurora*; but he also decided that the ships had only just arrived at De Castries Bay. There were two islands commanding the entrance to the inner harbour which he thought would be ideal for establishing fortified defending posts. That they were not so fortified led him to the conclusion that the Russians had not had time to do it. This did make sense in Russian terms, since it was their normal practice to establish batteries to defend coastal ports – Petropavlovsk was a case in point, and the same had been done with the ephemeral posts on Sakhalin; later the Russians would do the same elsewhere in these waters and in effect at De Castries Bay as well. But Elliot's reasoning was based on his assumption that the Russian ships were willing to fight, which they did not wish to do, and that they intended to stay in the bay while he was around, whereas they were in fact desperate to get out and away from the menace of Elliot's guns.

Elliot and his ships hovered outside De Castries Bay for the next two days, but this was clearly an uncomfortable situation. A blockade could not be maintained without organised reliefs and many more ships. On the evening of the 23rd Elliot met with Captains Vansittart and Forsyth to discuss the matter, with the result that *Bittern* was sent off that night to report to Stirling, carrying the two reports Elliot had written. He was also bound by his orders, which were to return to Hakodate by 31 May. *Bittern*, as it happened, reported in two days early.[17]

---

[17] ADM 53/6010, log of *Sibylle*, and 53/5614, log of *Bittern*, 20–24 May 1855.

Elliot concluded that either the Russian position at De Castries Bay would be fortified if it was not dealt with quickly, or that the ships would try to escape southwards. His dispositions while he waited for Stirling were therefore made to prevent this second possibility. He assumed that the escape route would be southwards through La Pérouse Strait, so he proposed to patrol a little inside the Gulf of Tartary in view of Cape Crillon (the southwest tip of Sakhalin) and to send *Hornet* to watch De Castries Bay periodically. A lookout post on the cape might also be established. An alternative position he suggested was off Cape Lamanon, halfway along the Sakhalin coast, where he had noted that the Gulf narrowed somewhat. This was all in the two reports delivered to Stirling by *Bittern*. In the event he chose to wait off Cape Lamanon, where he could watch both shores. Elliot's second report included an appeal to Stirling for assistance, and it was this which brought the admiral out of Hakodate on 30 May. He told the French Commandant de Montravel what he intended, asking him to come along; instructions were also left for the other ships which he expected to arrive, to either follow him or to wait at Hakodate.[18] Matters were not quite so easy in implementation as in planning, however. *La Sybille*'s crew was now quite seriously damaged by the outbreak of scurvy, and the ship stopped in Aniwa Bay to land a hundred of the sick men; seriously undermanned, and with the rest of the crew clearly in danger, the ship was then sent southwards, the belief being that a warmer climate would assist, and she would there have access to better supplies. The ship later enlisted a hundred Chinese sailors, but they were necessarily inexperienced, and were not likely to be capable of operating the guns, or willing to fight. The ship had to be counted out of the Allied forces for the present. In the circumstances de Montravel did not sail with Stirling.[19]

The squadron first went to the rendezvous off Cape Crillon, which was one of those Elliot had appointed. No doubt Stirling waited there for a time, but then he sailed on to the north towards the second rendezvous, off Cape Lamanon. He sailed in *Winchester*, collected *Spartan* as it arrived at Hakodate from Hoste's voyage along the Kuriles, and took *Bittern* north again. But he did not meet Elliot for several days.

[18] ADM 1/5657, 30 May 1855.
[19] Du Hailly, 'Une Campagne', part 2, 176.

Elliot had stayed at the northernmost of the two rendezvous he had suggested, off Cape Lamanon. He had just two ships to patrol a space a hundred kilometres wide, and had to sail back and forth to cover all of it. He spent the 25th and 26th doing this, sighting both shores regularly, the weather being 'light winds and calms', which made it unlikely that the Russians, five ships which were unable to sail fast in that weather, could have passed him. Either the ships had not moved from De Castries Bay, or the strait to the north existed and would allow their escape. If the latter, Elliot noted that a spring tide was due, and that the shoal-strewn area might therefore become passable. On the 27th he sailed north again to look into the bay, once more to check that the Russians were still there. Once again he left *Sybille* outside the harbour and took *Hornet* in to examine the anchorage. The Russian ships had gone.

Elliot spent the rest of the day examining the place. He landed and walked about, no doubt sending groups of his men to look at the various items. He was concerned that whoever had been in the place when the Russian ships had arrived had not gone far away, but were still nearby in the woods. No one appeared. The settlement does not seem to have caught his notice on the previous visit – at least he never mentioned anything on the land in his earlier reports; perhaps the line of ships hid the buildings from the sea, and anyway he was more concerned with them than the land; but now he found that it was in reality a considerable settlement.

There were several 'new' buildings, a store, a bakery, and no doubt other lesser buildings he does not mention. By 'new' he presumably meant built during that year. He concluded, from the remains spread about, from the quantities of goods in the store, and the hot bread still in the oven, that the evacuation was very recent, that it had in fact taken place when he arrived. At the same time the store suggested, from the presence of flour, peas, potatoes and army uniforms, that the settlement had actually been in existence and occupied for some time. He concluded, reasonably, that two evacuations had taken place: one by the ships, taking advantage of the south wind which had blown him northwards in the last two days, and one by land, by a stay-behind party which had left hurriedly when they saw *Sybille* and *Hornet* again.[20]

---

[20] ADM 1/5657, 7 June 1855.

When he rejoined *Hornet*, Commander Forsyth pointed out several floats of timber in the harbour which were made up of spars and masts from several ships tied together and held in place in the water by ships' anchors. Names on the spars confirmed his earlier conjecture as to the identity of the ships and gave names to them. He concluded that these floats had been jettisoned in clearing for action on his first visit, though in fact they may equally well have been dumped when the ships sailed away.

Next day Elliot sent Forsyth on shore with *Hornet*'s men and with parties from *Sybille* in that ship's cutters. The obvious recent occupation of the settlement meant that it seemed possible that the occupants had returned during the night, or were waiting to spring an ambush from the forest. Forsyth shelled the woods before landing. Two parties were put on shore, one of *Hornet*'s men under Lieutenant Bush, and one of *Sybille*'s men under Lieutenant Dent. They spent an hour or so destroying Russian government property, or bringing off what they felt was useful. The stores were interpreted as Russian-American Company property, and so destroyable. They noted some items which had clearly come from the ships. The visitation was completed and the men were recovered into the ships by 6 a.m.[21]

Elliot's conclusions were sensible: that the shore party had retired inland and that the ships had sailed off to the north. He instanced the south wind and the dense fog as reasonable evidence that the ships must have escaped him by going in that direction; he was adamant that they could not have passed him by going southwards. This led to two possible conclusions: either the ships were now hidden in another bay to the north, or they had got away though the shoals which might exist, and so through the supposed strait; just possibly they had separated and scattered, which might have allowed some to escape to the south, but this he considered 'improbable'. The obvious next step therefore was to examine the coast to the north, and to see if there really was a passage to the north through the sands. But the very weather which Elliot had adduced as favouring the Russian ships' escape prevented him from doing this: 'fog accompanied by a fresh gale from the south' was no weather in which to examine an unknown coast with shoals nearby.

[21] ADM 1/5657, 30 May 1855.

He 'reluctantly' gave up the idea in favour of returning south 'against fiery south winds' so as to report the new situation to Stirling, which he did by a letter on 5 June, enclosing reports by his officers of the landing on 30 May.

Elliot then retreated down the Gulf to Cape Crillon, where he met Stirling and the rest of the squadron on 7 June, presenting the Admiral with his report and the bad news. Five days later Stirling wrote a letter to Elliot acknowledging his report, expressing his 'approbation', and congratulating him on his 'hostile visit' to the Russian post and the devastation he had caused there.[22] But he cannot have been satisfied in any real sense. Elliot had been hunting a squadron of ships which had resolutely refused to face him. He had made ineffectual attempts to reach them, but on the one occasion when he came near them they were too strong and too well situated to be attacked. All this was clear and understandable, if not wholly pleasant. But Elliot had then lost touch with them. This had been his real mistake. He had at first, having sent *Bittern* off with the news, waited off De Castries Bay, in sight of the Russian ships, but he had then pulled back southwards a full day's sail or more. His true course should have been to stay on station outside (or even inside) De Castries Bay until Stirling arrived. He may well have been driven off station and lost the Russians in the gales and fogs, but by sailing away he had made it (relatively) easy for them to escape.

What had actually happened was simple. News arrived at De Castries Bay that the ice blocking the strait to the north had broken up. This came on 26 May by an officer who had been sent specifically to investigate the condition of the ice. It was not an open channel all the way as yet, but the way was more or less clear as far as the narrows at Cape Lazarov, a hundred kilometres to the north. That was where the sands began. The cape was a high point reaching 620 feet above sea level, and overlooking the narrow passage. This was only a few kilometres wide between the cape and the opposite shore of Sakhalin, and the fairway the ships had to use was narrower still. Next day, 27 May, in the dense fog which Elliot was also experiencing further south, the Russian ships left De Castries Bay.[23] The following day Elliot arrived.

[22] ADM 1/5657, 12 June 1855.
[23] Vladimir, *Russia on the Pacific*, 234.

The Russian squadron, beset by the bad weather, by the fog, and by a strong adverse current, took nine days to reach Cape Lazarov. So here was Elliot's second error. He had ships which were better sailors than Zavoiko's; above all he had *Hornet*, steam-powered and so largely independent of the awkward winds, and able to retrace its course southwards if the southerlies were blowing. Elliot should have, as he had originally intended, searched along the coast northwards for the Russians. It would have been difficult, certainly, given the weather, but the Russians were only a day ahead of him, and were making only an average of eleven or twelve kilometres a day, and no doubt they were anchoring at night. He would certainly have found them, probably within a couple of days. He had always been sceptical of the existence of the strait through to the Amur, but the accumulation of evidence, including the clear description by the Sakhalin native to Commander Vansittart, should, if it did not convince him of its existence, at least have persuaded him that it should be investigated. But it seems that he had it in his mind that the Russians had escaped some other way and that there was no way northwards.

As they crept north, the Russians found an American brig, the *William Penn*, loaded with 150 men from the wrecked *Diana*, anchored in a bay and waiting for the ice to break. They had chartered another American ship at Shimoda, the *Caroline E. Foote*, to take them to Petropavlovsk, which they reached on 22 May, after Zavoiko's evacuation, but before the British 'attack' under Admiral Bruce which took place a week later. Finding the place deserted, but finding the *William Penn* present, plans were changed. The master of the *Caroline E. Foote* had originally agreed to make three trips to Petropavlovsk, carrying a third of *Diana*'s crew on each voyage, but once was enough for him. *William Penn*'s master agreed to take the refugees to De Castries Bay instead. (The British ships which were nearby and waiting at the rendezvous knew nothing of either the *Caroline E. Foote* or the *William Penn* – but then they had been scattered by a storm for several days before entering Petropavlovsk harbour.) The *William Penn* had made its voyage by way of Hakodate, perhaps intending to land there for supplies, but seeing that the British ships were present in the harbour, the ship had sailed on. This was therefore the ship which had been vainly chased by *Hornet* and *Bittern* through the Strait of Sangar; it was also in all probability the 'two-masted ship' seen by the Sakhalinians heading north along the Gulf of Tartary several days before *Aurora* had passed. All the information gleaned from these people checked out; Elliot would have been well advised to pay them more heed. It seems that the master of the *William Penn* had decided to avoid De Castries Bay, perhaps bothered by his close escape at Hakodate, and had decided to wait for the ice to let him through to the Amur mouth. He now joined the Russian convoy. But the *William Penn* struck a rock and the crew and passengers were taken off by boats from the Russian ships. The *William Penn* sank, and Captain Carleton was later given a sloop – which *The Times* called the *Kamchadell* – by Admiral Zavoiko as compensation.[24] With a little initiative Elliot could have found this ship as well.

Admiral Stirling waited at Cape Crillon until 17 June, and then sailed north and took up a blockading and intercepting station at Cape Lamanon, where he spread his ships and waited to see if the Russians were coming south. In the meantime he asked Elliot to get Lieutenant Dent to write out a longer description of the condition of the settlement at De Castries Bay, which was dated 20 June.[25] Stirling sent *Styx* and *Tartar*, two of his paddle steamers, back to Hakodate on the 22nd, after they had been with him only five days, instancing the difficulties of the navigation in the upper part of the gulf. He gives no better explanation for this surprising decision, and he was later criticised for it, for these small steamers would have been very useful in exploring the shoals in the north. It was a similar ship, *Encounter*, which did the best exploring later.

A year later, however, he tried to answer criticism of his decision, saying that '*Styx* and *Tartar* had come up from Hakodate with a short supply of fuel, and the latter could not disconnect her paddle wheels'. As a result the sailing ships in his squadron were compelled to keep to easy sail to keep them in company. So he sent them back 'while they still had fuel enough to ensure their return'. This, it has to be said, is odd. He should have explained why it was thought necessary for the steamers and sailing ships to stay together; no one else bothered to do this. Even worse, though he could not know this, only three days' sailing to the north, at Jonquière Bay, there was coal outcrop-

---

[24] Lensen, *Russian Push*; *The Times*, 30 October 1855.
[25] ADM 1/5657, 20 June 1855.

ping which was suitable for the steamers to use. The log of *Styx* shows no serious difficulty with coal, and in fact the ship was under sail for much of the voyage north; *Tartar* did have to be towed at times (no log of this ship survives).[26]

Stirling waited three weeks at Cape Lamanon for the Russians to appear, and then finally sent Elliot in *Hornet* to look once more into De Castries Bay to make certain that the Russians had not returned, and then to do what neither had yet done, and examine the coast to the north of the bay. (The Russian ships had therefore had almost four weeks to get away.) When he reached the bay Elliot found that there were people at the settlement once more. They vanished as soon as *Hornet* appeared. He decided that the place had not been occupied in any strength – though he saw smoke from a fire in the forest nearby – and that, since the ships were not there, it was not worth further investigation. He clearly did not wish to land in the circumstances – he had only a single ship with him.

Then, at long last, Elliot sailed on northwards, through the usual 'rain and thick weather', but without serious difficulty he got to within '10 or 15 miles of the narrows', by which he will have meant Cape Lazarov. He found no ships, of course, for they had all gone further some time before. He did find that the water became shallow, and he was concerned, as before, that *Hornet* would run aground. The *Hornet* was a fairly large steamship, with seventeen guns, and took a fairly deep draught of fourteen feet at least. He found shoal water on both banks, with a 'very narrow channel' between them, which 'certainly could not be attempted without being previously buoyed'.[27]

Stirling had sent along on *Hornet* one of his own officers from *Winchester*, Commander Charles Fellowes, who made a separate report later. He was much more specific on the details. (This was thus the second special report Stirling had asked for to supplement one of Elliot's.) *Hornet* had sailed about thirty miles along the coast, sounding all the way, and periodically looking more closely at the land. A 'remarkable bay' was noted (no doubt the one in which the *William Penn* had waited), but the forest came right down to the shore, and there was no sign of human inhabitation to be seen. 'Had any boat or vessel been

---

26 ADM 1/5657, 2 July 1855, 1/5672, 13 February 1856, and 53/4915, log of *Styx*.
27 ADM 1/5657, 19 June 1855.

lying either at anchor or on the beach, they would have been distinctly seen from the deck of the *Hornet*', Fellowes wrote. This was exactly what Stirling wanted, and what Elliot had not said: no wonder Stirling needed a second opinion. Fellowes described the difficulties *Hornet* faced when the water shoaled.

> This ship ran from four fathoms into three, when the engines were ordered to be stopped. Two and a half fathoms was the least, with very uneven bottom, with hard mud, soft mud, and rock at times. The vessel was now backed out, stirring the mud up at the same time, and her head put to the eastward under slow speed. It was found necessary however to back out of similar difficulties twice.

These were conditions which would make the commander of any sailing ship shudder; again the versatility of the steamship was demonstrated. Fellowes' conclusion was, 'that in my opinion if any passage does exist it is a most intricate one, only to be navigated by small vessels assisted by the same passage being buoyed for guidance'. This was essentially the same conclusion Elliot had arrived at, but at least Fellowes gave the necessary details.[28]

And yet, despite these difficult sailing conditions, the Russian ships were nowhere to be seen, and one of them at least was of frigate size. They had not come south. If they had tried to do so, either as a squadron or singly, they would certainly have been seen. They had not hidden anywhere along the coast north of De Castries Bay, for they would have been found by *Hornet* on her voyage. Therefore they had gone north through the shoals. It was the only possible conclusion. Elliot may not have been willing to take his ship into the narrow intricate channel, but neither was he desperate to escape from his enemies – other than, perhaps, Admiral Stirling – but the Russians did have that edge to spur them on. Plus, of course, they already knew that the channel existed, and presumably had with them a pilot, or at least a man who had sailed the channel before.

On Elliot's return with his news, Stirling at last made up his mind. The whole squadron sailed back south, meeting the French frigates *La Sybille* and *Constantine* with de Montravel at Cape Crillon. Stirling had already given Elliot conditional

[28] ADM 1/5657, 6 July 1855.

orders to sail to the Sea of Okhotsk, and now he invited de Montravel to go along, who 'at once acceded to it in the frankest manner'.

Stirling laid out his reasons for withdrawing from the Gulf and investigating the Sea in his report to the Admiralty. If the Russians really had escaped south they would have been heard of in Japan, since there were only two or three ports they could use. If they had escaped through the strait to the Amur, as he must have assumed by then that they had, Elliot and de Montravel would find them in the Sea of Okhotsk or the Amur estuary, which was known to be accessible from the north. They might have gone to Petropavlovsk, in which case Bruce's force would catch them there. (He did not know Bruce had already left.) So he would take *Winchester* and the rest of the squadron back to Hakodate to investigate the Japanese possibility – it had suddenly become an advantage that Japan was so hostile to foreigners – and Elliot, with *Sybille*, *Spartan* and *Hornet*, and de Montravel, with *Constantine* and *La Sybille*, would examine the Sea of Okhotsk.[29]

[29] ADM 1/5657, 29 June 1855.

6

The Sea of Okhotsk

Elliot took his new squadron out of Hakodate on 10 July. He examined the former Russian post at Muravevsk, which the British called Aniwa, and which they at last realised was Russian – this was what had worried the Japanese – and saw that it was deserted. The Japanese village had been reoccupied even while the Russians were present.[1] The squadron then sailed north along the east coast of Sakhalin. Elliot took a week on the voyage, examining the coasts and bays in search of any more Russian settlements. None were found.

At the north cape of Sakhalin, Cape Elizabeth, Elliot met *Barracouta* and discovered that the Sea of Okhotsk had been under British investigation, even a distant sort of control, for the previous month. The captain of *Barracouta* was Commander F. H. Stirling, Admiral Stirling's son. He explained the situation to Elliot: the three ships had arrived at Cape Elizabeth on 24 June. This was long after the Russian ships had vanished from the north of the Gulf of Tartary, and while Elliot in *Hornet* was about to be sent to look into De Castries Bay again. Elliot included a paragraph in his report in which he argued that the timing of the arrival of the three ships from Petropavlovsk was such that the Russians could well have escaped southwards, through La Pérouse Strait and into the Amur from the north before these British ships arrived. He was in fact arguing still that the passage north from the Gulf of Tartary to the Amur did not exist.[2]

The three ships under Captain Frederick's command, *Pique*, *Amphitrite* and *Barracouta*, did in fact sail first of all towards the Amur. We have two firsthand reports on what happened, one by Frederick himself, the other by an officer, Tronson, on

---

[1] Atkinson, *Travels*, 121.
[2] ADM 1/5657, 28 July 1855.

board *Barracouta*, in a book he published four years later.[3] In addition Elliot included a paragraph in his report to Admiral Stirling; this is secondhand testimony, for no written report by Commander Stirling survives, though Elliot must have received one.[4] Frederick was concerned particularly to explain his doings at the river mouth, but Tronson remarked that they had earlier spoken to an American whaler in the area, who reported that he had been boarded by a Russian officer on 1 June, and that this officer was said to be from *Aurora*. This made their detachment into the area worthwhile, and they immediately approached the Amur estuary. This, after all, was the ship they had hoped to find at Petropavlovsk.

The approach to the river turned out to be as difficult from the north as Elliot was to find it was from the south at much the same time. The first problem was that the area was still encumbered with ice: 'heavy ice' to the north and northwest, 'broken ice' to the south. The light winds were of little assistance, and they were also held back by a strong current from the south. This current was also of fresh water, so they knew they were in the right area. After four days of this cautious approach, on 30 June the three ships sailed for the entrance, 'feeling our way with the lead'. They found, probably without surprise, that the water shoaled rapidly. The bottom was sandy mud, and they anchored in 5½ fathoms, probably in order to discuss what to do next.

There was no doubt that it was possible to sail into the mouth of the river; the problem was that it did not look as though these particular ships, with their comparatively deep draughts, could do it. They could not discern the channel, and the condition of the bottom – 'the sands lay loose and shifting' – was such that there was no guarantee that any channel they did find would still exist a few days later. They enquired of the ubiquitous American whaler men, who claimed that at that time there was not enough water for large vessels. These men were not necessarily to be believed, of course, but it was all that the British captains had to go on, and it tended to confirm what they had deduced from their discouraging soundings.

They stayed in the area until 4 July, sounding the area without discovering a usable channel. The freshwater current

[3] ADM 172/2/7, extract from Remarks by Captain Charles Frederick, 14 June 1855; Tronson, *Voyage*.
[4] ADM 1/5657, 28 July 1855.

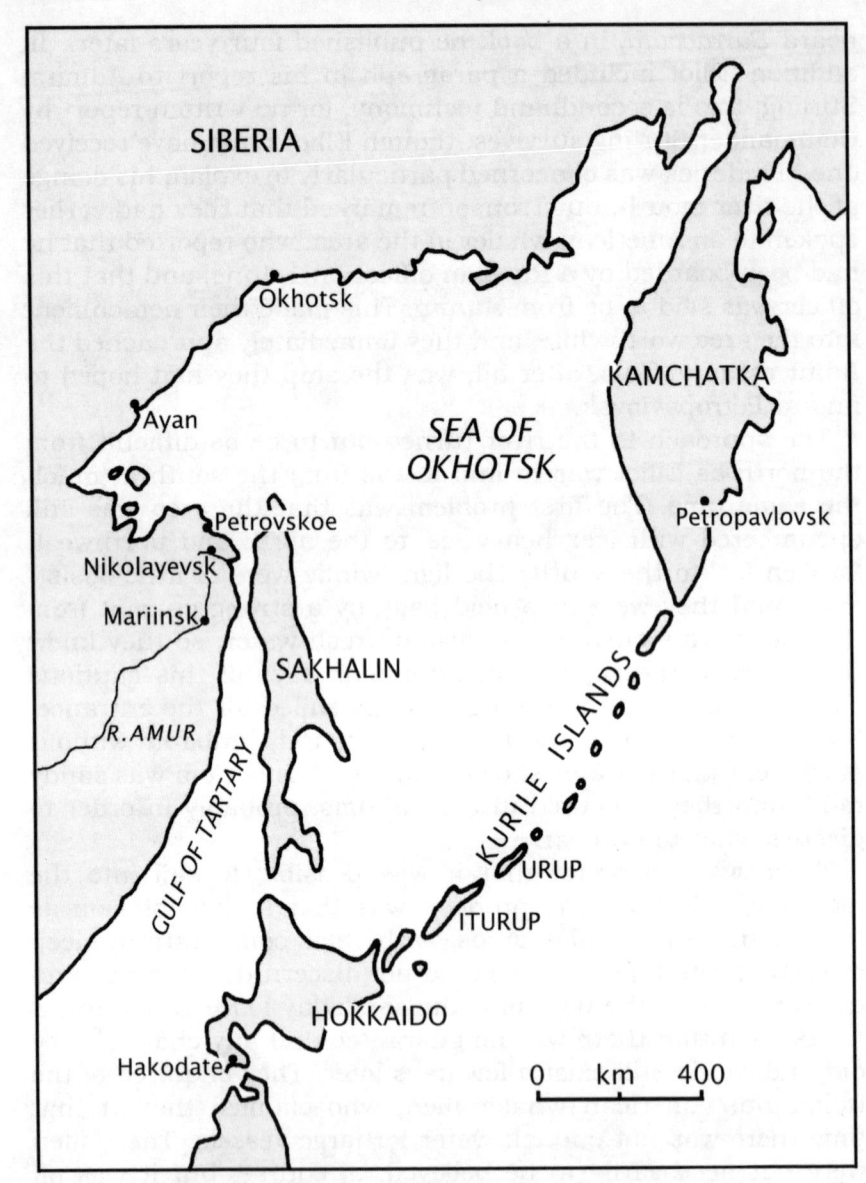

Map 3 The Sea of Ohkotsk and the northwestern Pacific

was measured at between 1 and 2½ knots, and the rise and fall of the tide at ten feet. The current was certainly due to the river emptying into the strait (there was an opposite current in the Gulf); its strength was presumably due to the release of water by the melting of the ice – the river froze along its whole length for up to eight months of the year. The current would surely be slacker later in the year. The size of the rise and fall of the tide was distinctly threatening, for a fall of such size could well leave any or all of these ships stranded. But, having spent nine days on the search, the captains could reasonably conclude that they were unlikely to find a channel without a long and systematic search.

By the time they came to this conclusion, the sea ice had retreated northwards substantially. The three ships sailed for Aian on the 4th, through loose ice, reaching the town on the 7th. *Barracouta*, the smallest, went into the bay, causing, so Tronson says, a 'commotion'.[5] This is explained in a more dignified way by the Russian side as an evacuation, repeating the tactic which was used at Petropavlovsk – and by the Russian squadron which had evaded Elliot in the Gulf.

It was two more days before Captain Frederick went on shore. The place was now deserted. Aian was known to be the collecting point for the furs acquired by the Russian-American Company, and a centre for the distribution of supplies, a place which was in contact with Kamchatka, the Aleutian Islands, the Kuriles, and Alaska. It was therefore somewhat disconcerting to see that it was no more than a village. There were a dozen houses, built of logs, several storehouses of the Company, and a scatter of cabins of the local natives. It was essentially undefended. An elaborate sketch plan is in the papers of Sir James Graham, First Lord until February 1855, showing three 10-gun batteries facing into the bay; in fact there was only one battery with no more than four guns. The source of this sketch is not known.[6]

There were two unfinished ships at the dockyard, and several guns were discovered. Frederick's main concern at first was to replace his ships' supplies of wood and water, which he swiftly did. The two part-built ships were examined. One was a wooden schooner, which was judged to be private property; the

---

[5] Tronson, *Voyage*.
[6] Tronson, *Voyage*, 238; BL Add. Mss 79696, 162.

other was an iron-hulled steamer. This was taken to be government property, and was destroyed by blasting. This distinction between private and public property had been observed also at Petropavlovsk; it was a reflection in part of the preoccupations of Victorian Britain, but it was also a consequence of the British belief that the war was between governments and not peoples. This was an interpretation which would change.

Captain Frederick realised that the inhabitants had not gone far from the town. He waited for a week, but no contact was forthcoming. He formally took possession in the name of the Allies, but he must have known it was an empty gesture, made into thin air. In the end there was nothing to do but sail away. It was understood that the Russians would simply return.[7]

Frederick took his ships back to Cape Elizabeth, and there he met Elliot coming from the Gulf of Tartary. *Amphitrite* was now sent back to the Pacific squadron, and sailed to join up with Bruce at Sitka. (Bruce in fact was still at Petropavlovsk, and would only leave a few days later.) It was at this point that the calendar on *Pique* was changed to China squadron dating, indicating that the ship was now definitively attached to Stirling's command.[8] This was all no doubt the result of Elliot's orders from Stirling.

Elliot received reports from Frederick before *Amphitrite* left, and despite hearing of the explorations already made, Elliot determined to try once more to reach the Amur area. He could argue that his earlier explorations of the Gulf had shown that there was no way through to the Amur from that direction, and that therefore there must be one – as the freshwater current showed – from the Sea of Okhotsk. The timing he worked out for the presence of Frederick's flotilla in the area seems to have persuaded him that *Aurora*'s squadron had escaped by sailing south and that he had missed them – and this despite his adamant belief, when in the Gulf, that the Russian ships could not have passed him. It followed that, having escaped by sailing south, they had reached the Amur area from where he was now. Therefore there was a channel from the north.

Elliot sent Commandant de Montravel with *Constantine* and *Hornet* off to explore the coast south of Aian and the Shantar

---

[7] Tronson, *Voyage*; Du Hailly, 'Une Campagne'; ADM 1/5657, 28 July 1855.
[8] ADM 53/5020, log of *Amphitrite*, and 53/6191, log of *Pique*.

Islands, and took *Sybille*, *Spartan* and *Barracouta* into the shoals to have another hunt for the passage to the Amur. A rendezvous was set for Aian.

Elliot's ships, having the advantage of the earlier explorations by *Barracouta*, were able to move straight towards the most likely place for the passage to be found. First, *Barracouta*, the only steamer, went in to examine a bay on the northwest corner of Sakhalin, Obman Bay, but it was shoal. Commander Stirling could see the whole bay, however, and there were no ships in sight, though he could see some buildings 'of a superior kind to those used by the natives', but of people, only natives, though Tronson suggests that these were spread along the coast as watchers and would pass the word along. Elliot had now sequentially examined the whole coast of Sakhalin from Jonquière Bay (opposite De Castries Bay, in the Gulf) south to Aniwa Bay, and north along the whole east coast; Obman Bay had been the last known bay in which the Russian squadron might have lurked. The only possibility now was the Amur and the sands.

Hornet and *Constantine* went off on their separate exploration. *Hornet*, as had been shown in the Gulf, was of too great a draught to be useful in exploring the shoals. *Barracouta*, a paddle steamer and smaller, was apparently more useful. And this proved to be the case here.

For the first time in his explorations-cum-campaign, Commodore Elliot found a Russian ship that he could reach. The three British ships anchored as close to the shoals as was safe. Further in they could see another ship, a brig. *Barracouta* was sent after her, but the water was too shallow even for her. Elliot decided he was seeing an armed vessel with stores, possibly carrying goods from Aian to the Amur, and that this was the ship which the American whalers had mentioned, perhaps even taking her, mistakenly or with intent to confuse, for *Aurora*.

Elliot sent *Sybille* and *Spartan* to search for the passage by sounding; *Barracouta* did likewise. For three days this went on, no doubt being watched with considerable interest by the men on the Russian brig. Elliot wrote a report on the 28th detailing his measures so far, and reported that all this effort had not found any passage. He reached the conclusion that, if the passage existed, it was too intricate to be followed, and that the strong northward current would prevent boats, even *Barracouta*, from getting through to the south and to the river mouth. He therefore reported that he intended to report back to Admiral Stirling at Hakodate on 15 August, and, unless ordered otherwise, to join de Montravel, who was due to meet *La Sybille* on the 20th, to have another look at the Gulf of Tartary.

Here again we have evidence from Elliot's own pen of a distinct lack of determination. Before his very eyes, for several days, there was a Russian ship, a brig, not especially small, and clearly stuck in the stands. It had obviously been attempting to sail through the sands, southwards. It would scarcely even attempt to do this without prior knowledge that a passage existed. Yet after three days' search, which had taken his boats nowhere near the Russian brig, Elliot was giving up. This was the same attitude which had lost him the chance of capturing the Russian ships in the Gulf. Even as he was writing the report, however, things changed.[9]

Commander Stirling, who was searching for the passage for the ships, took more decisive action. He had with him two cutters and a barge from *Sybille*, and the cutter from *Spartan* to do the sounding in search of the passage. The whole group moved to the west towards the Russian brig, though whether the intention at first was to attack or simply to go on with the sounding is not clear. The Russians on the brig clearly thought it was an attack developing, even though the British boats were several miles away – four or five miles, Elliot says. The crew of the brig abandoned their ship. They had watched the British activities for several days, while, as it had become clear, being themselves aground. The appearance and approach of all these boats clearly meant to them that they were about to be attacked, though in fact Stirling says that he was only doing more sounding. But once the abandonment was seen to take place, he sent the three cutters after the five Russian boats from the brig, adding one from *Barracouta*, and followed himself in the heavier and slower barge with *Sybille*'s gig.

The cutters had a long chase. The man in overall command was Lieutenant Robert Gibson of *Barracouta*, but it was the vessels from *Sybille* and *Spartan* which made captures. Two of the Russian boats were taken, one by Mr Hill, Master of *Sybille*, containing nine men, the other by Mr Sarratt, Second Master of *Spartan*, with five men. The chase involved 'a very severe day's work at the oars', as Elliot put it, and occasional

---

9   ADM 1/5657, 28 July 1855.

grounding so that the cutters had to be hauled over the sandbanks. The water, be it noted, was only just thawed; the men will have been very weary and very wet and cold when they finished. The Russians must have been shocked to find themselves captured after beginning the chase with several miles' start in these conditions; two or three of the Russian boats did escape, however, and they included the boats carrying the passengers and the skipper.

Stirling examined the brig. It proved to be the *Okhotsk*, a store and supply ship belonging to the Russian-American Company, armed with six guns, about 200 tons. It was destroyed, by fire and explosion, and the remains then sank. There was no loot, no prize money, no ship. But there were prisoners, and for the first time in the war in the western Pacific, the British were able to interview men who had useful information. It is surely probable that Commander Stirling had this in mind all along. And the information he acquired proved decisive.

Second Master Sarratt, who seems to have been a particularly useful officer at this point, was able to find out a good deal of information from his prisoners while ferrying them back to *Spartan*. He confirmed the brig's identity, though his rendering of the name was phonetic – 'Aheutsk' – reflecting the Russian pronunciation, and that it had a crew of twelve with four officers. It had been carrying six passengers. Of this total of twenty-two men, fourteen had been captured in the two boats. The ship had been trading along the coast from Aian southwards, sailing around the Shantar Islands and visiting Petrovskoi. This was the village established by the Russians a few years before on the southern shore of the Sea. Sarratt's report described it as a 'small village'; it had been one of the places Governor-General Muravev had virtually abandoned the year before.

The *Okhotsk* had, then, been trying to get into the Amur. It had left Aian on 29 June (while Frederick's ships had also been searching for the estuary). It had been wandering about the Shantar Islands while the British ships passed on their way to Aian, and when the British found her the ship had been trying for twelve days (that is, since 17 July) to get into the Amur. The crew were apparently unaware of the near presence of the British ships until an officer from Nikolaevsk reached the brig a few days earlier. He had warned them to keep watch for the 'English squadron', and had then taken his boat, a whaler manned by ten seamen and carrying ten soldiers, to Petrovskoi.

It seems likely that delivering the soldiers to Petrovskoi was his primary task, and that his visit to the ship was by chance.

He also mentioned, apparently in conversation, that the Russian squadron had already escaped from the British squadron, by sailing through to the Amur from the Gulf. They had done so by jettisoning their guns 'and afterwards weighing them by boats', that is, recovering the guns one by one.[10]

Captain Hoste confirmed all this by his own observations, and reported that his Royal Marine officer Lieutenant Stokes was able to converse with an officer prisoner in German (but he does not say how Sarratt conversed with the prisoners in the cutter). There is no mention of stores or refugees on the ships. He names the prisoner's source of information as a lieutenant Varanchikov, formerly of *Diana*, but now in command of the schooner Elliot saw in De Castries Bay; it was this man who had boarded the *Okhotsk*, adding the information that he had been attempting to pilot the ship into the Amur.

Hoste from his command perspective also found out more about the situation at Nikolaevsk. The Governor-General of eastern Siberia was there, as was the Governor of Kamchatka; they had 2000 troops, infantry and artillery, at the town. Admiral Putiatin – the only one of these commanders the British seem to have known of by name – had left for St Petersburg on a small steamer, steaming up the Amur, which was the Russians' means of communication along the river. They still had the *Vostok* steamer with them. The settlement was dependent for supplies on Irkutsk and the Amur route.

He could add more information also about Aian. The two ships on the stocks had both belonged to the Russian-American Company – so destroying one and not the other had been mistaken discrimination – and there had been 150 troops there, men of the Company. These had withdrawn into the interior, to a village called Nelkan. He does not indicate the distances, but the village was about 200 kilometres away, across the Dzhundzhur mountains. They were men who had earlier been evacuated from a place, apparently Aniwa, whose name nobody seemed to know – it was, of course, Muravevsk.[11]

The value of the capture of the brig's crew was out of all proportion to their numbers, or the meagre value of the ship

---

[10] ADM 1/5657, 28 July 1855.
[11] ADM 1/5657, 30 July 1855.

and its cargo, now destroyed. For the first time in this campaign, the British had some definite information to work with. The loquaciousness of the Russian prisoners was extremely useful. The crew are dismissed in one Russian account as 'Finlanders'. Captain Whittingham was more precise: Finns, Swedes and Germans, he says, and they were 'very communicative'.[12] But it was the officers (all Russians) who were the source of the most valuable information.

Several conclusions followed from Hoste's and Sarratt's evidence. First, of course, was the clear and definite confirmation that there really was a passage through between Sakhalin and the mainland. It could be travelled either from the south, as the Russian squadron had done, or from the north, as the brig clearly had intended. But neither passage was really practicable for anything larger than a boat of the brig's size – 250 tons, Sarratt reported – and even the brig had been stuck in the sands for nearly two weeks. It is also clear that the squadron, when it left De Castries Bay, was not overloaded. The Russian officer had reported only that the guns had been jettisoned. Nor were the ships still loaded with the Petropavlovsk refugees. They and the stores had been disembarked at the bay, as one would have expected. So Elliot's refusal to tackle a superior force when he faced it turns out to have been well judged.

There was also the new information about the troops at Nikolaevsk, which was evidently the main Russian base in the Amur mouth, and the rank and nature of the commanders there. They could understand the capability of the Governor of Kamchatka, from his defeat of the British at Petropavlovsk, and his evasiveness in the Gulf of Tartary. The rank of the commander at Nikolaevsk – the Governor-General – will have come as a surprise, perhaps, and meant that the garrison would be able to count on supplies and support from a wide area. The news of the presence of artillery troops and guns was not at all welcome. Yet a force of 2000 men consumed a lot of stores, food, spirits, ammunition, and if they were dependent on a supply line the length of the Amur River, they were still very vulnerable to sea power – if that power could be brought to bear in the river.

Elliot took a day or so to gather the information. Hoste's

---

[12] Whittingham, *Notes*, 132–133.

report is dated 30 July, and he had Sarratt's information by then also. Sarratt seems to have got the information while in the cutter, though it may have taken some time to persuade the officers of the *Okhotsk* to talk, and to find a common language. Then Hoste had to be told, and he had to write the report for Elliot, who then had to consider what he had been told, and had to check it over, perhaps with the Russians he was holding on *Sybille*. Hoste in fact had extracted enough information to be able to draw a plan of the area, with the positions of the Russian ships marked, though the plan shows the four ships lined up close to the Sakhalin shore: in fact they seem to have been inside the river estuary by this time.

Elliot took the point, and went a stage further. If what was understood from the prisoners was true – and he was still expressing some scepticism: 'too much reliance must not be placed' on the prisoners' stories, he commented – it would be necessary to check out what they said by exploring the head of the Gulf of Tartary once again. But he could not simply charge off to do this, since that would leave the northern exit, into the Sea of Okhotsk, available and unguarded. He was thinking, of course, in naval terms, that the Russians, having recovered their ships, would put to sea, perhaps to attack him. He therefore intended to make a demonstration again at the northern exit, to remind the Russians of his existence, and only then to sail south. He would need to be fairly obvious in his demonstration, and would need to be sure he was seen.[13] This was clearly not easy, since he had seen few Russians so far, and most of those were now his prisoners, though there certainly had been men watching his ships from the shore in Obman Bay. The solution to this little problem came unexpectedly.

The *Barracouta*, on her own at the time in the Sea of Okhotsk, 160 miles from Cape Elizabeth, met a brig flying American colours. The position was well away from any land, but the brig's destination could only be one of the Russian posts in the area. Any vessel so close to an enemy port – and it was clear by now that the Amur was a Russian port and base – was to be regarded with suspicion, and until proved otherwise must be suspected of carrying contraband. Commander Stirling stopped the brig, not without difficulty, and only after firing

---

[13] ADM 1/5657, 4 August 1855.

blanks twice. At that point the brig came to heel. Stirling sent his second-in-command, Lieutenant Gibson, to investigate.

Gibson met an evasive skipper. The brig was the *Greta*, from Bremen. Captain 'Thoulou', as Gibson calls him, claimed to be operating as an American vessel, but the documents he showed, from a Commodore Rodgers of the United States Navy, were not in any way legal, and anyway had expired. It seems likely the master could not understand the English of the document, or perhaps he expected Gibson to be wary of anything American. Gibson decided, not surprisingly, that this was all very unsatisfactory. He was not shown the manifest, for example, or anything referring to the cargo, which was what he had boarded the ship to investigate. There seemed to be an unusual number of men simply lounging about on the deck. The hatchways were open, which was hardly sensible at any time, and certainly not in the potentially stormy Sea of Okhotsk. Gibson asked the master to muster his crew, a group which evidently did not include the men he could see on the deck.

The master gave up. The men, he said, were Russians. Gibson got him to bring them all on deck, and soon found himself facing 277 of the enemy, eleven of them officers. They were survivors of the *Diana*. They must have been tempted to seize Gibson and the men with him (if there were any), but *Barracouta*'s guns were menacing, and they will have heard them fired twice already. The officers put to Gibson the case that they were heading for Aian, and were not intending to reinforce the Russian posts at the Amur, that they were not armed, and that they were shipwrecked sailors only asking to be landed at a Russian port. Gibson, who does not mention it but who must have been thoroughly apprehensive by now, and very grateful for the guns of the *Barracouta* pointing at the *Greta*, sensibly decided to pass the problem to his captain.[14]

Stirling, with his small steamer, could not possibly accommodate all these men. He brought the *Greta*'s master and the two senior officers among the Russians – Lieutenants Pushkin and Baron Schelling – onto *Barracouta* and explained that he would take them to Hakodate to let the admiral decide what to do with them. But he then rethought the matter. Hakodate was neutral territory; to go into Japanese waters might require

---

[14] ADM 1/5657, 1 August 1855.

him to release the prisoners; at the very least the Russians would claim that he should. And what of the reaction of the Japanese, who had only just got rid of these unwelcome shipwrecked sailors, and who were extremely loath to welcome any foreigners into their land? Further, if he went straight to the admiral he was cutting out his immediate commanding officer, Commodore Elliot, to go to his father. He does not write all this in his report, but simply says that, 'on a reconsideration of the subject', he told the Russians he would take them to Aian, 'which I considered better than the much longer voyage to Hakodate'.[15]

For Stirling and Elliot were now in a dilemma. Even when he had only fourteen prisoners from the *Okhotsk* on board his ship, Elliot was concerned that feeding them would reduce his stores to such an extent that he would have to shorten his cruise.[16] The ships had been at sea without replenishment, apart from wood and water collected at Aian, for well over a month, and if an extra fourteen mouths to feed caused him some concern, a further 277 rendered his squadron almost at once short of provisions, and made the ships unable to operate as warships. He had become, ironically, in a similar condition to Zavoiko's squadron as it had crept along the Kuriles and into the Gulf of Tartary – but one notes no sympathy being lavished on Elliot by the historians, and no concern that his accommodation of the prisoners made his ship *hors de combat*.

Commander Stirling took the *Greta* in tow and reported to Elliot. By now the time was approaching for the rendezvous with *Hornet* and *Constantine* at Aian, and that was where Stirling found *Sybille* and *Spartan*. Elliot wrote his report of Stirling's doings from Aian on 4 August. He was met with the same argument as Gibson and Stirling had faced from the Russian officers, that they were shipwrecked mariners and not prisoners of war. This was a clever point, playing on the fact that *Diana* had been on a diplomatic mission, and on the Victorian British impulse to categorise people and things into specific groups such as naval, military, civilian, diplomatic. And yet these Russian officers and men were sailors in their country's navy. They were emphatically not civilians. And they were, as Admiral Stirling later noted, prime seamen. Captain Whittingham remarked that 'the personal appearance of the Russians was soldier-like more

---

[15] ADM 1/5657, 21 August 1855.

than seamen-like; they were uniformly tall, strong, well-made men, who had served for seven to fourteen years'.[17] They may well promise not to engage in hostilities, but such a promise could be easily overruled by a higher officer. Their presence in eastern waters would hugely reinforce Russia's naval and military capability. It all made Elliot hesitate, and, like Commander Stirling, it led him to pass the decision up the ladder of responsibility to his superior, Rear-Admiral Stirling.

He made one concession. Several of the Russians were hurt or sick; he agreed, or decided, to land them at Aian along with their doctor and their priest, both from *Diana*. He also wrote a letter to 'the governor of the province of Yakoutsk', explaining what he was doing.[18] Aian had been reoccupied by some of its inhabitants after the original British visitation had ended. A new arrival was Archbishop Innokenti of eastern Siberia, who had assisted the refugees, and was now in the town. The return of the British ships sent the Russians fleeing once again.

When the British officers landed, therefore, they found the town again almost deserted. They noted that some of the houses and stores had been looted, which had not been done by their own men on the original visit; they tended to blame American whaler men, though it might just as well have been the local natives. They did find the local superintendent of the Russian-American Company, a man called Freiburg, and it was possibly he who told them that the archbishop was in the town. The officers called on him. By a clearly tendentious Russian account, they are said to have found him conducting a service in his church, praying that Russia be delivered from her enemies. The officers are supposed to have waited until he had finished, then announced they were arresting him; he saw the joke and went on board the ship – presumably the *Sybille* – where they toasted him in champagne, and released the sick, the doctor, and the priest into his custody. The Russian account is spoilt, however, by implying that '300' men of the '*Dvina*' were released.[19] Another author even claims that

---

[16] ADM 1/5657, 4 August 1855.
[17] Whittingham, *Notes*, 148.
[18] ADM 1/5657, 2 August 1855 (two letters).
[19] Atkinson, *Travels*, 134.

the British (he always says 'English') officers stole Freiburg's billiard balls.[20]

The Russian account is contradicted in its romantic details by the British accounts. Captain Whittingham agrees that the officers met the archbishop, but at his house, and Whittingham says that he showed them his church, and that it was the archbishop who produced the champagne. His toast was to a 'speedy peace'. This is a much more convincing account.[21] It is a mark of the difficulty of using Russian accounts in this study: they are suffused with nationalism, and tend to suffer a good deal of improvement and embellishment.

Elliot distributed the rest of the prisoners among the ships. The *Barracouta* kept 106 men and three officers; *Sybille* received 100 men and seven officers; forty men and two officers went on board *Spartan*. *Greta* was regarded as a prize; Lieutenant Gibson and a prize crew were brought on board to take her to Hong Kong where there was a Vice-Admiralty Court capable of jurisdiction – the master, of course, denied his prize status. *Barracouta* was sent off at once to report to the admiral at Hakodate. The prisoners on *Barracouta* soon showed incipient signs of scurvy. Their diet on *Greta* had perhaps not been of the best. Tronson reports that they were given tobacco and soap, and the scurvy soon cleared up – presumably through a better diet, not just the tobacco and the soap. Tronson also notes that the men seemed quite relaxed at being prisoners; it would seem that it was only the officers who were keen to get back to Russia and the war.[22]

Elliot now had to wait for *Hornet* and *Constantine* to arrive. *Hornet* entered Aian harbour on the 7th, but fog delayed *Constantine* until the 11th – further evidence of the versatility of the steamers. Commander Forsyth reported only largely negative results from his cruise. Beset by fogs, awkward winds and difficult currents, the ships had made only a slow exploration. *Hornet* had to tow *Constantine* more than once, and only *Hornet* could go in to explore some of the longer bays – de Montravel sometimes coming on board for the trip. They spoke to several whalers, who all had the story of the Russian squadron getting away through the sands to the Amur. One whaler's master, of

---

[20] Vladimir, *Russia on the Pacific*, 239–240.
[21] Whittingham, *Notes*, 148.
[22] Tronson, *Voyage*.

the *Endeavour*, claimed to have seen a Russian brig off Cape Romberg (the tip of the mainland at the northern edge of the strait) – this was obviously the *Okhotsk*. Other masters had also seen, or heard of, this brig, and all reported that it was headed for the Amur. The *Okhotsk* was on a more or less regular run between Aian and the Amur, so their comments were in the nature of commonplace remarks. The evidence of their frequent contact with one another, however, was a clear sign that it would be very difficult to attempt anything secret in this area. The evidence of their gossiping nature suggests that Elliot was sensible to be sceptical of what he heard from them.

The whalers were in the southern part of the Sea of Okhotsk because the ice was very persistent in the north: 'Heavy ice setting down the gulf on them', as Forsyth put it. He heard from the men of two boats, who had been blocked in for a fortnight by the ice and had spent part of the time hunting on land for food, that the land was low and swampy and virtually uninhabited. Lieutenant Bush was put ashore at one place to interview a party of native nomads, though he could get little from them; they had reindeer, but managed to move them away before Bush arrived, which shows both what they expected from a white man in a uniform, and their good sense.

The master of the whaler *Endeavour* had met the wife of the 'Governor of Petrovskoi', who spoke English. This was presumably Madame Nevelskoia, and she seems to have been as free with information as everyone else: merchant vessels had to be partially unloaded before getting into the Amur; the Russian squadron had 'warped' into the Amur from the south; the settlement at Petrovskoi was small and poor and inhabited by only a few people. And she was anxious to know whether the 'English squadron' had left, presumably asking for information in exchange for what she had said.

The news of the prevalence of ice – twelve whalers were reported to be blocked in at one area west of the Shantar Islands – as well as the fogs and general contrariness of the weather, persuaded Commander Forsyth that he was just wasting his time. De Montravel agreed. *Hornet* pulled *Constantine* into clear water, then headed for Aian.

This was final confirmation for Elliot. There was nothing at Aian, nothing in the southwest corner of the Sea of Okhotsk around the Shantar Islands, nothing on Sakhalin's east, south, north coasts, or most of its west coast. *Spartan* had found nothing in the Kuriles. Petropavlovsk had been evacuated. Wherever there was a small Russian settlement, the people moved inland as soon as British forces appeared, or in some cases the settlement was completely abandoned. He could be certain that the gossiping American whaler men would relay information to the Russians, whom they already had contact with, even more readily, and perhaps more accurately, than they did to the British.

Having reunited with *Hornet* and *Constantine*, Elliot went to Cape Elizabeth once more. There he met *Encounter*, which had come up from Hakodate and had brought welcome supplies of fresh food, including several live bullocks. He also received orders, for the first time since his expedition to the north had begun. He was to return to Hakodate, calling at Aniwa on the way. (*Constantine*, left at Aian to replenish with water and firewood and any food Commandant de Montravel could find, was already intending to call at Aniwa.) On the voyage south, Elliot set down his conclusions about the passage to the Amur, but noted that they had still not found the Russian ships. *Pallas* was reported to have been taken into the Amur, but she was also said to be in a bad condition and unserviceable, but the other ships remained a potential menace. He listed them, as much perhaps as a reminder to himself as for the admiral's information: *Aurora* (44 guns), *Olivutza* (24 guns; no one on the British side could ever get this name right), *Dvina* (20 guns), *Irtysh* armed transport, *Vostok* steamer, *Baikal* schooner, and another steamer operating along the river. In terms of European sea power, this was not much; in terms of sea power in the Pacific, it counted for a good deal, and in combination these ships would be formidable enough to give Elliot's or Stirling's separate squadrons a major problem.

Elliot, with *Sybille*, *Spartan* and *Hornet*, met *Encounter* again at Aniwa on 23 August. There he learned that Admiral Stirling had gone to Nagasaki and he was ordered to follow. This was not quite so easy to do. *Constantine* had not turned up yet, and *Sybille* and *Greta*, loaded with their prisoners, were in need of food and water. He would wait a week, he said, for *Constantine*, and then sail for Nagasaki.[23]

Rear-Admiral Stirling had based himself at Hakodate during the summer, joined by the French Rear-Admiral Guérin with

---

[23] ADM 1/5657, 7 August and 1 September 1855.

his ship, the *Virginie* (50 guns), and by the *Nankin* (50 guns), sent out from Britain earlier. *Nankin* was a brand new ship, only just completed, and manned by a crew easily recruited. It was reported at the time that she could have been manned several times over.[24] Along with *Styx* Stirling now had four vessels. He sailed at the beginning of August to examine the coast of Tartary, that is, the west coast of the Gulf which Elliot had not had time to look at. He had been joined also by *La Sybille*, remanned and somewhat recovered from the epidemic of scurvy, and by *Pique*, which had been sent across from Petropavlovsk by Rear-Admiral Bruce. So he now had so many ships that he could divide his forces. Most of the ships he took to the Gulf – *Winchester*, *Virginie*, *Nankin*, *Styx* – and the other two were detached. 'Upon a suggestion', as he puts it in his report – though whose suggestion it was he does not say – *Pique* and *La Sybille* were sent to 'take possession of' the Russian Kurile Island of Urup, the most southerly of that line of islands, which was in Russian possession.[25]

The purpose of this expedition, other than to take control of a piece of Russia, is not stated. It may be that Hoste in his report after *Spartan*'s cruise as far as the island earlier had reported that it had a worthwhile harbour – Port Tavano it was called – and that this could serve as a useful base from which to dominate the surrounding seas as far as Kamchatka and into the Sea of Okhotsk. Politically, Urup was the first of the islands which was Russian, when sailing northeast, those to the southwest having been settled by Japanese for three generations. The treaty which Admiral Putiatin had agreed with Japan had determined the boundary, and presumably Stirling knew of this. Geographically, it may well also have looked like a good notion. If a viable base could be established at Urup it would relieve the Allies of having to depend on Japanese goodwill, which by now – as the Japanese officials were at last coming to realise that their port at Hakodate was being used as a base in the war – was in distinctly short supply. Their forbearance at Hakodate was shortening. The island might be made into a possible coaling station, or so it has been suggested, though,

---

[24] *Illustrated London News*, 17 February 1855.
[25] ADM 1/5657, 1 October 1855.

like these other conjectures, this does not get a contemporary mention.[26]

Pique and *La Sybille* turned back to sail northeastwards along the Pacific side of Hokkaido. They were delayed for five days by bad weather and only reached Urup on the 26th, and then were delayed for another five days by thick fog and inconstant winds. Captain Nicholson of *Pique* then stood in to the harbour, under the impression – perhaps from Hoste's report – that it was large enough for his ship and *La Sybille* together. He was wrong. He moored, but on looking round decided that the space was far too confining, particularly in view of what he knew of the storminess of the region; he took his ship out again and anchored half a mile offshore. *La Sybille* had only been able to anchor several miles away, and Captain de Maisonneuve was spared the necessity of testing the harbour.

Whatever reasons had been put forward for this expedition, the failure of the harbour to provide decent accommodation for a relatively small ship – *Pique* was a 40-gun frigate – had already shown that the island was unsuitable. In such a geographical situation, only a decent harbour, large and well sheltered, with docking facilities, either available or to be developed, could justify possession by the Allies, since everything would have to be imported by sea, and the island's only value was that it was Russian, and that it was located in such a position that it could be used to dominate the local seas. Having come so far, however, it would have to be more comprehensively examined than Nicholson's brief encounter with the harbour had allowed.

On 2 September Captain de Maisonneuve was rowed to *Pique*, and the two captains then went into the harbour in their ships' boats. The two men carried out a ceremony of possession, taking the island in the names of both of their countries, an event which looks more like a lark than a serious political development. De Maisonneuve suggested that a more euphonious name would be appropriate: they renamed Urup 'L'île de l'Alliance'; the Kuriles were renamed, more sourly, 'Fog Archipelago'.

This ceremony was witnessed by elements of the local population, listed by Nicholson as three men, thirteen women, and many children. Tavano, now demoted to a village in his

---

[26] Stephan, *Kuril Islands*, ch. 2.

account, had a few wooden houses, some storehouses used by the Russian-American Company, some native huts, and 'a wooden battery with three small iron guns' facing the harbour entrance. This is a description which could have applied to Aian or to Okhotsk or to most other Russian posts on the coasts and islands between Sakhalin and Alaska. The only things missing, apart from a church, were the Russians themselves. The people Nicholson and de Maisonneuve saw were Ainu, with 'a broad Tartar cast of countenance, with prominent cheekbones'. The children, he noted, 'were remarkably fat and chubby'.

Over the next two days, the men of the village drifted back, till there were about forty of them. They explained that there had been three Russians there, but they had left just before the Allies landed; the brief appearance of *Pique* in the harbour will have been sufficient warning. As at Aian and Petropavlovsk, the Russians will not have gone far, but Nicholson and de Maisonneuve did not have the time, resources, or inclination to search for them. The resources of the island consisted of fish, which abounded in the harbour, and a few roots and herbs. Rye flour was supplied by the Russians periodically. The island was visited about once a month by a Company ship from Sitka, no doubt one such as the captured *Okhotsk*. The storehouses showed what was collected: skins, salted fish, salted seal meat. The rye flour, sugar, salt and oil were given to the natives in exchange for these goods.

Nicholson and de Maisonneuve went through with the charade of taking possession, though they surely knew that it was never going to be a usable base, at least not for the Allies. A man was selected as the chief and appointed as 'governor', three of the storehouses were burnt, and the battery was destroyed. (This will have told the new governor that his new masters were not intending to stay in the place, for why destroy what is now yours?) A notice, in English and French, was fixed to the largest house (which was no doubt the one the Russians lived in), signifying the island's possession by Britain and France. The captains then departed. No one present, other than the invaders now leaving, could read the notice.

Lieutenant Mansel of *Pique* was meanwhile dispatched in a boat to examine the coast to the northeast of Tavano. He sailed parallel to the shore for twelve miles, but at only one place could he land; elsewhere 'the rocks and surf, which extend about half a mile offshore, the whole length of the coast', prevented any approach. He did spot a cutter and two whale boats in a bay, and came back next day together with a French boat under Lieutenant Sibour. They managed to get ashore to remove the boats, and found a few huts nearby, from which the inhabitants had fled. They took the boats, which were regarded as Russian government property and therefore lootable, back to their ships. The victors divided the spoils. The whale boats were allocated, one to *Pique* and one to *La Sybille*; the other, described by Nicholson as a 'sailing vessel' (Mansel called it a cutter), was scuttled; Nicholson in the event did not want his allocated whale boat and gave it to de Maisonneuve. In Mansel's brief report of his fruitless exploration he added a postscript which in effect summed up the result of the whole expedition: 'I observed no appearance of any harbour or anchorage.' Without either, for the Allies the island was useless.

Nicholson added some 'remarks' about the island, but these are essentially sailing directions, and a brief geographical description. It is replete with comments such as 'the constant prevalence of fogs', 'numerous rocks scattered along near the shore', and 'there is no firewood at Tavano', all of which would be quite sufficient deterrence to discourage anyone, particularly a sailor, from visiting. Nicholson's description of how to get into the harbour is hair-raising; and once inside, the ship was exposed to a heavy swell and to strong winds. A few names were bestowed which summed up as bleakly as Lieutenant Mansel's comments the non-attraction of the island: the Pique Rocks at the entrance to the harbour, and Cape Sybille, whose offshore rocks mean that it 'should not be approached too closely'.[27]

The two ships returned to Hakodate by 12 September, after a voyage of five weeks. By that time even *Pique*'s company were showing symptoms of scurvy – one wonders how *La Sybille*'s company were faring. Fresh vegetables purchased at Hakodate stayed the symptoms quickly enough, and the two ships sailed again on the 21st. They parted from each other in fog and rain soon afterwards. *Pique* arrived at Nagasaki on the 29th.

While this little expedition was going on, Stirling had taken his own force, *Winchester, Nankin, Virginie* and *Styx*, to investigate the coast of the mainland, the area Elliot had never been

---

[27] ADM 1/5657, 29 and 2 September 1855.

able to look at. No report on this seems to have survived. It was probably in a letter which Stirling wrote to the Admiralty dated 15 September in which he 'detailed proceedings of Her Majesty's Squadron in the exploration of a portion of the coast of Tartary', but this is not in the Admiralty archives. The logs of the ships, however, noted that the squadron reached the mainland on 23 August. They then explored along the coast to the north before heading for Nagasaki.

What they had 'discovered' was the bay earlier called Broughton Bay by William Broughton, who had explored this area half a century before, and which is now Zolotoy Bay, the Golden Horn, at Vladivostok. Later Stirling was to wax lyrical about its attractions, both as a place and as a possible naval and commercial base. The squadron had some fun naming the islands and harbours they located, some after their ships – Nankin Harbour – some politically correct – Victoria Island, Napoleon Harbour – and some named after individuals – Port Bruce, named after the captain of *Styx*, which was used to explore much of the area.

Sailing north they found and named Alliance Bay and Guérin Bay, but were unable ever to make these names stick. Turning south the squadron sailed along the east coast of Korea, just as Admiral Putiatin had done a year earlier in the opposite direction. Stirling sent a letter to the governor of Fusankai – presumably Fusan, on the south coast – explaining that ships of the Allies had come into his harbour in search of Russians and looking for refreshments. In neither case were they successful. Korea was not about to be opened up yet. The squadron sailed for Nagasaki.[28]

On 1 October, Admiral Stirling, surrounded in Nagasaki harbour by eleven British warships, plus the French *Virginie*, wrote a summary of his squadron's achievements over the previous summer. The seas and coasts from Japan to Kamchatka had been examined, the maritime power of Russia was exposed in these seas as minimal, several Russian vessels had been destroyed and many of *Diana*'s men had been captured, Urup Island had been acquired. But he could not claim that his primary mission, which was to destroy the Russian ships, had been successful, nor had he destroyed or even harassed the

---

[28] ADM 53/4915, log of *Styx*; 53/5634, log of *Winchester*, 23 August–3 September 1855; 50/278, Stirling Journal, 15–29 September 1855.

Russian posts on land, though he could claim that it was an advantage that relations with Japan had allowed its Hakodate port to be used as an Allied naval base.[29] Nor could he claim to have either investigated or located, still less destroyed, the Russian base said to be at the mouth of the Amur River.

What Stirling did not do in this summary, though his next actions imply that he did appreciate what had occurred, was to report on what he understood the Russian actions to mean. Someone else did draw up a set of conclusions, however, though the paper is both incomplete and anonymous. It consists of a copy made in the Admiralty for a file containing a variety of accounts of places around the world. One of these, for example, is by Captain Frederick of *Amphitrite* concerning the Sea of Okhotsk. The next one in the file refers to the dates at which Aian and Petropavlovsk are likely to be free enough of ice to be visited (June), and notes that they are likely to be closed again by early October. It then goes on with a paragraph on the situation as perceived by the writer in political terms:

> It seems more than probable that the intentions of the Russians are to establish themselves in force and permanently, to form as soon as they can a strong hold on the island of Saghalien which would not only give them easy access to Japan and the Chinese ports, but perhaps also in the course of time an occasional preponderance in the North Pacific and the Sea of Japan, especially if they happened to be in concert with the United States and the United States held the Sandwich Islands ...[30]

The document breaks off at this point, in the middle of the sentence. It is clearly written from the point of view of a British naval officer on the China Station who had experience in those seas in the previous months. Elliot, perhaps, or Stirling, or one of the captains, could have written it. It is also a fairly accurate summary of the information gathered with such difficulty over the summer of 1855. And this is what Stirling appears to have understood also. He had just about one more month in which to do something about it, before the ice closed in again.

And while he and his ships had been searching the seas

---

[29] ADM 1/5657, 1 October 1855.
[30] ADM 172/2/7, 'Sea of Okhotsk'.

between Kamchatka and Korea for Russians, the Russians themselves had been consolidating their hold on the posts they had established on the mainland. The two were at last about to collide.

7

The Amur Estuary

Governor-General Muravev planned a second expedition down the Amur River for 1855. He sent a note to Peking to that effect on 2 March. No doubt he was much encouraged by the success of his expedition of the previous year, and by the successful defence of Petropavlovsk, which had been largely due to the soldiers he had sent there from the Amur in August. The Russian position at the Amur had thus, to some extent, proved its value even in 1854. He set 28 April as the date on which the expedition was to sail.

This new voyage was to comprise a much larger company than that of the previous year, and was to be divided into three successive sections. Muravev would conduct the first himself, consisting of twenty-six barges carrying half a battalion of Cossacks; the second group, of fifty-two barges, would carry the 15th Line Battalion; the third, with thirty-five barges, would have on board half of the 14th Line Battalion. All these units would be accompanied by the wives and children of the soldiers, and by cattle and horses, and would carry with them supplies and ammunition. For Muravev, perhaps the most important part of the cargo was forty heavy guns, made in the Ural iron foundries in the past year and moved with infinite effort all the way across Siberia. Loading them onto the rather fragile barges was not easy. They were intended to be Muravev's key elements of power at the Amur estuary. Under the guise of fighting the British and French, he was intending to establish a military colony.

Such a huge expedition took more organisation than he had time to give it, and almost inevitably it was not ready in time. Muravev was, of course, annoyed. He had intended his first section to be at Lake Kizi, that is, the post at Mariinsk, and therefore close to De Castries Bay, by 18 May, but it was only on the 14th that he was able to set off from Nerchinsk with just half of the first section, thirteen barges. He had in fact been very optimistic in hoping to begin the voyage before May, since the frozen river rarely thawed before that month.

The Chinese replied to his earlier note with a proposal for a meeting in order to determine the boundary. This had been their standard tactic, for the determination of the boundary would mean the acceptance by Russia of the terms of the old Treaty of Nerchinsk by which the boundary had been located well to the north of the Amur. By the same token Muravev had always evaded that issue, emphasising the need to defend Russia against British and French attacks, in order that the Nerchinsk terms should be overruled. He had also opposed the search by Colonel Akhte for the Chinese boundary markers, since if they were found, he was in trouble: Muravev knew he was on very shaky legal ground. His earlier message said that he was taking reinforcements to help defend the Amur estuary against the attacks of the Allies, even though none had taken place, and none were even threatened. He described the repulse of the Allies at Petropavlovsk, which, of course, was irrelevant, but he could be fairly sure that the Chinese government had no idea where the place was.

On this second voyage down the river he met four Chinese ships, carrying a group of officials towards Gorlitza, the meeting place which the Chinese had suggested for the boundary delimitation. Muravev put them off with the same argument, then suggested a meeting at Aigun, and further suggested that they wait there to receive more instructions. The two parties passed each other, going in opposite directions; there would be no boundary negotiations for some time, but the Chinese and officials did not give up.

Again Muravev passed Aigun, giving the governor the same explanation as the year before, and remarking that many more boats would follow him, carrying, so he said, 8000 people and much material – once again deliberately exaggerating his numbers. He requested, politely, that they be allowed to pass. The governor, faced by such numbers, could not possibly demur; but now, for the first time, a Chinese official realised the sheer scale of the Russian expeditions. It scarcely looked like a defensive military operation. The Russian purpose was at last appreciated: it was to establish a new settlement, in some numbers, on Chinese territory.[1]

1 Quested, *Expansion of Russia*, 48–51; Vladimir, *Russia on the Pacific*, 235–237; Semenov, *Siberia*, 271.

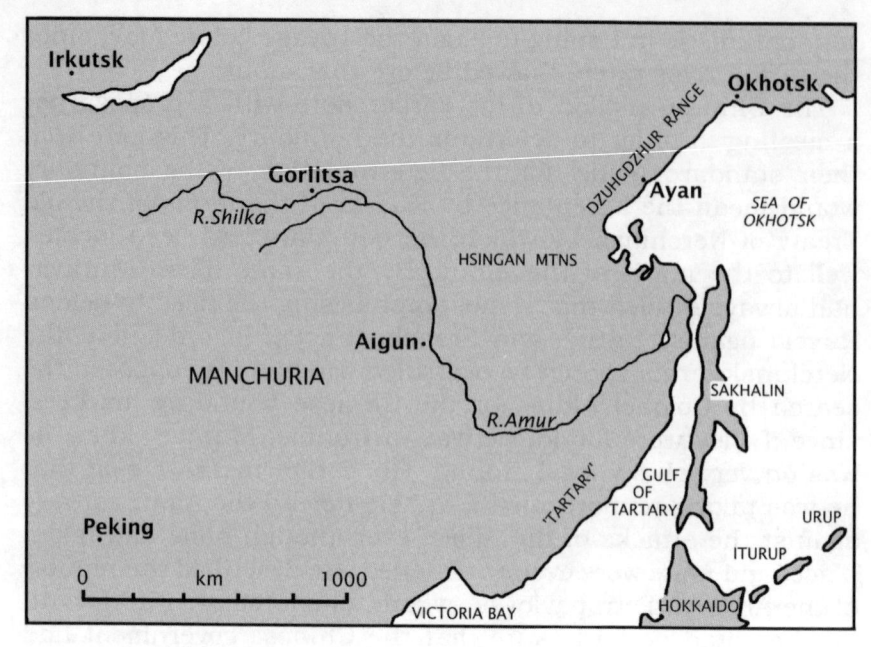

Map 4 Eastern Siberia and the Amur River

The journey down the river was easier this time for Muravev and his comparatively small advance group. The following sections had a more difficult time of it, encumbered with women, children, stores, and the forty artillery pieces. Some of the cattle died, because food for them had been stored on different barges. Typhus broke out and several of the victims died. And yet most of the colonists survived and reached their destination.

The civilian settlement was to be the charge of Prince Volkonski, who travelled with the settlers. They arrived late in June, and Volkonski inspected the suggested sites for the settlements, but at once rejected them as unsuitable. The sites had been chosen by Nevelskoi, whose priorities were military. A committee of senior peasants looked at all the possibilities and chose the sites likeliest to be agriculturally successful. Volkonski, Muravev and Nevelskoi had the good sense to accept their recommendations.

No less than five places were chosen, four on the right bank, given the names Irkutskoi, Bogorodskoi, Mikhailovskoi and Novo Mikhailovskoi, and one, called Sergeievskoi, on the less hospitable left bank. These were scattered along the length of the river between Mariinsk and Nikolaevsk, and were chosen for their agricultural potential rather than their defensibility or tactical use. Only one of Nevelskoi's original suggestions was included. The grandees' acceptance of the suggestions of the peasants is another clear sign that the settlement, as Muravev all along had intended, was to be permanent and eventually civilian in character. He was a coloniser and imperialist.[2]

Muravev had already been in the area for some time when this took place. He arrived after the British had discovered Zavoiko's squadron at De Castries Bay, but at about the time Zavoiko escaped into the Amur sands. Zavoiko, true to his dual experience as an army officer who had transferred to the navy, went as far as Cape Lazarov, and there he landed, bringing up some of his guns from the ships – they could not be carried through the shallows anyway – and began to fortify the headland. It seems that the guns from *Pallas* had already been landed there, and the ship sent back to Imperatorskaia Gavan. The strait between the cape and the Sakhalin shore was only four kilometres wide at that point, and the narrow channel rendered the high cape a very defensible post. Any ships trying to get through would become very vulnerable to bombardment, all the more so if they were sounding and searching for the channel. The guns would be firing from a firm foundation at ships which may well be stuck in the sands; it would be an artilleryman's dream.[3]

Muravev, however, was not concerned about defending the strait. What he intended was to defend his settlements along the river, and that meant Nikolaevsk, Mariinsk and De Castries Bay – though it seems that this last was probably expendable. It is unlikely that the new peasant villages established under Volkonski's guidance were included in the defensive system. Muravev himself took overall command of all his forces; he appointed Nevelskoi as his chief of staff, and Zavoiko was put in command of all the ships and crews. Muravev placed his headquarters at Mariinsk, the best communication centre from which to reach the other two main posts. When the guns arrived on the barges from Nerchinsk, they were placed to defend Nikolaevsk,

---

2 Vladimir, *Russia on the Pacific*, 234.
3 Vladimir, *Russia on the Pacific*, 234.

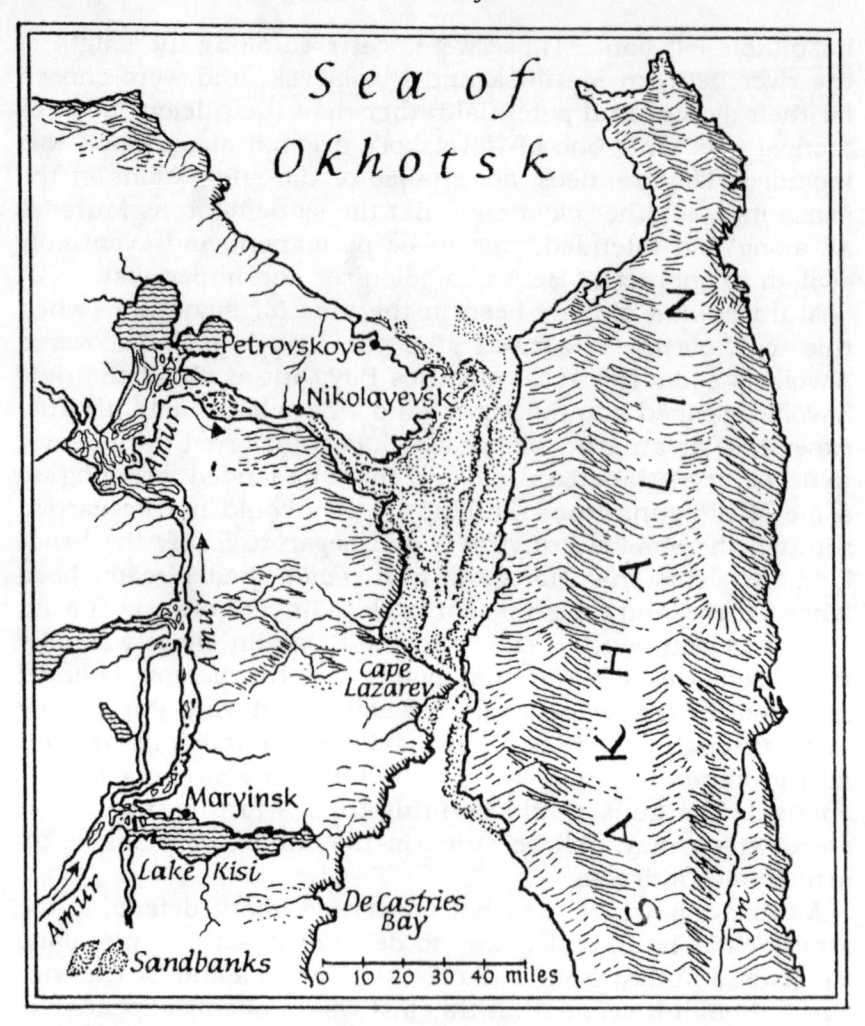

Map 5 'The Riddle of the Mouth of the Amur' (from Y. Semenov, *Siberia, its Conquest and Development*, trans. J. Foster, London 1965, p. 265)

for Muravev expected the Allies – he repeatedly referred to them as 'the English' – to attempt to destroy his posts by sailing up the river, and the experience of Zavoiko at Petropavlovsk was that the ships could destroy land batteries unless the latter were concentrated and well fortified. The visits by the British to De Castries Bay will have convinced him that he was right, and their examination of the Sea of Okhotsk would seem to be further confirmation that they were actively searching for his bases. De Castries Bay, where there were several buildings, was to be defended by his force of 500 Cossacks. These were, in effect, light infantry, for they had not been able to bring a full complement of horses in the barges. They were, therefore, skirmishers, and they were obviously intended only to delay any serious attack and harass any invasion, fighting from the forest, until a larger and better-equipped force could move in from Mariinsk.

Muravev's strategy, therefore, had changed since the year before. He had at first intended to defend all the main posts, as exemplified by his dispatch of a large part of his disposable force as reinforcements to Petropavlovsk. Perhaps he thought that the Allies would therefore concentrate on that town, and it could therefore be a post from which all the other places could be defended. At the same time he had then withdrawn the smaller posts such as those on Sakhalin, which were manifestly indefensible against even the smallest Allied naval force. Petropavlovsk with a thousand men, an admiral in command, and numerous batteries, seemed to be defensible; Muravevsk in Aniwa Bay, with a score of men and a small battery, was not worth holding. In fact, however, the fighting at Petropavlovsk had almost been disastrous for the Russians. A continuation of the first plan of attack – Price's plan – would have seen the ships destroyed or taken, and perhaps the town itself captured. After just one day's bombardment, the crucial batteries had been suppressed; but for the Allies' switch to a landing, the town might well have been itself battered to destruction. But what Muravev never seems to have understood was that the Allies were mainly after the ships, not his landward posts. On the other hand, he was fixated on the idea that the 'English' wanted the Amur estuary for themselves, and any warlike actions and developments by the Allies were interpreted by him in the light of that idea.

He had now decided to concentrate all his defence in a relatively small area, the lower course and estuary of the Amur. Whether he took into account the difficulty of an approach by sea through the sands is not clear, but any sailor – Zavoiko, for example, or Putiatin – could have pointed it out. Under the new strategy, even well-established places such as Petropavlovsk and Aian had become expendable; defence was wholly concentrated at Nikolaevsk and Mariinsk, with forward posts at De Castries Bay and perhaps Petrovskoi.

For Muravev was, as before, playing a triple game. He used the quite evident threat of Allied sea power to gull the Chinese into thinking he was conducting a forward defence of his area of command, taking full advantage of the preoccupation of the imperial government with the huge Taiping rebellion. In this he was greatly assisted by the inability of the Manchu provincial governors and commanders to do anything without instructions from Peking, though, to be fair, the governors and commanders in Manchuria had had to give up large parts of their armed manpower to help fight the rebels elsewhere. None of them had enough men to be able to stop any of Muravev's expeditions.

Muravev was thus playing off China against Britain (he always ignored the French in all this), knowing full well that Britain was a power detested by the Manchu government for having defeated it in war and having forced the opening of several ports to foreign commerce. For all we or he knew, the emperor may have believed he was playing a subtle game in having two of China's enemies, Britain and Russia, fight each other. The emperor was, of course, profoundly ignorant, as were all his officials, about the size, capabilities, wealth, even geographical position, of the two.

Muravev could also be given an almost up-to-date briefing on the results of Putiatin's negotiations in Japan, and the fate of the *Diana*. The admiral's stay in the Amur region overlapped with Muravev's for a month or so, and he could also give Muravev some idea of the capabilities of the Allied forces, particularly those in Chinese waters. Muravev may well not have considered the sheer quantity of sea power involved, but he surely understood the implications of Stirling's agreement with the Japanese that he could use Hakodate as his forward base. He and Putiatin could also rely on the officers at Shimoda filling Japanese ears with stories of Russian power. Indeed these officers did make good use of world maps to contrast the size of Britain and France with that of Russia, and the distance of Britain and France from Japan by comparison with the closeness of Russia.[4]

Putiatin, no doubt almost as committed as Muravev to

---

[4] Lensen, *Russia's Japan Expedition*.

the extension of Russian territory in the Far East, began his return journey to St Petersburg on 4 July, embarking on one of Muravev's steamers, the *Nadezhda*, to steam up the Amur. By this time Muravev will have heard that his tsar, Nicholas I, had died in March, but he could rely on his successor, Alexander II, with whom he had had good relations for some time; and in July he received a message from the new tsar's brother, Grand Duke Constantine, which encouraged him to continue his work. The fighting in the Crimea was going badly enough, and the threat of Allied sea power in the Baltic was even more potent, so that the imperial government would wish to encourage any development anywhere which looked as though it would redound to Russia's advantage.

Muravev had passed the Chinese delegates who proposed to meet him at Gorlitza on the Shilka River, and they had gone on there, perhaps hoping someone else would turn up with whom they could negotiate. When he heard of this, the Xianfeng emperor ordered them to go after Muravev, and they finally caught up with him at Mariinsk on 20 September. By this time the settlements had been founded, the guns emplaced, houses begun, and some cultivation prepared, as Elliot's men were to discover a little later at De Castries Bay. Muravev may well have appreciated by this time that the Allies were not actually preparing an armed attack, at least not yet, and that his conquest was secure, at least militarily for this year.

That is, Muravev's delaying tactics had once again blocked any Chinese counter moves. But now, at last, he had to meet with the group of Chinese officials who were prepared and empowered to negotiate. He hijacked the conference by issuing a set of demands which had only marginal relevance to the actual reason for the meeting, which was supposed to be frontier delimitation. He set out three demands: that all the territory from the Hsingan mountain range southwards as far as the left (that is, the northern) bank of the Amur be recognised as Russian; that the Russians be permitted to navigate the whole of the Amur – thereby effectively making the boundary the right (the southern) bank – and that the posts at Mariinsk and elsewhere be kept by Russia, even though these were largely on the right bank; and thirdly, that the Fei-ya-ha (or Feiyko), the local tribe, and others in the area, be resettled elsewhere in China.

The Chinese delegates argued, pointing out that this was not what the conference was supposed to discuss, and referring to the original Russian note of June 1853 which had asked that the actual frontier be marked. That is, they quite rightly pointed out that Muravev was breaking the diplomatic rules. Muravev simply repeated his list of demands, knowing full well that the Chinese would never be able to accept them and that they would need to refer back to the emperor on the subject. The conference was therefore short and wholly unproductive. The Chinese wrote a memorial for the emperor, reporting on the conference, and, proving that they had kept their eyes open, describing the Russian establishment at Mariinsk as having nearly a hundred buildings, with artillery emplacements; it was evident, they said, that the Russians intended to seize control of the area. As Muravev no doubt hoped would happen, this memorial did not reach the emperor until the beginning of December. By that time any reaction by the emperor and by the Chinese government as a whole would not eventuate until the next spring. Further, late in December the Russian government sent a note to Peking endorsing Muravev's demands.[5]

How much Muravev knew of the internal Chinese situation is unclear, but he obviously knew of the great Taiping rebellion, which in 1855 was in control of much of the south of the country, and had been threatening to extend its conquests into the north for some time. He probably did not know that the Yellow River had again burst its banks during the year, flooding immense areas, and eventually changing its lower course drastically. He presumably understood that it was exactly in such circumstances that an autocratic government is at its most vulnerable – after all, he was a subject of an autocrat himself – and that the bureaucratic system in China required constant reference back to the emperor in person for major decisions. And from the state of the country he had passed through, and its sheer size, it was obvious that any decisions would be slow in coming.

To the Xianfeng emperor the events in the north were of minor importance compared with the loss of control of the south and the destruction in the Yellow River valley. The very fact that Muravev and his explorers met no Chinese officials, or even merchants, in the Amur valley, except at Aigun, indicates

---

[5] Quested, *Expansion of Russia*, 53; Lin, 'Amur Frontier Question', 12–13.

the lack of any real interest in the area on the part of the imperial government. When Muravev first passed along the river, the emperor had minuted that he should be allowed to go and fight his enemies. He surely understood the feeling.

Muravev's assumption that the Allies intended to attack his posts, which we must accept that he believed since this is what he consistently said, was, of course, quite wrong. The Allies had only become involved because of the presence in the Pacific of the *Aurora* and the *Diana*. If they had not been around, or if they had been intercepted off the coast of South America, or somewhere else in the Pacific, it is very doubtful that the Allies would have bothered with such places as Petropavlovsk or Aian or the Amur estuary. But once *Aurora* reached Petropavlovsk the chain of events unfolded inexorably. Even so, the Amur was all Muravev's work. If he had not deliberately attracted all the local Russian power to the Amur, in effect thereby emphasising his presence, the Allies would not have paid him any attention.

The various expeditions and surveys by the Allies – the British were clearly the driving force – have attracted some adverse comment. One account scornfully claims that the capture of the *Okhotsk* was 'the great achievement of the naval campaign in the Pacific'.[6] This is of course ignorant nonsense. Stirling had used his ships to systematically investigate the whole immense area where the Russians might be found, and he had done it within a single sailing season. It was only in the previous winter that he had been told to do this, and only since May that he had been able – because of the weather – to carry out the task. It was the only approach which made naval strategic sense: that is, investigating the possible places where the Russian ships might be, eliminating them one at a time, and then deducing that whatever was left, however unlikely, must be their refuge. By the end of September this refuge was narrowed down to the area of the Amur estuary. So that became Stirling's next task.

Yet he still needed further information, and he had to bear in mind the Admiralty's contradictory instructions to harass and/or destroy the Russian posts and settlements, and yet not to get involved in any armed landings. Stirling was, of course,

---

[6] ADM 1/5657, 1 October 1855.

not just concerned with Muravev's doings. In his report to the Admiralty on 1 October he listed the ships in Nagasaki harbour and described the scene with the substantial fleet at anchor there as an 'exhibition of force'. The British ships were *Winchester, Sybille, Nankin, Pique, Encounter, Spartan, Hornet, Barracouta, Styx, Saracen* and *Tartar*. In addition there was the French *Virginie*. The only Russian ship to reach Japan had sunk. As an exhibition of power it was very convincing.

Stirling referred to this in the context of the war with Russia, but it was also relevant to the implicit competition with the United States in relation to Japan, for Stirling's eleven British ships were a much more convincing 'appearance of menace' – which he deemed was necessary in the negotiations with Japan – than anything Commodore Perry had produced, which was a maximum of four ships. But then the Japanese were already fully aware of British power in the area; it had been the British defeat of China in 1842 which had been the real beginnings of the argument within Japan which ultimately led to the opening up of the country, the Meiji Revolution, and the country's subsequent 'modernisation'.

And in the back of Stirling's mind there was also the issue of China. His command was, after all, the 'China and East Indies Command', and it stretched from Africa to Australia to the Sea of Okhotsk and east to longitude 170°E, halfway to America. In all that huge territory it was relations with, and the future of, China which was the real ongoing problem. The war with Russia was no more than a mere brief interruption. Stirling's vessels would need to be prepared to deal with a Chinese difficulty at any time. Probably Stirling and the Xianfeng emperor would have agreed on the unimportance of Russian activities, had they ever met; they were both mistaken.

Then there was Stirling's most difficult and dangerous problem: his relations with the Admiralty in London. He now had to deal with the new First Lord, Sir Charles Wood, who, like his predecessor, used a series of private letters to supplement and amplify and correct the official letters which came from the Board. The result might well be awkward and confusing. Wood had, for example, made the Russian war Stirling's priority, in a private letter of 19 March, and had claimed that there was a group of Poles exiled at Okhotsk who might be induced to rise in rebellion against Russia in the Allies' favour. In June he had suggested expelling Russian settlers 'from the islands'

– he was not specific, though he evidently meant the Kuriles – which could then be handed to the Japanese, thus, he thought, 'making the Japanese friends' of Britain. (It was more likely to horrify them; they were becoming fully aware of the complications which the war was bringing to their neighbourhood by now, far more so than was the Manchu government in Peking.) Wood had added, in contradiction to earlier messages to Bruce and Stirling prohibiting landings, that he might be able to arrange 'aid with some force from India', and perhaps Manchu forces could assist, and so deal with the Russian settlements, if Stirling could not reach them from the sea.[7]

This letter is a most interesting formulation of Stirling's possible future conduct, and it fits in well with traditional British military strategy. In the Crimea, the great majority of soldiers were French, Turkish, or Sardinian, with no more than a quarter being British. In the Baltic and the White Sea the naval burden was to some extent shared, but the majority of ships and men were British. Back in the Napoleonic Wars, which was the last time any of the generals and politicians had been involved in a great war against a major European power, the British forces had similarly been a relatively small proportion of those fighting to bring down Napoleon – even the Waterloo army was no more than a quarter British, when the Prussians are included. And now Wood was suggesting using these same methods in the Far East: make friends with Japan, enlist Manchu help, use forces from India.

Stirling, therefore, had to juggle several competing priorities and demands. He could be certain that, despite Wood's assurance that the war should be his priority, if trouble developed in China he would be expected to be on the spot to deal with it. Meanwhile, he had a month or a little more to accomplish something in the Gulf of Tartary, now that it was certain there was a passage to the north, and that the Russian ships had escaped in that direction. From the end of October he could not be sure of being able to operate in that area due to ice; from the beginning of October he could be sure that most of the Sea of Okhotsk would be inaccessible. On the day he finished his Admiralty letter, 1 October, he gave instructions to Commodore Elliot to go again to the head of the Gulf, determine the nature

---

[7] BL Add. Mss 49562, 4–6, 9 March 1855, and 49563, 21, 9 July 1854.

of the passage north, and find the Russian ships. Elliot was allocated his own ship *Sybille* and no less than three steamships – *Hornet*, *Encounter* and *Barracouta* – for the Gulf; *Barracouta* was sent on ahead. Elliot was to stay as long as he could, considering the health of his men, the state of the weather, and the quantity of stores he had. And on his return, Stirling had jobs for him in China.[8]

Meanwhile Stirling had to deal with the *Greta* prize and the Russian prisoners. *Greta*, still with her prize crew on board, had been sent on to Hong Kong to be adjudicated in the Vice-Admiralty Court. Neither *Sybille* nor *Barracouta* could go on their voyage into the Gulf carrying their quotas of prisoners. The newly arrived *Nankin*, a large frigate, received a hundred men and two officers – which looks like the men from *Sybille*, less some of the officers, possibly those left at Aian. Other ships going to Hong Kong, such as the *Winchester*, no doubt took on *Barracouta*'s contingent.

Nankin reached Hong Kong on the 11th. *Greta* had arrived in mid-September and at once went to the Vice-Admiralty Court for adjudication, but the prisoners were a problem. Sir John Bowring claimed that he could not allow them to be landed on the island, given the precarious state of affairs involving Britain, Russia and China, and the Taiping rebels, though he did accept the officers' paroles, and let them live in the town – while also instructing the Superintendent of Police to watch them. He reported all this in a letter to the Colonial Office, and meanwhile he was waiting, no doubt with some apprehension, for the rest of the prisoners to arrive. But by keeping them on board *Nankin*, he effectively left them to be dealt with by the Navy.[9]

Stirling sent *Barracouta* first to Shanghai, where the new captain took over. This was Commander Fortescue, and Stirling's son now reverted to his original post as commander in the flagship. Commander Fellowes, on the end of the line, had to go, discharged on half pay. (He went to Hong Kong on his way home, and there found a position as commander of *Rattler*, a small steamship which operated on the Canton River.)[10] After a couple of months young Stirling was sent to Britain carrying

---

[8] ADM 1/5657, 1 October 1855.
[9] ADM 1/5666, 13 October 1855.
[10] ADM 53/278, Stirling Journal, 28 December 1855.

The Amur Estuary

mail and messages for the Admiralty. His presence there will concern us later. *Barracouta* reached Shanghai on 4 October and sailed again on the 8th, heading for the Gulf, but did not make the full journey. In the middle of the Sea of Japan, Fortescue turned back; it was clearly not possible for him to get through to the Gulf in time to be of any use. He was back in Shanghai on 21 October. So Elliot's little fleet was reduced by a quarter.

Elliot himself, with *Sybille, Encounter* and *Hornet,* sailed from Nagasaki, but did not reach De Castries Bay until the 15th. Once at the bay he found that things had changed. In the first place there was a ship in the bay discharging passengers and cargo. Perhaps Elliot at first thought he had found his quarry, but it turned out to be the *Behring,* the American ship out of Boston whose owner had been sending a ship or two every year for the past dozen years, carrying supplies to Kamchatka and other areas, and receiving furs and so on in exchange. It had already been at Petropavlovsk where no market existed, and had come to De Castries Bay with a varied cargo.

We are fortunate in this case that Elliot's official report can be supplemented by an account given by the supercargo on the *Behring,* George Cushing, which he gave in to Consul-General Miller at Honolulu in December (and which Miller sent to the Foreign Office; this has already been referred to in connection with the events at Petropavlovsk after Admiral Bruce had departed). *Behring* had brought Madame Zavoika, the admiral's wife, her children and servants from Petropavlovsk, under a safe conduct pass from Captain Houstoun of *Trincomalee,* and had put them ashore at De Castries Bay on 2 October, a fortnight before Elliot and his ships arrived. They had then, Elliot was told, gone inland to the Amur. The ship had been unloading freight ever since. *Behring*'s captain appears to have been as free with information as anyone else in this situation, and Elliot learned that a Russian officer from *Pallas* had been in charge at the bay.[11]

So, as soon as he had spoken with the captain of *Behring,* Elliot knew that De Castries Bay was once again under Russian naval or military control, and that there was a reasonable road connecting it with whatever settlements there were inland

---

[11] ADM 1/5672, 25 November 1855, and 1/5677, 5 December 1855.

and on the river. When he repeated the visual inspection he had made five months before, he could also see that substantial changes had been made, changes which implied a better defence than had been the case earlier. The buildings which he had inspected near the shore on his original visit had been dismantled and rebuilt 500 yards inland, 'behind a woody ridge which hid from our view all but their roofs'.

Elliot was quite sure all this indicated a more substantial Russian investment in the place as a base and as a port than earlier; the question was whether the Russians were present this time in sufficient numbers to attempt a defence if he landed. For he had to land, if only to gather the usual fresh water and firewood, but above all to make a proper inspection and to see what else lay behind that ridge; he also had to test the Russian position. So much for the Admiralty's instructions.

Lieutenant Dent was once again put in command of the landing force, divided among six boats, cutters, a barge and a pinnace, from all three of the ships, and manned both by sailors and by the marines, forty in number, from the ships. The landing was hampered by the interference of the captain of the *Behring*, who informed Elliot, no doubt with a mixture of apprehension and indignation, that the goods he had landed were not yet sold, were therefore still his (and American) property, and that he had thrown American flags over them. This may have restricted Elliot's options, since a preliminary bombardment would have been a sensible move. So Dent and his landing force did not have that protection. On the other hand, Elliot made ready to bombard the shore anyway, in case resistance appeared.

It was now early afternoon – 1 p.m., Elliot says – and the several British boats approached the chosen landing spot, no doubt well spread out. At 200 yards from the beach, *Sybille*'s cutter was fired on. Dent had a brief warning of this, for some men had appeared near the huts just before that, and then the fire came from two or three artillery pieces, firing both round shot and grape, and from riflemen, armed with Minié rifles, who were spread along the edge of the forest.

Fire was returned from the boats' guns, from the rocket-firer on *Hornet*'s cutter, and from the men in the boats. In all cases the distance was far too great for it to be effective – the other boats were some way behind *Sybille*'s cutter, and the Russian soldiers were well back from the beach and well hidden. Dent ordered his boats to pull back, and *Encounter* fired over their heads. *Encounter* and *Hornet* then steamed in closer and kept up 'an occasional fire', as did *Sybille* from further out. In the whole affair, which cannot have lasted long, the British suffered only five men wounded.

One Russian account claims that there were 400 men in the landing force, and only seventy, and two guns, in the defence.[12] But, since it also claims that the British ('English') actually landed, it is hardly reliable, though it does admit to one Russian soldier killed and one wounded. The commander of the garrison had apparently just gone inland to Mariinsk, and he turned back as soon as he heard the news, and brought reinforcements with him. The 500 Cossacks Muravev had posted to defend De Castries Bay were in fact scattered along the route from Mariinsk to the bay, though some were within about twenty miles. By the day after the attempted landing, the Russian commander had arrived, and a day later most of the Cossacks were also present. The Russian account may be deficient in detail, and inaccurate in parts, but it is quite correct in commenting that 'the slender chances of success the English might have found on the first day were rapidly diminishing' in the days after.

Yet Elliot's purpose, according to his instructions, was not actually to land or to conquer, but rather investigation, and by detecting that a substantial Russian force was available to defend De Castries Bay he had completed part of his task; the absence of any Russian ships was also significant, as was the presence of the American importer. During the night Elliot sent the masters of the ships in the boats to sound the entrance to the bay and to investigate the mouth of the creek which he thought might be big enough to conceal a ship; the water was only two or three feet deep at the mouth, so he could write off that possibility as well. In the morning Dent was sent out again with four of the squadron's boats to make a more careful search of the harbour. He discovered a partly built log building 'loop-holed for musquetry', close to a watering place; on a low point to the north there was an unfinished 'gabionade' which was placed to dominate the entrance to a creek.

The boats then trailed their coats, moving close to the landing

---

[12] Vladimir, *Russia on the Pacific*, 240–244.

place in a menacing way. Sure enough, the Russian guns opened fire. The ships were thus able to register their guns on those positions; shrapnel was fired, and shells, and 'the guns were soon silenced, and the enemy must have suffered severely'; this is when one Russian died and one was wounded. Bullets from the Russian riflemen were dug out of the sides of the boats and recognised as Minié bullets from their distinctive shape. Elliot then knew, if he had not already realised it, that he was facing government troops, probably regular soldiers, for a substantial force armed with Minié rifles could only be soldiers. It was one more item to add to the tally; the Russians were at De Castries Bay in strength, and nearby inland in considerable numbers. It had not actually been necessary to land to discover all this.

This part of his work having been accomplished, Elliot sent *Hornet* north, arguing that Forsyth and the ship had already partially explored the area, and that he could take up where he left off earlier. He added one of his lieutenants, Alston, and one of *Sybille*'s cutters, to assist. *Encounter* was sent in the other direction to look at the coast to the south. The Americans in *Behring* had talked of half a dozen boats having been seen before Elliot's squadron arrived; *Encounter* went to check this to see if they were nearby. *Sybille* stayed in De Castries Bay, occasionally lobbing a shell at the Russians so as to annoy them and interrupt their work. Some boats were spotted on the beach; *Sybille*'s boats went off to shoot holes in them – from a distance, of course. In this case one of the Russian guns fired at them, from a new position. Elliot could do that too, and while waiting for *Hornet* and *Encounter*, he kept changing *Sybille*'s position, sending boats about the harbour, and firing at the shore. He was, that is, harassing the Russian settlement.

Encounter returned on the 19th, after a voyage of three days. Captain O'Callaghan had found nothing but a few native huts, having sailed as far as Cape Duchie, keeping close to the coast. He had found no landing places or possible harbours, and there were steep and rugged mountains close behind the coast.[13] He was then sent north to help Forsyth and *Hornet*. *Encounter* was a smaller, lighter vessel, drawing much less water than *Hornet*, and would clearly be useful in the shoal waters. He found that Forsyth claimed to have found the channel, and was about to

---

[13] ADM 1/5672, 19 October 1855.

return to De Castries Bay in order to be there by the 23rd, as his orders stipulated. But Elliot had told O'Callaghan that he could take longer if he wished. So on the 22nd both steamers sailed north to the point which *Hornet* had earlier reached. The weather was startlingly clear and the ship was in thirteen fathoms. *Hornet* had not in fact sailed along the channel, but had merely located its southern end; it might therefore not actually be the channel, but only a cul-de-sac.

O'Callaghan was much more adventurous and determined than Forsyth – or than Elliot, for that matter. He assumed that the channel led along close to and parallel with the Sakhalin shore, but on searching for it he found that it shoaled comparatively quickly. He sent out his boats to sound, found the channel, and travelled along it for eight miles. He described the channel as 'apparently broad ... with deep water, but on either side banks'. It turned out, though, that he was not in the main channel after all, and his boats found that it shoaled to two fathoms not far ahead. Then *Hornet* ran aground. The cutter under Lieutenant Alston explored, and found another ten fathom area to the west.

By observation O'Callaghan determined that he was about thirty miles from the mouth of the Amur. 'We could see the high land about it, and I feel quite confident none of the enemy's ships were anywhere in the area.' He was well north of Cape Lazarov by this time and would have been a prime target for Zavoiko's guns had they still been there, as the two ships slowly and carefully edged their way along. The passage through to the Sea of Okhotsk was, however, still another fifty miles (eighty kilometres) away.

Meanwhile *Hornet* remained stuck on her sandbank for thirty-six hours. Forsyth had veered, thinking *Encounter* had herself run aground, only to do so himself. It was only after most of her guns, all her water, and much of her ballast were removed that the ship was eventually floated off. 'His position', O'Callaghan comments, 'was becoming hourly most critical, as the sand and mud was forming around her.' It was a point which had also been made earlier when *Barracouta* was searching for Amur's northern exit – that the sands shifted all the time, and no channel, once located, could be relied on to be still navigable even a few days later.

The two steamers did manage to get five or six miles to the south, but they were clearly not following the deepish channel they had used on the way north. O'Callaghan stopped and sent boats out sounding while he returned the guns and so on to *Hornet*. The masters found the channel for several miles, but the north wind then blew up, snow fell, and 'the land being obscured the whole day it was impossible to move the ship with any prospect of safety'. It was not until the morning of the 29th that they were able to move, and they got back to De Castries Bay late that afternoon.[14]

In the course of his report O'Callaghan claimed twice to have located the channel. But he added a postscript before handing it in to Elliot, dated Hakodate on 3 November. This time he suggested that a different route be tried, 'from the north point of Cape Wood to North Point'. But this is developed from the idea that the river would deposit its mud 'on the opposite shore', not from direct observation, sounding, and sailing. (Rivers deposit their load when the velocity of the flow is checked, and so usually at the point the river water reaches the sea; hence the bars commonly found at their mouths.) What O'Callaghan had done was to show that there was a strait between the mainland and Sakhalin, and therefore that, in all probability, there was a channel for shallow-draught ships. That the Russian ships, by the sort of drastic lightening which had been used with *Hornet*, had got through was thus demonstrated as being very probable.

By the time the two steamers had returned to De Castries Bay, Elliot himself had gathered more information. On the 26th, a flag of truce was displayed on the land. Elliot sent 'a boat with a lieutenant', to see what was required. He found that the 'mercantile agent' on *Behring* had returned from a journey inland. Elliot had been successful in his manoeuvres in the bay, one of the intentions of which was to prevent the master of *Behring* from communicating with the shore. No doubt he assumed that the skipper would be as willing to give information on the British to the Russians as he had been to give it on the Russians to Elliot; hence the need for the momentary truce with the Russians.

Elliot exploited his opportunity. The lieutenant was to put on a most elaborately polite act, asking whom he was addressing – for it was the Russians with whom he had to speak first – intro-

[14] ADM 1/5672, 29 October 1855.

ducing himself, and so on. And it was also by way of Elliot's ship that the American agent was to be returned to *Behring* – but only after he had revealed his information to Elliot. This was, in fact, the same man, George Cushing, who later told his story to Miller in Honolulu, so we may be reasonably sure that he told Elliot much the same, perhaps with more immediacy and in more detail.

The commander of the Russian forces was Colonel Gleskhavin, according to Elliot (or Sestavine, according to Miller – neither was probably accurately transcribed), and the lieutenant also met Captain Rimskii-Korsakov, who had been the captain of the *Vostok*. (He was the father of the future composer, who was himself a naval cadet at this time.) Since Rimskii-Korsakov had had to take over *Vostok* at Portsmouth, no doubt he spoke some English, and Cushing will have had at least some Russian, so communication was not difficult. There were several other Russian officers present, but the lieutenant noted particularly that they wore almost the same uniform as the private soldiers.

Cushing described his journey. He had landed Madame Zavoika and her party on the 2nd, and Colonel Gleskhavin organised a passage for them inland. Cushing went along, partly to make sure that he would be able to sell his goods, partly no doubt out of curiosity, and partly because the Russians wanted to thank him properly. He described a journey of fifty or sixty miles, taking three days, staying overnight in requisitioned native huts, in order to reach the river. 'There was no regular road', he commented, but it is clear that the party was not cutting its way through the forest; the way had been cleared, though streams and rivulets had to be crossed by canoe or on horseback. The distance of this stage of the journey is consistent with their reaching Mariinsk, though he does not say anything about the place.

Then they embarked on boats and sailed down the Amur for about 200 miles to a place he calls 'Keey', but which was evidently Nikolaevsk, a 'Russian military settlement and town', where he met Admiral Zavoiko, Governor-General Muravev, and the captains of *Diana* and *Olivutza*, together with a group of naval and military officers. He noted the existence of other Russian settlements on the left bank – he had this wrong, and he also claimed that 'Keey' was on the right bank – and he named two of those small settlements. 'From the information I obtained, as well as from what I saw, I should calculate the number of Russians on either bank ... to be not under 10,000, including from 3000 to 4000 soldiers; they have well-constructed batteries with heavy guns mounted.' These figures are somewhat exaggerated; maybe Cushing was fed such numbers by Muravev and his staff, just as the numbers on the river migration were exaggerated so as to impress and intimidate the Chinese officials. Or maybe his civilian eyes simply perceived the fortifications and numbers to be greater than they really were.

Cushing was much less informative about the Russian ships, but Elliot surely questioned him on this. He knew the names of the ships but not, it would seem, their locations. He did mention that *Pallas* was 'quite unseaworthy', but could not say where she was. Elliot noted that she was said to be in the river, but he also recorded that he had hints of her being dismantled in some place south of De Castries Bay.[15]

This was the sort of information which the British were after. Elliot was now able to estimate the military and naval situation much more accurately than before. De Castries Bay had some troops in garrison, and more within reach, a day or two's march away, but the place was not yet properly fortified; there were guns 'mounted about the place'. Along the Amur, batteries had been erected at strategic places, 'heavy guns and mortars', which had been brought from Irkutsk. The area was being supplied with food by way of the river, including flour and beef, in the hope that it could be made independent of supply from the United States, which had not been the case with Petropavlovsk, for example. But the presence of *Behring* and the disembarkation of her goods rather suggested that local supplies were still poor, and that those coming down the river were intermittent.

Elliot also heard, no doubt from Cushing, but this was not mentioned to Miller at Honolulu, that Muravev was doing all this without Chinese consent, 'after years spent in ineffectual endeavour to get China to come to some arrangement about it' – a formulation which suggests that Cushing heard it directly from Muravev. And he related that a Chinese envoy had recently

---

[15] ADM 1/5672, 25 November 1855, and 1/5677, 5 December 1855.

appeared to demand an explanation. 'But the reply it was said was given by significantly pointing to the shipping, guns, and several thousand troops around.' Again this must be Muravev, giving a partial and distorted account of the meeting, for this is not what it had been about, nor what had really happened, and there seems to be no mention of such a gesture from the Chinese side.

Muravev was again playing Britain and China off against each other. He will have known that Cushing would report to the British – he had agreed before he sailed from Honolulu in the summer that he would see Miller again when he got back. The 'several thousand' soldiers was a deterrent message to the British as much as to the Manchu government. The lack of information, even the disinformation he purveyed, about the Chinese negotiations implied that the Chinese had accepted the situation, which was anything but the truth. His remark about having spent several years trying to get Chinese agreement neatly glossed over the fact that the 'agreement' he sought was a Chinese humiliation and a repudiation of the old Treaty of Nerchinsk.

Elliot had got the information he had been sent to find out: a reasonable idea of the Russian position in the area of the Amur mouth; the absence of any Russian occupation of any part of Sakhalin; the existence of a channel for shallow-draught ships between the mainland and Sakhalin. In addition he had now confirmed that the whole Russian position was organised under the command of the Governor-General of eastern Siberia, a rather higher authority than the Russian-American Company which had been the previous political authority in the area. And he now knew that this had been done despite Chinese objections, and that the Chinese government was informed of the problem and concerned about it.

Elliot, overcome by the same winter weather which nearly trapped O'Callaghan and Forsyth to the north, left the bay on 28 October; he left a 'memo' for O'Callaghan, presumably with the master of *Behring*. *Encounter* and *Hornet* arrived next day, and all three ships were reunited at Hakodate on 3 November. Pausing only to collect a group of prisoners from *Constantine*, Elliot sailed directly to Hong Kong with *Hornet*. *Encounter* followed later. Captain O'Callaghan had spoken with the master of *Behring* in the bay and had gathered a good deal of information; this he summarised in a few terse sentences for

Admiral Stirling. Elliot meanwhile was busy writing the same information at greater length and in much greater detail on his voyage to the south. Elliot also made some further suggestions as to the next year's campaign.

8

Plans

Commodore Elliot finished his report on his second expedition into the northern part of the Gulf of Tartary, in which the extent of Russian settlement on the Amur River had become much clearer, by suggesting that this would be a secure base for the development of Russian naval power. Behind the shoals and sands, but on a navigable river, 'the extension of her naval power in the east should not be overlooked, nor can its importance be overrated'. Indeed, though he did not spell it out for lack of precise information, that naval base already existed, with a frigate (*Aurora*), a steamship (*Vostok*), and assorted smaller craft, all armed and present. If the Allies withdrew – as in fact they did, from Hakodate to Hong Kong for the winter, these Russian ships became the strongest naval force in the North Pacific, with other bases available as far east as Sitka in North America. On the other hand they could not get to sea until the ice melted in May.

Elliot added some comments on what naval force would be required for further operations. He thought in terms of either getting ships into the river, or setting up a blockade. In either case it would be steamers, of a shallow draught, which would be required. And if a blockade was imposed – he seems to have assumed that this was what would happen – there would have to be two forces, for the northern and the southern entrances to the strait. Sailing ships were especially awkward in the Gulf of Tartary, because of the lack of sea room, the absence of harbours, and the poor weather – predominantly southerly gales and intermittent fogs. And he was the commander with most experience of both entrances, so he could be sure he would be listened to.[1]

---

[1] ADM 1/5672, 25 November 1855.

The future was something Stirling also had to consider. The length of time it usually took for letters to reach him from Britain meant that he could only be given the most general instructions. The First Lord, Sir Charles Wood, had written on 9 October, commenting that it was disappointing that the Russian ships had escaped (this was clearly referring to the events at the end of May) and remarking that Elliot should have left a ship to watch the bay; this was scarcely a helpful comment, nor was his conclusion that 'at present you are quite at a loss to know where they are gone to'. His next letter to Stirling was sent at the same time as an official Admiralty letter dated 8 December, which was critical of the conduct of both Stirling and Elliot over the events in May. And this was said, despite also acknowledging Stirling's later letters. Wood in his private letter did comment that the Russians 'seemed to have managed their affairs very adroitly'.[2]

None of this was of any use at all to Stirling in deciding what to do next. His instructions still were to seek out the Russian ships, and to harass and destroy their posts and settlements, but not to attempt a landing, even though Wood had mused in letters earlier in 1855 that there were reported to be Poles at Okhotsk who might rise, and it might be possible to get an army detachment from India. Since these points were made in private letters he was clearly leaving it to Stirling to make an official request for military help. Yet the time scale involved – Stirling would write to London, London would write to India, India would send the troops to Hong Kong – was clearly very long, even if the India Office in London and the Governor-General in Calcutta could be brought to agree to such an expedition. Not only was the time scale long, but there were great opportunities for bureaucratic delays at all the official stages involved. And many of the European troops stationed in India had been taken off to fight in the Crimea, so that the ratio of European to Indian soldiers in India itself was now very low, to the Governor-General's alarm. This clearly concerned the Governor-General above all, and he was highly unlikely to agree to send any more European troops off to fight in the North Pacific, wholly unacclimatised as they were. It seems that Indian troops were simply not to be considered, though

---

[2] ADM 2/1704, 8 December 1855; BL Add. Mss 49564, 168–170, 9 October 1855, and 49565, 56–60, 8 December 1855.

a few years later they were employed in China in the Second China War.

However, it was now winter in the north, and this gave a breathing space for London and Hong Kong to coordinate their ideas, even at two or three months' postal distance. In his letter of 9 December, Wood asked for Stirling's ideas on how the Russians were progressing. Wood expressed the belief that the Russian purpose was to develop a naval threat to India, a reversion of the idea Stirling had put forward a year before of a large Russian squadron loose in the Pacific, ranging over the ocean as far as Australia. This was, of course, British naval thinking in operation; there was in fact absolutely no evidence that the Russians intended to use their ships for any intelligible naval purpose; Wood was merely reflecting the Admiralty's normal anxieties.

Wood soon received more information, for Stirling had sent his son, Commander Stirling, home with the Japanese treaty ratification,[3] and had written also about the prisoners. He had decided that, now that he had another frigate, *Nankin*, he would send *Winchester* home carrying the prisoners. The ship, he thought, needed attention it could not be given in China, and this therefore, he thought, solved two of his problems in one.[4] Commander Stirling could also explain the situation with regard to Russia in more detail than Stirling could express in his letters, and in terms which the First Lord and the Admiralty Board might understand. It must have been clear to Stirling, from their letters, that both were reacting to Stirling's reports by merely criticising; no help had been forthcoming, either in words or deeds, or in the sending of any useful instructions. And by January it will have become necessary for Stirling to consider what he was to do in the next campaigning season even if no new instructions arrived from London.

This is not so easy to discern, for Stirling appears to have decided by December that he would be replaced, and sent few letters. He complained of ill health, presumably in a letter in December which is not preserved, for Wood wrote on 9 February 1856 promising that a successor would be sent.[5] Perhaps it was

---

[3] BL Add. Mss 49565, 88–90, 9 January 1856.
[4] ADM 1/5672, 1 November 1855.
[5] BL Add. Mss 49565, 130–132, 9 February 1856.

Stirling's son who carried an oral message; whatever was said and however it was delivered, it was obviously persuasive. But at the same time, both in private and in public letters, Wood and the Admiralty had made it clear that they were unhappy with the results of the naval campaign conducted by Stirling in the past year. If Stirling had not requested relief he might well have been, like Pellew, replaced anyway.

In the end Stirling decided not to send *Winchester* to Britain with the prisoners. Instead he used three smaller ships, *Styx*, *Rattler* and *Grecian*. He had devoted a long letter in mid-November to discussing how to get rid of the prisoners: they could not be released, since they were prime seamen and would be a significant naval reinforcement to the Russians in the east; they could not be kept in Hong Kong, for there were neither prisons nor guards to hold them – as Bowring had pointed out earlier; they could not be kept on board several ships, presumably at Hong Kong, since this would immobilise the ships and the crews, and would probably result in the unnecessary deaths of numbers of the prisoners from illnesses. So he would pack them into *Winchester*, which needed, he said, to be 'docked, repaired and recoppered', and this could only be done at Bombay or in Britain. He would shift his flag to *Nankin*, taking with him his Flag Captain and staff;[6] but this caused a further problem, since *Nankin*'s captain, the Hon. Keith Stewart, would need therefore to shift to *Winchester*, and he was only recently appointed.

Nankin had been Stirling's flagship on his voyage into the Gulf of Tartary in October, and it seems that he and Stewart had not been too friendly. Stirling had carefully passed on comments from the Admiralty that Stewart had signed on two seamen in Britain who had earlier deserted from some other ship, and now wanted explanations. And at the end of the cruise, as they all reached Nagasaki, Stirling had written an official notification to the effect that he considered that Stewart was too free with punishments for *Nankin* to become a happy ship.[7] Above all, perhaps, Stirling will have enjoyed *Nankin*'s newness after the age and stink of *Winchester*.

His rather pathetic letter about sending *Winchester* home was superseded by some unknown means a month later.

6 ADM 1/5672, 11 November 1855.
7 ADM 50/308, Stirling Journal.

Stirling presumably had second thoughts on the matter. It was, after all, a curious decision to send his flagship halfway round the world as a transport for unwanted prisoners of war, just before a new campaign was to start. *Nankin* and *Winchester* both stayed at Hong Kong, while the three smaller ships took the prisoners to Britain; *Winchester* was repaired at Whampoa. It took some time to gather all the prisoners at Hong Kong. Some were on the French ships, which tended to be based at Shanghai. Elliot had retrieved one group from *Constantine* when he met her at Hakodate, and he only reached Hong Kong late in November.

But one would suppose that the real obstacle to Stirling's plans was Captain Stewart, who could quite legitimately put up strong arguments: that he had only just been appointed to the *Nankin* by the Admiralty, and that it was unreasonable that he should be shifted. If this argument became heated it would soon become clear that the two men could not work together at all easily, and they had clearly not done so earlier. Meanwhile the situation in Chinese waters was becoming difficult once more. The absence of many of the Allied ships in northern waters during 1855 had encouraged the revival of Chinese piracy – and Sir Charles Wood had remarked on it from the distance of Britain in his letter of 9 October.

By 12 December, Stirling had received letters, public and private, criticising his handling of the campaign, the prisoners had been gathered at Hong Kong, and, presumably, Stewart had made his case, no doubt in the strongest terms. By that date Stirling had completely changed his mind, and he had sent *Styx*, *Rattler* and *Grecian* with his prisoners to Britain, and he had also developed ill health to such an extent that he had requested to be replaced.

Stirling's letter about the prisoners and *Winchester*, dated 11 November, will have reached the Admiralty in January – possibly carried by Commander Stirling. Although Admiral Stirling had changed his mind by then, it cannot have created a good impression. By early February Wood was writing his letter promising that a replacement would be sent out. On top of the Admiralty's dissatisfaction, the unpleasant letter from Stirling proposing a fairly drastic change in the Admiralty's own dispositions may well have been the final straw. At the least it will have shifted opinion away from any sympathy for the man.

The problem is that his period of command had in fact been well conducted and generally successful, and in the matter of the ships he was right. *Winchester* was a powerful ship, but in the context, both of the war with Russia and the problem of Chinese piracy, the three smaller ships, all steamers, were more useful. There was still the problem of Stirling's return, for it was normal for a retiring commander-in-chief to travel home in his flagship, and for a new commander-in-chief to arrive in its replacement. The Admiralty wanted *Winchester* to stay in China, and in February, when Wood wrote to Stirling in effect accepting his resignation, he had to tell him not to bring *Winchester*, his flagship, home, but to travel, as he puts it, 'overland' – that is, by commercial shipping from Singapore and across Suez.

In the meantime Stirling had also been attempting to make plans for the 1856 campaign against Russia. He had received Elliot's report in which the possibility of an attack along the Amur was mentioned, but where a blockade was regarded as much more likely; he had also received O'Callaghan's summary of what he had learned from the American skipper of the *Behring*, and this was much more daunting and considerably less subtle and nuanced than Elliot's more considered approach. The effect of O'Callaghan's blunt words may well have been the stronger. In short, single-sentence paragraphs he had summarised the Russian achievements:

> There are posts every 20 miles on the coast from Castries Bay to the Amur where troops are stationed.
> The Russian squadron was up the Amur and dismantled.
> They had a large launch on the coast.
> That the Russians had suffered to some extent by our force at Castries Bay.[8]

In actual fact, none of this was accurate, and it will be as well to explain why, since O'Callaghan's pithiness makes his points very quotable, and one would not wish other accounts to use it by mistake. There were no posts on the coast between De Castries Bay and the mouth of the river; the ships had not been dismantled, though *Pallas* had been abandoned; if there was a launch near the coast, it was of little importance; and

---

[8] ADM 1/5672, 30 November 1855.

the Russians had suffered not at all from the De Castries Bay bombardment. But the total effect of O'Callaghan's emphatic interpretation was to imply that the Russians had abandoned naval warfare, for the present war at least, but had built up a formidable military presence. So, ironically, the net result of O'Callaghan's letter was correct, despite all his errors. In this at least O'Callaghan's implications were generally accurate, even if his facts were wrong.

If, therefore, the Allies, specifically the British, were to actively oppose the Russian power on the lower Amur, they would need to introduce their own power into the river area itself. At the same time, the Russians, by Muravev's strategy, had in fact rendered themselves very vulnerable to a single knockout blow. As Stirling pointed out to the Admiralty in his letter of 11 December, and as O'Callaghan and Elliot had earlier noted, by Muravev's strategy they had effectively abandoned 'Petropavlovsk, Okhotsk, Aian, and the several settlements upon Saghalien'.[9] A crippling blow aimed at the new settlements on the Amur would therefore drive Russian power back, all the way to Irkutsk. Only trappers would be left in a huge area of eastern Siberia; and the Russian-American Company, unable to communicate by sea for fear of losing its ships, would be emasculated; its one remaining base would be Sitka.

Muravev's strategy in effect had removed all the subsidiary supports from his main centre, and that centre – the river from Nikolaevsk to Mariinsk – depended totally on supplies arriving from Irkutsk, or on the import of American supplies by sea. Interrupt one or both of these supply routes and the settlements in the Amur, newly established and unable to grow their own food for some time, would be extremely vulnerable to starvation. It was this aspect which Stirling and his captains did not yet understand, though there had been several comments relevant to it in their various remarks. Still, the obvious way to attack the settlements – to harass and destroy them, as his instructions demanded – for Stirling and the Admiralty, was to gain access to the Amur for the Allied warships. If the ships survived the Russian batteries, they would inevitably cut the Russian settlements' lifelines simply by sailing up the river beyond Mariinsk.

9 ADM 1/5672, 11 December 1855.

The discovery by Forsyth and O'Callaghan of the passage between the mainland and Sakhalin now provided the necessary means of access to the local Russian power centre for the Allied ships. From George Cushing's account, it was clear that there were just two places to be concerned with: Nikolaevsk and Mariinsk. All the rest were dependent on these two, as Elliot's experience at De Castries Bay had shown, for it was from Mariinsk that the bay was actually being reinforced and therefore controlled.

It is from the correspondence of Sir John Bowring, the British Superintendent of Trade at Hong Kong, that we can get some idea of the discussions on what to do in the next fighting season which went on under Stirling's aegis during the last couple of months of 1855. As background it is worth recalling those comments by Sir Charles Wood in his letters to Stirling during that year: there were Poles at Okhotsk who might be prepared to rise; if land operations were necessary, it might be possible to bring troops from India.

Behind all of this was the war in Europe. The Allied landing in the Crimea and the siege of Sebastopol had almost monopolised attention in London and Paris. The Russian evacuation of the city in September 1855 reduced the importance of the conflict in the Black Sea area, but left both sides without the possibility of a victory. And at the same time the costs mounted, in men and money, so that the need for victory also mounted.

There was another aspect of the war in Europe which by the winter of 1855–1856 had become dominant: the Baltic. In Britain the country's industrial power had been exerted to build a great new fleet, later described as the Great Armament, which was developed specifically for the campaign in the Baltic. It was intended to bring Allied sea power right to the very doorstep of the tsar. During 1854 and 1855 it had been demonstrated that the Allies, mainly the British, could move a large fleet to within a few miles of St Petersburg without any significant Russian opposition; and it had been demonstrated that the forts which were expected to defend the approaches to that city were vulnerable to the guns of the fleet: both Hangö and Bomarsund had fallen to bombardment very quickly.[10] The only fort left to protect the capital city was Kronstadt, and it was

---

[10] Lambert, *Crimean War*; B. Greenhill and A. Gilford, *The British Assault on Finland, 1855–56*, London 1988.

clear that it could be destroyed by the Allies, if they could bring against it a large enough force. After that the city of St Petersburg itself would be open to bombardment, not to mention the imperial palaces along the shore. (It was this threat, exemplified in the Great Armament, which helped to bring the tsar to negotiations, together with the prospect of wars with Austria and Sweden. The Great Armament was displayed in a great review to celebrate the peace.[11])

In considering what happened in the winter of 1855–1856, and the next year, it is necessary to avoid falling into the trap of assuming that discussions and plans were unimportant because the war ended early in 1856. It was in fact only in late February that it became likely that the war would end with a peace conference. It was only in March that the peace was agreed, and April when it was signed, and it was only late in June that word reached the Far East that the peace had been concluded. For those involved in the Pacific theatre, the war therefore went on until June, and the plans the British made for dealing with the problem they had uncovered are therefore of some interest. Had the peace conference dragged on into, say, late April or May, there would certainly have been fighting in the Amur region.

It also has a wider relevance. One of the crucial elements in the Russian decision to seek peace was the naval threat to Kronstadt and St Petersburg, a threat which the British scarcely bothered to keep secret. Thus the potential bombardment and possible destruction of the enemy capital would mark a distinct escalation in the war. But Lord Palmerston had more than once discussed the possibility of going on with the war until Russia was broken, and there were several areas – Poland and Finland were usually mentioned – which could be detached into independent national states.[12] The future campaigns in the Far East might well reflect this attitude. Japan and China had already been mentioned as possible beneficiaries of the drastic reduction in Russian power; the United States was known to wish to acquire Alaska. Driving Russian power back from the Pacific shore all the way to Irkutsk would be a British war

---

[11] This is the argument of Lambert, *Crimean War*, chs 21 and 22; see also W. Baumgart, *The Peace of Paris 1856*, trans. A. P. Saab, Santa Barbara, CA, 1981, 68–80.

[12] Baumgart, *Peace of Paris*, 13–15.

aim which may well have been approved by all these countries, and would certainly be in consonance with Palmerston's programme. The later history of the Far East would have been very different had this taken place.

The Allies had, at least publicly and technically, gone to war to protect the Ottoman Empire from Russian attack. But their appetites had grown as the investment in money and men had increased. In Britain the diplomatically inclined, limited war administration of Lord Aberdeen had been replaced by the fire-breathing, ambitious Lord Palmerston. Palmerston's administration had not been very firmly based at first, but with success, notably the bombardment of Bomarsund, and the capture of the city of Sebastopol, had come support, internally in Parliament, and externally by the addition of Sardinia to the anti-Russian alliance. By late 1855 both Sweden and Austria were almost persuaded also to join the Allies. Spain was sympathetic for reasons of her own. Sweden in particular was interested in recovering Finland, lost in 1809 (though how keen the Finns might be was not considered). Austria would be interested in reducing Russian power, though not necessarily in acquiring territory. Further afield the Ottoman Empire was keen to recover territories lost in the past century, notably in the Caucasus, but maybe including even the Crimea; Persia had suffered repeatedly at Russian hands. And in the Far East, both China and Japan were apprehensive and feeling threatened by Russian advances in the Amur and Sakhalin. There was plenty here to make for a drastic peace involving a serious reduction in both Russian territory and Russian power, if the war went on.

How much of the ambition and aggressiveness of Viscount Palmerston had seeped through to the commanders in the East is impossible to say. It was not an attitude shared even by all of Palmerston's ministers. But several of the comments by Sir Charles Wood – the Poles, troops from India – had indicated that a more vigorous pursuit of the war in the East would be welcomed in London. The Admiralty's criticism of Elliot's conduct in the Gulf of Tartary would certainly have stung, and was clearly shared to a degree by Stirling – who ultimately carried the responsibility. His sending of Elliot back into the Gulf in October indicates his own sensitivity on the matter: 'I think fit that the conduct of the aforesaid service [the new voyage into the Gulf] should be entrusted to you', he wrote, pointedly, in Elliot's instructions. And the longer the war went on, the more action would be expected of the Royal Navy.

The discussions at Hong Kong about the future direction of the campaign inevitably involved Sir John Bowring. In the process Bowring spotted a chance to develop 'a better understanding with the Court of Peking'. As with the international alliance which formed the coalition against Russia, so with the cooperation of Bowring and Stirling, each man came to the discussion with his own agenda and his own set of priorities, and Bowring's priority was not necessarily to assist in the defeat of Russia. Stirling had been clearly discussing a blockade, as Elliot had outlined, but he had not excluded the possibility of more aggressive action. Bowring, perhaps for the first time, and perhaps alone amongst the men involved in the East, understood that the new Russian posts were actually in what was generally assumed to be Chinese territory – he referred to 'the Russians in Chinese Tartary'. He knew nothing of the repeated exchanges between Muravev and the Chinese officials in the north, nor of the imperial policy which had acquiesced in Russian encroachments, nor of Muravev's repeated assurances that he needed to sail down the Amur in order to fight the British. But Bowring thought he saw an opportunity, not just for improving his contacts with the Chinese government, but also for possible joint action involving Britain and China.

Sir Charles Wood had raised the possibility of sending troops from India to assault the Russian positions, though in the same letter he had remarked that they were unlikely to be available. The prospect of bringing China into the anti-Russian coalition raised the possibility in Bowring's mind that Chinese forces could be employed.

Bowring first reported to London, to the Foreign Secretary, the Earl of Clarendon. He had received a letter from Stirling with one from Elliot enclosed, giving him a clearer idea of the situation in the north, he reported. Conventionally disclaiming any expertise in military or naval affairs, and specifically in the matter of the blockade, he then went on to argue forcefully that Russia had to be stopped. 'Every day's delay in opposing some barrier to her pretensions will help to forward her views and to consolidate her strength.' He then argued that China – 'looked at as she is and not as she might be', an indirect reference to the Taiping rebellion, presumably – was not capable, at present at least, of mounting or organising any serious opposition to the Russian advance. At least China could not do so alone, 'but I cannot doubt that the notification from Peking assisted and backed by European influences would be respected by the Tsar'.[13] He was obviously ignorant of the powerful anti-British feelings in the Manchu ruling class which would block any Anglo-Chinese cooperation. Therefore suggesting that China join in the anti-Russian alliance was highly unlikely to succeed. But Bowring could not escape the mind-set which he and other Europeans and Americans brought to relations with 'Oriental sovereigns'. There was no question of persuasion and patient diplomacy: he would force China to become an ally.

Superficially this policy had its attractions. In Europe, Sardinia had been recruited to the alliance, and Sweden almost so. Each country did so for its own reasons, which had no real relevance to those which had brought Britain and France to declare war in the first place. And Britain and France were as much competitors and rivals as they were allies. The Admiralty in particular was building warships more with a view to a future possible war with France than to the present war with Russia. So recruiting Chinese support would make sense. It had also been observed that Japan was apprehensive of Russian advances; one earlier suggestion was that an island – possibly Urup, perhaps Sakhalin – should be handed to Japan as a prize for joining in on the Allied side. What Bowring and Stirling quite failed to appreciate was that, of all the European and American states with whom China and Japan had had contact, it was Britain whom they most distrusted and feared. It was Britain which had fought and defeated China and forced that proud empire to admit unwanted foreigners to its ports and territory, and to accept the detested opium. It was the British Navy which the Japanese had seen quite clearly was the greatest sea force in the East (despite the fact that the first treaty with a foreign power had been made with the United States), something which had been emphasised by the fleet Stirling had assembled earlier in Nagasaki harbour, and by the busy activity of his ships during the 1855 campaign. (The American consul at Shimoda, Townsend Harris, was in the habit of threatening the Japanese government with the power

---

[13] ADM 1/5677, 10 December 1855.

of the Royal Navy, not that of the, mostly absent, United States Navy, in his frequent disputes.[14])

Bowring used the reports he had received on Russian activities to try to warn the Chinese. His channel to the Peking Court was through the Viceroy of Guandong and Guanxi, Ye Minchen. It was also through him that news of events in Europe was passed to the Court. Bowring wrote on 27 November explaining what he had heard.[15] If it was passed on, this information will have arrived in Peking sometime after the memorial about the abortive negotiations at Mariinsk, which, after a long delay, finally reached the emperor on 24 November. In theory, therefore, Bowring's note should have reinforced the unease the Chinese authorities will have felt when the nature of Muravev's demands was known.

On the other hand, Ye's message probably arrived along with an account of the progress of the war in Europe, as Ye understood it. He reported that the British and French forces had invaded the Crimea, but that this had been followed by a Russian raid on Britain which had caused much destruction; Queen Victoria had fled the country on a steamer, to seek help in France and America.[16] The Chinese government had been in receipt of other, similarly misinformative, bulletins, which might have come from almost anyone. Ye's account sounds like Russian boasting, along with a misunderstanding of the queen's state visit to France, but there seem to have been few Russians who were in contact with Ye. There is no sign that the Manchu Court seriously understood anything about the war. Ye's story may, indeed, have been no more than wishful thinking on his part, or on that of his Chinese informants. Anything which suggested a diminution of British power would clearly be welcomed by any Chinese official.

Meanwhile Muravev had sent a note to Peking claiming that he had suffered many casualties in fighting the British (no French were mentioned), and asking for help from the authorities along the Amur to get his wounded men back to Russian territory by land. The sub-text here was that the Russians were valiantly defending both themselves and China against

[14] Beazley, *Great Britain and the Opening of Japan*, esp. ch. VII.
[15] ADM 1/5677, 14 December 1855.
[16] Quested, *Expansion of Russia*, 56.

the violence of 'the English'. It was, of course, a lie; Russian casualties in all the fighting had been very few.

It was also a cover for the Russians who were now travelling by land along the Amur, using the northern bank only. This took them through lands opposite the Aigun fortress which had long been settled by Chinese and Manchu peasants. The commander of the Aigun fortress, quite unable to resist this movement, instead assisted it by providing horses and provisions, presumably on the grounds that this would both protect the peasantry and get rid of the travellers all the quicker. He claimed to have stopped Russian ships and to have delivered protests, and to have attempted to stop the travellers by force, though this is probably not true. But he had no authority to use force, and he reported that the protests were ignored – likely enough if they were ever made – and that the Russians had threatened to kill him, so he gave in.

Muravev's story of his men having suffered casualties was also, of course, not true. This story of casualties helped to support his story that he had sailed down the river to fight Russia's enemies, and provided verisimilitude to his claim to be fighting. It relied, as before, on the profound Chinese ignorance of this part of their empire, a reliance which was not misplaced.[17]

Amid all this confused misinformation, disinformation, and plain lies, it is unlikely that Bowring's message made much impact, even if it ever got through to the Court by way of Commissioner Ye. Muravev, whatever the imperial response to his note might have been, had made the journey back up the Amur River before then, having paid a quick visit to Aian.[18]

Muravev was conscious of the vulnerability of the Russian settlements, but he assumed, as did most of those involved in the East, that the war would go on into 1856, and that therefore he would have the backing to reinforce and relieve the settlers during the next summer. The nearest Chinese governor, Chingshun at Kirin in Manchuria, during the winter made enquiries about what was going on. His report to the emperor was vague: he could find out nothing about any Russian settlements other than that at Mariinsk, where the abortive frontier conference had been held, but he explained that the area was

[17] Quested, *Expansion of Russia*, 55–56
[18] Semenov, *Siberia*, 272.

only a wilderness inhabited by a couple of tribes, and it was all far away from any Chinese military posts.[19] It seems unlikely that anyone in the Chinese government felt that such territory was worth a fight, particularly when they were faced by a huge rebellion in the interior.

Sir John Bowring therefore was unlikely to be able to persuade China to join Britain in an assault on the Russians at the Amur in the immediate future. And yet he noted in his report on this to the Foreign Secretary that 'the Amoor is accessible to ships of considerable draught of war', though what his source for this was is not clear, and it was not really correct. But he implied that, if Stirling wished, he could clearly get even his frigates into the Amur, and certainly some of his smaller steamships, and this was probably the case.[20]

Stirling had discussed the prospects of a new campaign in a letter to the Admiralty on 4 December. He repeated his views of the Russian situation: they had abandoned their outposts and had withdrawn to the Amur as a sort of central citadel. There they had also concentrated their surviving ships, and, given their enclosure in the ice and the dismantled condition of the vessels, there was nothing to fear from them for the next six months. After that Stirling proposed to mount a blockade. Elliot would command, with five ships – *Sybille* and *Pique*, and the steamers *Encounter*, *Hornet* and *Barracouta* – all positioned at the head of the Gulf of Tartary early in May in time to block the exit southwards when the ice broke up. The blockade would then be conducted, however, 'by a squadron anchored within the channel recently discovered at the head of the Gulf of Tartary'.

The rest of his force he proposed to distribute from Shanghai to the Straits (of Malacca), with the preponderant power – *Winchester*, *Nankin* and *Coromandel* (a steam tender) – at Hong Kong. 'India must be left to the Bombay Marine and Australia must trust to the squadron at present stationed there.' This disposition would, he thought, protect 'our sea-borne commerce and the valuable cargoes conveyed by our ships' from any cruisers, Russians or privateers or pirates.

He then discussed the chances and purposes of an attack which might be launched against the Russian settlements. He

---

19 Quested, *Expansion of Russia*, 57–58.
20 ADM 1/5677, 10 December 1855.

made a sensible estimate of the Russian manpower – 3000 to 4000 soldiers and 1200 sailors – and noticed that they were all concentrated within a hundred miles of the coast. But he got some aspects wrong. He knew they were in contact with Nerchinsk, but showed no appreciation of the fact that this was at least a month away by the river route. And he imagined that 'the Russians have no view to a permanent residence upon the Amur'. That is, no clear idea of Muravev and his purposes had yet penetrated to the British high command in the East.

Stirling estimated that to destroy the Russian settlements 'would require an expeditionary army of seasoned troops, and a squadron of at least a dozen steamers of heavy armament and light draught of water'. This would need to be mounted between June and the early part of September, the only guaranteed ice-free periods. But he also now made a further error in his estimates. He commented that this could be only a temporary achievement, since the British forces would have to be withdrawn for the winter; therefore, he implied, the Russians would be able to return to reoccupy their settlements as the British evacuated them. It was certainly correct that the British would need to leave when winter came, but again he did not take into account the huge inland distances involved. Muravev was never able to leave Nerchinsk or thereabouts before mid-May, and the journey was a month or so long, so he could not reach the lower Amur until mid-June. The British, approaching by sea, could be in the Amur area two or three weeks earlier than that, and even before that if they landed at De Castries Bay, which was ice-free late in April or earlier, and then marched inland from there. (This, of course, may well have been appreciated by Muravev, and he was quite right that the only possible competition he had to face for control of the Amur was from the British.) One gets the impression that Stirling was emphasising the difficulties, but, reading between the lines, he also appreciated the possibilities of the situation.

Stirling had thus stated his intention to set up a blockade, and having argued somewhat ambiguously the case for an expeditionary force to take the settlements, he then made an alternative suggestion, which again was a curious mixture of prescient observation and error. He suggested that, if it was intended to block Russian expansion in the area, southern Manchuria was the key region, and that an alliance 'with the Manchoo Tartars' was the best approach. This is presumably in part the result of his discussions with Sir John Bowring, whose similar notion went to the Foreign Office a week later, at the time of his attempted alerting of the Chinese government through Commissioner Ye. Stirling pointed out that the lower Amur is very inhospitable country: 'it is inaccessible for eight months of the year, it is incapable of great prosperity'. Therefore, he argued, the real aim of the Russians was further south, where the land and climate were more welcoming, and he suggested that 'the south of Manchuria' was the area they were really after. He pointed out that no serious opposition could be expected from the empire of China. He was in effect suggesting that the British ally themselves with the local people of the area, 'the Manchoo Tartars', who were the very people Muravev had demanded to be 'relocated' in his discussions with the Chinese at Mariinsk. The area identified by Stirling, the southern part of Manchuria, has also of course turned out to be the key geopolitical region in the century and a half since he wrote, the object of Japan, Russia and China ever since, and fought over repeatedly since 1895.[21]

Stirling was certainly thinking as a naval man throughout this document. He claimed to have located a suitable island, which would be 'a very advantageous site for a naval station', an island, 'fertile, wooded, and well watered ... about the size of Malta', in the Gulf of Tartary. He claimed it had places where ports could be developed, and that it 'might become a centre of extensive commercial operations'; clearly he was thinking of a whole series of successful British coastal foundations, from Bombay to Perth to Singapore and Hong Kong and onwards. The island had been named Victoria Island, in Victoria Bay; he was clearly pressing all the right buttons. He had 'found' it during his cruise along the mainland coast of the Gulf of Tartary in September; the mainland became the site of Vladivostok.

This letter was written on 4 December. It will have taken two months to reach London. There was certainly time for a decision on an expedition or a blockade to be made and transmitted to Hong Kong by April. But by February, as Wood wrote to Stirling in giving him the news that he would be replaced, a peace agreement was under discussion, and seemed likely to result in an end to the war. This prospect, together with

[21] ADM 125/1, 4 December 1855.

Stirling's explanation of the difficulties involved in either an expedition or a blockade, was the basis for Wood's own conclusion that the Russians 'are evidently constructing a place of refuge for themselves in Manchuria up the Amur where they will be quite inaccessible hereafter'.[22] This, of course, did not preclude an expedition if peace did not result, but it certainly made it very difficult to organise one during 1856, given the geographical and climatic constraints. On 1 April Wood was writing to Admiral Bruce that the Russians 'had made themselves very secure on the Amur, too high for us to get at them'.[23] But a different view was possible, had peace not been agreed three days later.

[22] BL Add. Mss 49565, 130–132, 9 February 1856.
[23] BL Add. Mss 49565, 196, 1 April 1856.

9

The Victims

The conclusion of a peace treaty was notified to all commanders-in-chief of British naval stations by a circular letter from the Admiralty dated 4 April 1856.[1] It had been well signposted in advance, and had been expected in Europe at any time from February onwards. This expectation had diffused outwards, and was received in the Pacific and China commands by April, though the official news did not arrive until early in June and did not reach the Allied naval forces until the beginning of July. This uncertainty made it impossible to do more than make preparations in case no peace was made, which cannot have been very inspiring.

Admiral Stirling took his ships to winter in China, the British at Hong Kong, and the French at Shanghai. His concern returned to the problem of Chinese piracy, but he also felt he had been maligned by some criticism from a man called 'Mr Phin'. He wrote to the Admiralty justifying his conduct in the search for the Russian ships, explaining why he sent *Styx* and *Tartar* back to Hakodate, and giving chapter and verse for his original belief that there was no strait separating Sakhalin from the Amur. (The Admiralty drafted a reply, which may or may not have been sent, but which maintained the old criticism of him: he had in fact attacked the naval bureaucracy, and that was a fight no one could win.[2])

By the time his letter was at the Admiralty, he had been retired. His successor was Rear-Admiral Sir Michael Seymour, who had made a name for himself in the Baltic campaign, in part because he had lost an eye in the fighting, so receiving much public sympathy. He was appointed on 19 February and set off by Royal Mail steamer at once, reaching Singapore on 20 April,

---

[1] ADM 125/1, 4 April 1856.
[2] ADM 1/5672, 13 February 1855, and draft reply.

where Stirling was awaiting him. He took over command two days later. In accordance with Wood's order, Stirling and his staff, who had heard only on 30 March of his replacement, went home by another Royal Mail steamer. Seymour reached Hong Kong two weeks later, and on 11 May issued orders to Commodore Elliot for another examination of the shores of the Gulf of Tartary. This was not actually unusual naval efficiency, but Seymour obeying orders from the Admiralty.[3]

In fact Elliot had already gone. Stirling had sent him off from Hong Kong on 16 March to examine once more the Gulf coasts. It is probable that the trigger was a report Elliot received from a sailor on *Pique* who had got into conversation with a Russian midshipman, one of the *Diana* prisoners. The sailor, Master's Assistant Benjamin Jackson, had elicited a description of the passage through the shoals, and of the entrance to the Amur. It turned out that the passage lay along the Sakhalin side, and was said to be 'deep enough for their frigate', meaning presumably *Aurora*. There was also information about the fortifications on the Amur and at Nikolaevsk.

This information was passed by Elliot to Stirling in a letter 'with a statement from Jackson' on 12 March. It made it clear that by sailing along the mainland side, the British explorations had missed the main channel. Stirling reacted by giving Elliot instructions on 16 March to investigate. (Two weeks earlier the Admiralty wrote to Seymour, by then on his way east, giving similar instructions.)

Elliot was once again to make Hakodate his forward base. He took a month to get there, *Sybille* having a damaged bowsprit on the way. Even so *Sybille* arrived on 12 April, and *Pique* only three days later; *Barracouta*, slower than the sailing ships, arrived on the 27th. Elliot was conscious that there was to be a change of command and clearly hesitated to take further action without Seymour's authority, but, 'judging that nearly a month must elapse before further instructions could reach me', he decided to spend the month exploring. He could, of course, have headed straight for the passage Jackson had reported, but that would have led him to the Russian fortifications at the Amur, and he would need more ships for this, and a better authority before engaging in a battle.

---

3 ADM 50/280, Seymour Journal; ADM 50/278, Stirling Journal; ADM 125/1, 3 March 1856.

So he decided to search the mainland coast, only parts of which had been explored by the British so far, the north by Elliot himself, the southern part by Stirling in *Nankin*. The three ships sailed on 4 May. He spoke to American whalers, who said that La Pérouse Strait had been blocked by ice until three days before, so no Russian ships could have got through. He was concerned to follow up earlier hints that *Pallas* was somewhere south of De Castries Bay. He took his ships across to the mainland, to where Stirling had turned south the year before. On 10 May they were near Suffren Bay, one of La Pérouse's discoveries, and turned north, *Barracouta* inshore.

The next day, 11 May (coincidentally the day Seymour sent Elliot his new orders), *Barracouta* found the bay which the Russians called Imperatorskaia Gavan, and which the British now named Barracouta Harbour. This coast had been looked at before, but *Barracouta*, closely watching the shore, which on the charts showed no bay at all, discerned, as du Hailly said, 'to the great surprise of the steamer's sailors' (*'au grand étonnement des marins du vapeur'*), a wide basin of calm waters. It proved to be a set of three large bays, all with deep water.[4] The disintegrating remnants of *Pallas* were found, together with an abandoned village and two batteries. It was another minor settlement which the Russians had determined not to defend. But it was an important discovery for the Allies. Stirling's Victoria Island may not have been as wonderful as he had made it seem, but Barracouta Harbour, as the Russians had found, was a very useful harbour indeed. It would form a good base from which the British ships could conduct the blockade, which otherwise would have had to be run from Hakodate.

Names were busily awarded: Pique Bay, Tronson Point, Sybille Point, Ice Harbour, Fortescue Island, and so on. In one bay they saw 'a Greek cross planted on a rising ground or hillock', which 'gave evidence of the presence of Russians at not too distant a date'. Next day they landed and discovered the Russian settlement, which consisted of 'two batteries, some log-houses, and a burial place'. Elliot got *Barracouta* to tow *Sybille* into the harbour and began investigations. He deciphered the dates on the graves, and concluded that the Russians had left very recently. And *Pallas* was finally discovered, a burned-out

---

[4] Du Hailly, 'Une Campagne', part 2, 189.

wreck imprisoned in ice in what was now called Pallas Bay. The local natives described how the Russians had left the previous autumn, with some of the men on sledges, going by land. Elliot did not wholly believe that the Russians could have made the entire journey by land, but was finally convinced when the same story was told to Fortescue further north.

Elliot spent five days revelling in his discovery, then sailed on, northwards along the mainland coast as far as De Castries Bay. This completed the exploration of both shores of the Gulf of Tartary, with the sole, and crucial, exception of the strait into the Amur, which they had all been searching for all the time. But Elliot had now located the best harbour, and the Allies were now thus well-prepared if a full campaign of blockade became necessary.

Elliot brought his three ships back to Hakodate, arriving there on 30 May. It must have given him considerable satisfaction to arrive at the same time as Seymour's letter. These orders, he must have been relieved to discover, were to do what he had just been doing, and so, having replenished his ships, he sailed again for the Gulf on 4 June, believing, of course, that Britain and Russia were still at war.[5]

The Allies sent other naval forces into the Gulf of Tartary and used Barracouta Harbour as their base. Two of the French ships, *Virginie* and *La Sybille*, sailed north as far as De Castries Bay, reaching it on 9 June, but made no hostile moves. By now there were strong suspicions on both sides that peace had been made. A flag of truce went ashore, but there was nothing to discuss; the Russians clearly had no definite news yet either.[6] Both sides observed an unofficial truce, except that if any Russian ships had appeared, the truce would clearly have ended at once. The Allied ships were obviously positioned to impose a blockade on the Gulf if necessary, and the French ships will have ascertained whether the ice had yet broken in the passage to the north.

Muravev had mounted a third expedition down the Amur, but this time he was not in personal command. He had instead gone to recover from his exertions at Marienbad. In his winter visit to St Petersburg he had discovered that the peace was

[5] Tronson, *Voyage*; ADM 125/1, 2 June 1856; ADM 53/6011, log of *Sybille*.
[6] Atkinson, *Travels*, 137.

near, and presumably therefore assumed that the pressure on his settlements was reduced. Captain Rimskii-Korsakov was in command this time, and left again in May, passing the Chinese fort at Aigun on the 21st. This time there were 110 boats in the convoy, and they carried over 1600 troops, plus their families. The officials at Aigun made the usual token protest, but they were outnumbered and outgunned, also as usual. Rimskii-Korsakov comfortably exaggerated his numbers, and those who were at the Amur settlements. The Manchu officials seem to have been quite unable to form any clear estimate of the numbers who passed by for themselves; and by accepting the Russian exaggerations they could justify to their superiors their inactivity.

Muravev had as usual given warning of the expedition, pointing out that the Allied ships were wintering at Shanghai and Canton (presumably meaning Hong Kong) and that they would certainly return to the attack in the spring. In addition the Chinese received reports from a Chinese Muslim spy about Russian preparations and intentions. All this information was with the emperor by late February. There was a certain scepticism over Muravev's claims by now, but it all made no difference. The officials at the frontier posts could not stop the expedition, so it was best to let the Russians through.[7] China was still racked by the Taiping rebellion, and relations with Britain were becoming very difficult. The provisions of the treaty of 1842 were unravelling, and later in 1856 another war broke out with Britain. A fight with Russia at the same time as all this was not to be contemplated.

In terms of timing, therefore, it would have been possible to mount an expeditionary force as far as De Castries Bay well before 9 June, when the French ships were there, and into the Amur estuary well before the third Russian expedition down the river arrived. Elliot had reached the bay in mid-May, having sailed without hurry from Hong Kong. The Russians were far fewer in strength than the '10,000' Rimskii-Korsakov claimed to the Chinese, and probably considerably fewer, after a hard winter, than the 5000 Stirling assumed. Their reinforcements from Irkutsk, by the third expedition, did not arrive until mid-June at the earliest. It would have been possible for the Allies to establish control of the river mouth and the area of the

---

[7] Semenov, *Siberia*, 272; Quested, *Expansion of Russia*, 58–59.

Russian settlements with armed steamers – a dozen would not have been needed – and to take over the De Castries Bay base and Mariinsk before Rimskii-Korsakov's people arrived. And by controlling the river, those barges and rafts could have been intercepted well before they reached the settlements.

This, of course, did not happen. The news of the peace reached the squadron in Barracouta Bay on 1 July, and on the 24th HMS *Pique*, captained by Nicholson, sailed into De Castries Bay carrying the last of the Russian prisoners, ninety-six men and two officers, who had been part of the crew of *Diana*. They were landed next day.

Nicholson looked about with a keen eye and an inquisitive tongue, just as he had at Urup Island. Despite the only Russian officer on the spot having only 'a few words of indifferent French', and the fact that other officers were 'peculiarly reserved on all matters concerned with the Russian settlement in the neighbourhood', he came away with a clear and reasonably detailed dossier of information on the Russian position.

The base at De Castries Bay was half a mile inland, as Elliot had found, and was defended by a breastwork of 'sandbags, gabions, and bushes' along what Nicholson called 'low cliffs' and which is no doubt the low ridge Elliot had seen. Two breastworks dominated the landing place. This was all more or less as Elliot had discerned on his October visit the year before, perhaps a little further on in construction, though it was by no means yet complete. Nicholson, however, penetrated further inland than Elliot, confined to his ships, had been able to do. Nicholson found a second clearing with houses capable of holding 1500 men and officers, and a corduroy road which connected De Castries Bay with the base at Mariinsk. That the settlement was permanent was indicated both by the buildings, and by the fact that some ground had been cleared for cultivation, where potatoes and cabbages and oats were growing. This second clearing with the barrack buildings was apparently unoccupied, and the garrison he saw was no more than fifty men. But, again as Elliot had found, reinforcements were available and the whole settlement showed that a much larger force could be housed and sheltered at short notice.[8]

Nevertheless it would not be correct to take the Russian preparations as absolutely forbidding any successful assault. Elliot

---

[8] ADM 1/5672, 1 August 1856.

in the previous year had not made a serious attempt to land, being mainly concerned, as were all the British expeditions in 1854 and 1855, with locating the Russian ships. His threat at that time was less to make an attempted landing and more to conduct a reconnaissance so as to provoke the Russians to reveal their strength. Nicholson's estimate of a garrison of fifty men is probably accurate enough, and such a force would have been swamped easily by a large Allied force armed with the guns in the ships and prepared to accept a few casualties in landing. Once a sufficiently strong Allied force was ashore, De Castries Bay could be maintained against any force the Russians could bring forward along the rough road, where the streams were unbridged, from Mariinsk.

Nicholson also found out about Mariinsk and Nikolaevsk (which he refers to as St Nicholas), their distances, and the times of journeys, but he noted that the journey between the two was only twenty-four hours by steamer. Nikolaevsk held soldiers, infantry, and guns of heavy calibre, up to '120' of them in batteries, though this is certainly an exaggeration; Muravev had brought only forty down the river the year before, and no more seem to have arrived with Rimskii-Korsakov. De Castries Bay, Nicholson found, was going to be further developed as a base, with still more batteries. The width of the entrance to the bay was to be reduced by connecting the islets with the mainland, and building a breakwater. One is reminded of Elliot's conclusions after his first visit, that the bay had not been occupied for very long because the islands in the bay had not been fortified. Elliot's naval eye was closely complemented by the Russian military eye in this case.

The Russian naval squadron was to be increased, so Nicholson was told, by the arrival of 'several vessels, one of which is to be a screw frigate of 300 horse power'. Unkindest cut of all was the news that *Aurora* and *Dvina* were expected soon, and that *Aurora* was to sail to Japan, taking a diplomat to exchange ratifications of Putiatin's treaty. Whether these ships had been 'dismantled' in 1855 or not, as the various reports received by the British had suggested, they were not sufficiently rendered useless as to be unrecoverable, and so the Admiralty's priority in getting Price and Bruce and Stirling to search for them had been quite correct – but the Russians had foiled the search by reacting in a landlubberly fashion, by withdrawing the ships from all possible contact.

As to the difficulty of reaching the Amur, Nicholson was told that an American schooner from Hong Kong, the Ge*neral Pierce*, had reached Nikolaevsk after lightening her load. (And next year, there was sufficient traffic for the United States to appoint a consul at the place.[9]) Nicholson also discovered, apparently by meeting him, that Captain Chichagov, an aide to Muravev, had sailed across to Jonquière Bay in Sakhalin the day he arrived, taking with him a naturalist and another Russian officer. Their purpose was to begin examining the coal supplies available at what had been and became again Alexandrovsk. This would be a supply of fuel for the steamers when they arrived.

So Stirling was being proved wrong in some respects. The Russians had not made their settlements merely on a temporary basis, but with permanent intent. Muravev had now been appointed to a newly constituted province, which included Kamchatka, the coast of the Sea of Okhotsk, and the Amur settlements. This amounted to the annexation of the land as far as the Amur, without any Chinese agreement. And, of course, some of the Russian settlements, including Mariinsk and De Castries Bay, were south of the Amur, while the Russian use of Imperatorskaia Gavan (Barracouta Harbour) could certainly be assumed; it was too good a harbour to be ignored. This all implied a Russian ambition to extend their powers southwards along the coast from the Amur, both along the mainland and in Sakhalin. So here Stirling had been shown to be more or less correct in his interpretation

Along the river itself intermediate posts were developed, with small settlements established at Khabarovsk and Blagoveschensk, so that the Russians in effect controlled the whole of the river, with the single exception of the Chinese fort at Aigun. With the ending of the war against Britain and France, and thus the reopening of the seaways to Russian shipping, commerce was encouraged and the resupply of the Amur estuary became easier and less dependent on the river passage; it could also take place over a longer period, for the post at De Castries Bay was open for a month or more longer than the river mouth, and Imperatorskaia Gavan for even longer.

---

[9] E. Griffith, *Clippers and Consuls: American Consular and Commercial Relations with Eastern Asia, 1845–1860*, Ann Arbor, MI, 1936, 17–18.

A steamer was built in the United States, with a draught of only nine feet, and she was thus able to enter the river without having to be lightened first: she was named *Amerika*. The clipper *Europe* brought out the parts for two more small steamers; *Amerika* towed her up the river, and during the winter of 1856–1857 the two small steamers were constructed. This pattern was repeated next year, 1857, by which time Count Putiatin was in Peking attempting to negotiate a treaty-port agreement similar to that which the Chinese had made with Britain and France several years earlier. Muravev, at Aigun in 1858, concluded a boundary treaty with China at last, and at about the same time Putiatin also got his treaty-port agreement. The northern boundary Muravev demanded was different from that he had asked for at Mariinsk in 1855 – for he now wanted the long stretch of coast south of the Amur which was already partly settled by the Russians, and which included De Castries Bay and Imperatorskaia Gavan. Muravev had eventually to threaten war to get an agreement, though he did so in a vague, if menacing, way. The treaty of Aigun was the result, which appointed the Amur as the boundary between Russia and China, but neither side either honoured or implemented it.

In effect Muravev was again using Britain to further his own designs. Whereas in his first expeditions he had claimed that he was merely defending Russia against attack – an attack which had scarcely taken place – this time he was using British attacks on China to extort his agreements from the Chinese government. In effect, he was threatening to join in the British assault on China. In 1860 the Russian negotiator Ignatev, present at the Peking Court to exchange the ratifications of Putiatin's treaty, acted as an intermediary between the British and French invaders, who had occupied the city, and the Peking Court, which had withdrawn into the interior in Jehol. And Ignatev incidentally got the ratification of the Aigun treaty, but on rewritten, that is, Russian, terms, not the original terms. This new treaty assigned the coast of the Gulf of Tartary as far as Broughton Bay, the future Vladivostok, to Russia.[10]

Nicholson's news of the development of Russian naval power in the Amur and at De Castries Bay was a confirmation of

[10] Semenov, *Siberia*, 273–276; Quested, *Expansion of Russia*; Lin, 'Amur Frontier Question'; Graham, *China Station*, 421.

that generally expected by the British. It had been in part brought about by the activities of the British and French along the northwest Pacific coast of Russia during their war. That is, the British had helped to bring into existence themselves that which they had feared had already existed, and then the Russians had used British attacks on them to confirm and extend their gains.

But what is especially noticeable is that in this war between Russia, on the one hand, and Britain, France, the Ottoman Empire and Sardinia on the other, the principal victims, apart from the soldiers, were China and Japan. The number of Allied casualties in the Eastern war was only a few more than those received at Petropavlovsk in September 1854; the Russians, on the other hand, had suffered considerably more in their dangerous expeditions along the Amur, which must be considered as campaigns of that war. Even so, the total number of dead was probably no more than a hundred or so, minimal compared with the casualties in the Sebastopol siege. It is also an example of a campaign which, despite a few fights, had very large consequences.

It was as a direct result of the war between these European powers that China lost a huge area of territory to its north and northeast (though, to be sure, Chinese 'possession' had been really no more than theoretical); and it was as a direct result of the war that Japan was opened up to Western influence. Of course, it was a United States mission which acquired the first treaty, but it was British, and to a degree also French and Russian, maritime activity in the waters around Japan – off China, in the Gulf of Tartary, in Sakhalin, the Kuriles, Kamchatka, the Sea of Okhotsk – which brought home to the Japanese government the real dangers of their isolation. Stirling's gathering of the eleven Allied warships in Nagasaki harbour was very convincing, as he understood.

If naval powers based in the North Atlantic, as all four of them were, could campaign in the waters around Japan, using Japanese and Chinese ports as their bases, then Japan itself was clearly under threat. And indeed, it was only another eight years before a joint task force made up of ships of three of these powers launched a naval attack on the Japanese port of Shimonoseki. The 'Crimean' war had surely provided Japan with sufficient warning.

Japan's victim status in 1854–1856 was not directly

damaging to the country, except to her pride; but China was cut to the heart. Not only did Russia take advantage in all sorts of open and underhand ways to expand its territories at Chinese expense, but one of the side effects of the European conflict was the diversion of European naval vessels away from pirate suppression. This has to be one of the elements which led to the conflict over the *Arrow* and so to the Second China War, with its appalling humiliation to them of seeing foreign troops in occupation of the imperial city. (Had the 'Crimean' war continued longer, this might also have been the fate of St Petersburg.) The prestige of the Manchu dynasty never recovered, just as, in Japan, the authority of the Shogunate suffered a disabling blow by the Western treaties and the bombardment of Shimonoseki. One result of this war was the early death of the Xianfeng emperor, still in virtual exile in Jehol; he died in 1861; his successor, his six-year-old son Tongzhi, was the son of Cixi, later notorious in the West as the 'Dowager Empress', who thus began her long career of dominating Chinese politics.

Conclusion

The geopolitical results of the campaign in the Pacific were crucial to the future development of the whole region, and their effects are being felt even now in relations between Japan and China, China and Russia, and Russia and Japan, with the United States intervening. It was one of those moments in history when one is very tempted to discuss 'what if' things had happened otherwise – what if, the war continuing, the British had invaded the Amur; what if the Manchu emperor had been more alert, and had responded to the tentative British offers of an alliance; what if the Japanese government had objected loudly and strongly either to the Russian encroachments, or to the British use of its ports for what were in effect warlike purposes, or both? But it is certain that in these three years the history of the region was wrenched out of one set of tracks and put on another route, altogether rougher and more dangerous.

None of those involved, except one, gained anything from the events. The commanders and politicians in all the involved states found no advantage to be gained from their work – excepting, of course, Muravev, soon ennobled as Count Muravev-Amurski, certainly a distinction well earned in terms of contemporary estimates of success, but one which tended to glorify, by recognising his achievement, his rather unpleasant methods. A close examination by the tsarist government would surely have elicited cries of alarm at the way he had made imperial policy on his own, presenting a *fait accompli* to the government in St Petersburg which it could not disavow, and threatening war with China. This was, of course, a danger in every empire, and the British and French had their share of such men – men who acted in what they claimed to be the 'mother-country's' best interests, but without considering consequences beyond their own small area of activity.

Muravev was extremely close to involving Russia, already undergoing an agonising defeat in Europe, in a war with a great empire in Asia. It was to control such men that the Russian government had become a bureaucratic entanglement. Muravev's achievement, in breaking out of such an entanglement and acting essentially alone for a decade, was as impressive as the geopolitical results he achieved. But it was infinitely dangerous. One only has to consider the results of the career of a similar local power-broker in the British Empire – a man such as Cecil Rhodes, for example – to see just how lucky Russia was.

The British commanders faded away into retirement and death. Price was already dead, Stirling died only a few years later, Bruce and Seymour not long after. Elliot floated up the naval ladder of promotion to the top, becoming Admiral of the Fleet for a couple of years before he died late in the century. Sir John Bowring tried too hard to be an independent power, but the Second China War was, quite rightly, his undoing; he was removed from Hong Kong and not employed again.

At home, Palmerston's career survived the war, and he died, still Prime Minister, in 1865, technically a Liberal, but by then a notorious block on any sort of liberal reforms. Sir Charles Wood also survived, as a second-rank politician, and achieved the rank of Earl of Halifax some years later. The emperor of China died in 1861, leaving as his successor his six-year-old son, whose mother's strong will and determination held the empire together for several decades; when she died, the Manchu dynasty and its imperial system lasted only three more years.

Only ten years after the end of this Pacific war the United States purchased Alaska. This was clearly one of the main consequences of the war, for it had been shown to the Russian government that, in any Pacific conflict, Alaska was undefendable. By 1867, the year the transfer was completed, Japan was developing into a regional power of some significance, and the United States, having gone through its civil war, was revealed as a power of global importance, if it chose to exert itself. Unless the tsarist government chose to expend scarce resources on fortifying Alaska, it would be better to be rid of it. The development of the Far Eastern provinces would be more worthwhile.

The Royal Navy maintained a presence in the Pacific for the next century and a half, but the surrender of Hong Kong to China removed its final justification. And the Hawaiian kingdom succumbed to an American filibustering coup in 1893, which led to its annexation to the United States five years later. The scene was set for the confrontation between the United States and the Japanese Empire which became the Second War in the Pacific.

Every now and again, when they wish to be particularly difficult, the Chinese Communist empire's politicians complain that its northeastern provinces have been illicitly removed, and ask for them back. Russia, an anti-imperialist empire as it still is, disdains to answer.

Sources and Bibliography

Sources

British Library

BL Add. Mss 47549, 47555, 49562, 49563, 49564, 49565, 49632: Halifax Papers of Sir Charles Wood.
BL Add. Mss 79612: Papers of Sir James Graham.

National Maritime Museum

94/009 Burridge Journal.
LOG/N/10/1 MS 9297 Maccall Journal.

The National Archives (Public Record Office)

ADM 1/5629, 5630, 5631, 5656, 5657, 5661, 5677, 5692: Admiralty In-letters, China, Pacific.
ADM 2/1611, 1612, 1697, 1698, 1699, 1702, 1704: Admiralty Out-letters, China, Pacific.
ADM 50/260, Journal of David Price.
ADM 50/278, Journal of Sir James Stirling.
ADM 50/280, Journal of Sir Michael Seymour.
ADM 50/308, Journal of William Bruce.
ADM 53/4915, log of *Styx*.
ADM 53/5020, log of *Amphitrite*.
ADM 53/5614, log of *Bittern*.
ADM 53/5634, log of *Winchester*.
ADM 53/5743, log of *President*.
ADM 53/5881, log of *Spartan*.
ADM 53/5961, log of *Encounter*.
ADM 53/6010, 6011, logs of *Sybille*.
ADM 53/6189, 6191 logs of *Pique*.
ADM 53/6292, log of *Hornet*.
ADM 172/2/7, Pacific reports.

Printed Sources

Illustrated London News, 1855.
Nautical Magazine 1854–1856.
The Times, 1854–1855.

T. W. Atkinson, *Travels in the Regions of the Upper and Lower Amoor and the Russian Acquisitions on the Confines of India and China*, London 1860.

B. Dymytryshyn, E. A. P. Crownhart-Vaughan and T. Vaughan, *The Russian American Colonies, 1798–1867*, Oregon Historical Society 1989.

E. Du Hailly, 'Une Campagne dans l'Ocean Pacifique', *Revue de Deux Mondes*, 1858 (in two parts).

S. S. Hill, *Travels in Siberia*, London 1854.

M. Lewis, 'Eye-witness at Petropavlovski, 1854', *Mariner's Mirror* 39, 1963, 265–272.

R. O'Byrne, *O'Byrne's Naval Annual of 1855*, London 1855 (reprinted 1969).

E. G. Ravenstein, *The Russians on the Amur*, London 1861.

H. A. Tilley, *Japan, the Amoor, and the Pacific*, London 1861.

J. M. Tronson, *Personal Narrative of a Voyage to Japan, Kamschatka, Siberia, Tartary ... in HMS Barracouta*, London 1859.

P. B. Whittingham, *Notes on the late Expedition against the Russian Settlements in Eastern Siberia*, London 1856.

Bibliography

Admiralty, Naval Intelligence Division, *A Handbook of Siberia and Arctic Russia*, 3 vols, London 1918.

R. W. van Alstyne, 'British Diplomacy and the Clayton-Bulwer Treaty, 1850–1860', *Journal of Modern History* 11, 1939, 149–183.

M. Bassim, *Imperial Visions: Nationalist Imagination and Geographical Expansion in the Russian Far East*, Cambridge 1995.

W. Baumgart, *The Peace of Paris 1856*, trans. A. P. Saab, Santa Barbara, CA, 1981.

W. G. Beazley, *Great Britain and the Opening of Japan*, London 1951.

K. J. Bertrand, 'Geographical Exploration by the United States', in H. R. Friis (ed.), *The Pacific Basin: A History of its Geographical Exploration*, New York 1967.

W. R. Brock, *Conflict and Transformation, 1844–1871*, Harmondsworth 1973.

W. R. Clowes, *The Royal Navy*, vol. 6, London 1901.

J. S. Curtiss, *Russia's Crimean War*, Ithaca, NY, 1979.

G. G. van Deusen, *The Jacksonian Era, 1828–1848*, New York 1959.

Dictionary of National Biography.

A. Dowty, *The Limits of American Isolation: The United States and the Crimean War*, New York 1971.

P. E. Eckel, 'The Crimean War and Japan', *Far Eastern Quarterly* 3, 1944, 109–118.

J. Forsyth, *A History of the Peoples of Siberia, Russia's North Asian Colony, 1581 – 1990*, Cambridge 1992.

J. R. Gibson, 'Russia on the Pacific: The Role of the Amur', *Canadian Geographer* 12, 1966, 15–27.

J. R. Gibson, *Feeding the Russian Fur Trade: Provisioning of the Okhotsk Seaboard and the Kamchatka Peninsula, 1679–1856*, Madison, WI, 1969.

F. A. Golder, 'Russian-American Relations during the Crimean War', *American Historical Review* 31, 1925, 462–476.

I. Goncharov, *The Voyage of the Frigate Pallada*, trans. N. W. Wilson, London 1965.

B. M. Gough, 'The Crimean War in the Pacific: British Strategy and Naval Operations', *Military Affairs* 37, 193, 130–136.

G. S. Graham, *The China Station*, Oxford 1978.

G. S. Graham and R. A. Humphreys (eds), *The Navy in South America, 1807–1823*, Navy Records Society 1962.

M. Greenberg, *British Trade and the Opening of China*, Cambridge 1951.

B. Greenhill and A. Gilford, *The British Assault on Finland, 1855–56*, London 1988.

E. Griffith, *Clippers and Consuls: American Consular and Commercial Relations with Eastern Asia, 1845–1860*, Ann Arbor, MI, 1936.

J. T. de Kay, *Chronicles of the Frigate Macedonian, 1809–1922*, New York 1995.

H. I. Kushner, *Conflict on the North-West Coast: American-Russian Rivalry in the Pacific Northwest, 1790–1867*, Westport, CT, 1975.

R. S. Kuykendall, *The Hawaiian Kingdom*, vols 1 and 2, Honolulu 1938 and 1953.

A. D. Lambert, *The Crimean War: British Grand Strategy 1853–56*, Manchester 1990.

G. A. Lensen, *Russia's Japan Expedition, 1852–1855*, Gainesville, FL, 1955.

G. A. Lensen, *The Russian Push Towards Japan: Russo-Japanese Relations, 1697–1875*, Princeton, NJ, 1959.

T. C. Lin, 'The Amur Frontier Question between China and Russia, 1850–1860', *Pacific Historical Review* 3, 1935, 1–27.

H. M. MacPherson, 'The Interest of William McKendree Gwin in the Purchase of Alaska, 1854–1861', *Pacific Historical Review* 3, 1934, 28–38.

S. G. Marks, *Road to Power: The Trans-Siberian Railroad and the Colonisation of Asian Russia, 1850–1917*, Ithaca, NY, 1991.

W. A. McDougall, *Let the Sea Make a Noise*, New York 1993.

D. W. Mitchell, 'A Forgotten Naval War in the Pacific 1854–56', *American Neptune* 31, 1971, 268–274.

D. W. Mitchell, *The History of Russia and Soviet Sea Power*, London 1974.

S. R. Okun, *The Russian-America Company*, ed. R. D. Grekov, trans. C. Glasberg, Cambridge, MA, 1951.

V. N. Ponomarev, 'Russian Policy and the United States during the Crimean War', in H. Ragsdale (ed.), *Imperial Russian Foreign Policy*, Cambridge, MA, 1993.

H. M. Potter, *The Impending Crisis, 1848–1861*, New York 1976.

R. K. I. Quested, *The Expansion of Russia in East Asia, 1857–1860*, Kuala Lumpur 1968.

A. Seaton, *The Crimean War, a Russian Chronicle*, London 1977.

Y. Semenov, *Siberia, its Conquest and Development*, trans. J. Foster, London 1965.

J. J. Stephan, 'The Crimean War in the Far East', *Modern Asian Studies* 3, 1969, 257–277.

J. J. Stephan, *The Kuril Islands, Russo-Japanese Encounter in the Pacific*, Oxford 1974.

J. J. Stephan, *The Russian Far East*, Palo Alto, CA, 1994.

P. A. Tikhmenov, *The History of the Russian-America Company*, trans. and ed. R. A. Pierce and A. S. Donnelly, Seattle 1978 (originally published in 1861–1863).

Z. Vladimir (Z. Volpicelli), *Russia on the Pacific*, London 1899.

Index

Ships names are in italics and their nationality is indicated by letters – F: French; R: Russian; RN: British; US: United States.

Aberdeen, Earl of, Prime Minister 71, 170
Admiralty, British 7, 9–11, 29, 33–4, 42, 62–3, 72–4, 148–9, 162–3, 170, 172, 179
Aian, Siberia 17, 18, 20–2, 35, 117–18, 121–2, 125–8, 133, 136, 143, 150, 167, 174
Aian (R) 79
Aigun, Manchuria 22, 25, 54–6, 139, 146, 174, 183, 186, 187
Ainu, inhabitants of Kuriles 89, 133
Akhte, Lieutenant-Colonel 22–3, 25, 139
Alaska (*see also* Russian America) 16–18, 21, 57, 133, 169, 191; neutrality of 31–3, 47, 64–5, 84
Albazin, Siberia 54
Alceste (F) 66, 76–7, 79–80, 82–3
Alcock, Rutherford, British Consul 62
Aleutian Islands 117
Alexander II, Tsar 71, 145
Alexander Liholiho – *see* Kamehameha IV
Alexandrovsk, Sakhalin 96, 186
Alston, Lieutenant 154–5
Amerika (R) 187
Amphitrite (RN) 8, 10–1, 33–4, 76, 81–2, 84, 100, 114, 118, 136

Amur River 19–23, 25, 70, 122–3, 145; British concerns 88, 161, 167; mouth of 21, 23, 53–4, 60, 62, 67, 82, 90, 113, 129, 136, 155, 186; Muravev's expeditions 53–58, 158, 173–4, 186
Amur Strait 96, 107–19, 112–20, 123, 141, 154–6, 159, 168, 180, 186
Anadis (R) 46, 80
Anderson, George, execution victim 80–1
Aniwa, Sakhalin 114, 122, 130
 – *see also* Muravevsk
Aniwa Bay, Sakhalin 25, 95, 99, 105, 119, 143
Anson, Admiral 3–4
Argun (R) 54
Arica, Peru 28
Arrow (RN) 189
Artémise (F) 33–4
artillery, Russian 138
Aurora (R) 29–30, 33–4, 38, 43, 47–8, 57, 70, 78, 80, 83–4, 89, 98–9, 101–2, 104, 110, 115, 118, 130, 147, 161, 180, 185
Austin, Rear-Admiral Charles 12, 14, 50
Australia 1, 14, 72, 148, 163, 175
Austria 168, 170

Index

Avatcha Bay, Kamchatka 36, 37, 42, 46, 77

Baikal (R) 21, 57, 98, 102, 130
Baikal, Lake 20, 25, 53
Baltic Sea 62, 145, 149, 168, 179
Barracouta (RN) 66–7, 74, 76–9, 82, 87, 92, 98, 114–7, 119–20, 124–6, 128, 148, 150–1, 155, 175, 180–1
Barracouta Bay 181, 183 – see also Imperatorskaia Gavan
Batavia, Java 58–9
Behring (US) 83, 151–2, 154, 156–9, 166
Bering, Vitus 20, 37
Bering Strait 9, 11, 17, 28–30, 33
Berkeley, Rear-Admiral Maurice 15–16
Bittern (RN) 90, 92, 94, 96–7, 102, 104–5, 108–9
Black Sea 33, 62, 149, 168
Blagoveschensk, Tartary 186
Bogorodskoi, Tartary 140
Bolsherets, Kamchatka 18
Bomarsund, Finland 168, 170
Bonin Islands 51
Bounty (RN) 34
Bowring, Sir John, Superintendent of Trade at Hong Kong 12, 59, 61–2, 150, 164, 168, 171–5, 177, 191
Brisk (RN) 76, 79, 81–2, 84
British Columbia 5, 10
Broughton, William 89, 135
Bruce, Rear-Admiral Henry William 62, 64–6, 70, 71, 73, 75–6, 178; at Petropavlovsk 76–83, 90, 93, 109; at Sitka 84–5, 118
Buenos Aires 2
Burma 6, 12–13, 24
Burridge, Captain RN 8, 31, 44, 49
Bush, Lieutenant 107, 129

Caldera, Chile 28–9
California 5–6, 9, 11, 28
Callao, Peru 28–30, 33, 53, 65–6, 75–6
Canada 6, 85
Canton, China 1, 11, 13
Cape Horn 1, 3, 5, 51
Cape of Good Hope 51
Cape Town 1
Caribbean Sea 6
Carleton, Captain 110
Caroline E. Foote (US) 109
Ceylon 14, 58
Chekiang, Archbishop of 59
Chichagov, Captain 186
Chile 3, 8, 64
China 1, 3, 6, 11, 12, 14–15, 19–20, 24, 28, 188–9; and Britain 148, 163, 169–72, 183; authority absent in Amur valley 21–3, 25; Muravev and 53–5, 59, 138–9, 145–6, 158–9, 173–4, 183
China Sea 60
Chincha Islands, Peru 64–6
Chingshun, Manchu governor of Kirin 55, 174
Cixi, 'Dowager Empress' 189
Clarendon, Earl of, Foreign Secretary 16, 171
Cockatrice (RN) 8, 28
Colbert (F) 52, 91–2
Collier, Rear-Admiral 12, 50
Collinson, Commander Richard 16
Constantine, Grand Duke 145
Constantine (F) 87, 91–3, 112–13, 118–19, 126, 128–30, 159, 165
Cook, Captain James 4, 37
Coquimbo, Chile 28, 30
Coromandel (RN) 175
Cossacks 138, 143, 153
Crillon, Cape, Sakhalin 93, 105, 108, 110, 112
Crimea 71, 145, 149, 162, 168, 173

Index

Cushing, George, American merchant 78, 83, 151, 157–9, 168

Darien (Panama) 66
De Castries Bay 23, 25, 51, 52–3, 56–7, 61, 96, 97–100, 104–11, 114, 138, 141–3, 145, 151–4, 158, 166–8, 181–4, 186–7
de la Grandière, Captain 45
de Maisonneuve, Captain 131–4
de Montravel, Commandant 92, 105, 112–13, 118, 120, 128–30
Dent, Lieutenant 107, 110, 152–3
Deshima Island, Nagasaki 60
Diamond (RN) 9
Diana (R) 29–30, 33–4, 38, 43–4, 47, 51, 57, 59–61, 70, 147; sailors from 91, 95, 109, 122, 125–7, 135, 150, 157, 159, 164–5, 180, 184; wreck of 67–8, 87–9, 95, 104
Dido (RN) 8, 77, 79–80, 82, 84
Drake, Sir Francis 3
Duchie, Cape 154
du Hailly, Edmond 35, 79, 181
Dutch factory in Japan 50, 59, 60–1
Dvina (R) 38, 43, 57, 78–80, 98–100, 102, 130, 185
Dzhundzhur Mountains, Siberia 18, 122

East India and China Station – see Royal Navy, China Squadron
East India Company 1
Edo, Japan 15, 51–2, 58, 94
Edo Bay, Japan 60
Elizabeth, Cape, Sakhalin 114, 118, 124, 130
Elliot, Commodore the Hon. Charles 67, 90–2, 191; at De Castries Bay 99–113, 145, 168, 184–5; in Sea of Okhotsk 114–30; voyage in Gulf of Tartary 92–8, 149–60, 161–2, 165–6, 170–1, 180–3
Encounter (RN) 14, 66–7, 74, 76–9, 81–2, 87, 92, 98, 110, 130, 148, 150–1, 153–5, 159, 175
Endeavour (US) 129
English Channel 7
Essex (US), 4
Europe (US) 187
Eurydice (F) 33, 81, 84

Farrer, J. W., British consul in Manila 58
Fearless – see *Vostok*
Febvrier-Despointes, Rear-Admiral 30, 33–4, 38–40, 42–5, 47–9, 60–1, 66, 71
Feiyko, Tartar tribe 145
Fellowes, Commander Charles 111–12, 150
Finland 169–70
Formosa 91
Forsyth, Commander 97, 104, 107, 128–9, 154–5, 159, 168
Fortescue, Commander 150–1, 182
Fourichon, Admiral 66, 70, 81–2, 84
France 3, 7, 11, 19, 30–31, 50, 69, 144, 172, 188
Franklin, Sir John 9
Frederick, Captain Charles 81, 114–15, 118, 136
Freiburg, superintendent 127–8
Fuji, Mount 68

Garland, William, released prisoner of war 81
Gavrilov, Ensign Aleksandr Mikhailovich 21–2, 34
General Pierce (US) 186
Gibson, Lieutenant Robert 120, 125–6, 128
Giliaks, Siberians 21
Gleskhavin, Colonel 157
Gorlitza, Siberia 139, 145

Graham, Sir James, First Lord of the Admiralty 74, 117
Grecian (RN) 164–5
Greta (Bremen) 124–6, 128, 130, 150
Guerin, Admiral 91, 130

Hakodate, Japan 15, 52, 61, 68–9, 82, 88, 90–6, 104–5, 109–10, 113–14, 120, 125–6, 130–1, 134, 144, 156, 159, 161, 165, 179–80, 182
Hamburg, consul of, at Shanghai 35–6
Hamilton, Captain William 73
Harris, Townsend 172
Hawaiian Islands 3, 6, 10–11, 15, 28–9, 34, 51, 63, 82, 86, 191–2
Heda, Japan 68
Heda (R) 68
Hill, S. S. 37
Hill, Master of *Sybille* 120
Hokkaido, Japan 52, 61, 89, 93, 95
Holme, Rev. Thomas, chaplain 39–40, 41
Hong Kong 3, 11, 13–16, 51–3, 90, 94, 128, 150, 159, 161–5, 168, 171, 175, 180, 183, 191
Honolulu 11, 28–9, 30, 33–4, 36, 64–6, 75–6, 78, 81, 100, 151, 157–8
Honshu, Japan 95
Hornet (RN) 90, 94, 96, 97–8, 101–2, 105–7, 109, 111–14, 118–19, 126, 128–30, 148, 150–6, 159, 175
Hoste, Captain Sir William, Bt 91–2, 93, 99, 122–4, 131–2
Houstoun, Captain William 30, 78, 82, 151
Hsingan Mountains 145
Hudson's Bay Company 5, 10, 31–2
Husunpu, Deputy Commander at Aigun 55

Iakutsk, Siberia 18
Ignatev, Russian envoy in China 187
Imperatorskaia Gavan, Tartary 25, 56–7, 60, 100, 141, 181–2, 186–7 – *see also* Barracouta Bay
India 1, 12, 149, 162
Indian Ocean 1, 74
Innokenti, Archbishop 127–8
Irkutsk, Siberia 19, 25, 53, 78, 158, 167, 169, 183
Irkustskoi, Tartary 140
Irtysh (R) 25, 57, 98, 100, 102, 130
Iturup, Kurile Islands 89, 91, 93

Jackson, Master's Assistant Benjamin 180
Japan 15, 24, 50, 91, 188–9, 191; and Britain 60–1, 69, 92, 144, 148–9, 163, 169, 172–3, 188; and Russia 51, 60, 68, 87, 89, 131, 144, 170, 172, 185; and US 52, 61, 188; settlers in Sakhalin 25; traders 23
Java 59
Jeanne d'Arc (F) 91
Jonquière Bay, Sakhalin 96, 110–11, 119, 186
Judd, Gerrit, 29

Kamchadell (R – US) 110
Kamchatka 17–18, 21, 35–6, 58, 60, 62, 89, 99, 117, 131, 136–7, 151, 186, 188
Kamchatka (R) 30, 34, 58, 84
Kamehameha III, King of Hawaii 29, 34, 65, 71
Kamehameha IV, King of Hawaii 65, 82
Khabarovsk, Siberia 186
Kiakhta, Siberia 19, 20
Kirin, Manchuria 55, 174
Kizi, Lake, Tartary 56, 138
Kniaz Menshikov (R) 51, 57

Kodiak Island, Alaska 35
Kolosh, Alaskan tribe 85
Konstantin (R) 21
Konstantinovsk 25
Korea 52, 53, 59, 135, 137
Kostromotinov, Russian Consul at San Francisco 31
Kronstadt, Russia 50
Kunashira Island, Kuriles 89
Kurile Islands 88–9, 91, 93, 99, 105, 117, 130, 149, 188
Kyushu, Japan 58

La Forte (F) 30, 33, 35, 40–1, 45, 81–2, 84
Lamanon, Cape, Sakhalin 105–6, 110–11
Langlois, Pierre, released prisoner of war 81
La Pérouse, Captain, French explorer 23, 37, 100, 181
La Pérouse Strait 93, 95, 99, 105, 114, 181
La Sybille (F) 87, 91–3, 105, 112–13, 131–4, 182
Lazarov, Cape, Tartary 93, 108–9, 111, 141, 155
Lena River, Siberia 18
Lima, Peru 28
Line Battalions, Russian, 15th 138; 14th 138
Lobscheid, Rev., interpreter in Japan 87, 89
Lopatha, Cape, Kamchatka 89, 91

Macedonian (US) 4
Maia River, Siberia 18
Maimiya Renzo, Japanese explorer 23
Malaya 1, 12
Manchuria 67, 144, 176–7
Manila, Philippine Islands 52, 58–9, 91
Mansel, Lieutenant 133–4
Mariinsk, Tartary 56–7, 100, 138, 141, 143–6, 153, 157, 167–8, 173–4, 177, 184–5

Marquesas Islands 33
Marshall, Commander Edward 10, 44
Martinov, Captain, aide-de-camp to Muravev 78, 81–3, 98
Matsmai, Hokkaido 94
Mediterranean Sea 7–8, 14
Mexico 5, 8, 10, 20
Mikhailovskoi, Tartary 140
Miller, William, British Consul-General at Honolulu 28–9, 35, 65, 78, 151, 157–9
Monarch (RN) 63–4, 76, 84–6
Moresby, Rear-Admiral Sir Fairfax 7, 8–9, 11, 28, 34
Muravev, Governor-General Nikolai Nikolaievich 19, 28, 186, 190; Amur expeditions 25, 53–9, 70, 72–3, 75, 122–3, 138–47, 157, 167, 176, 182–4; and exploration of Far East 20, 21–3; and Petropavlovsk 37–8, 60, 78–9, 83; and relations with China 22, 53–5, 59, 138–9, 145–6, 158–9, 171, 173–4, 183, 187, 190–1; fear of Britain 19, 24, 26, 53, 73, 144, 159
Muravevsk, Sakhalin 25, 88, 95, 114, 122, 143 – see also Aniwa
Nadezhda (R) 145
Nagasaki, Japan 50–2, 59, 60–1, 68, 71, 91–2, 95, 130, 134, 135, 148, 151, 164, 172, 188
Naiad (RN) 8, 66
Nankin (RN) 13, 67, 131, 134, 148, 150, 163–5, 175, 181
Nanking, China 59
Napoleon III, emperor 52
Napoleon III (F) 68
Nautical Magazine 35
Nelkan, Siberia 122
Nerchinsk, Siberia 20, 54, 138, 141, 176
Nereus (RN) 8, 29, 64

Nevelskoi, Captain-Lieutenant Gennadi Ivanovich 21–3, 56, 100, 140–1
Nevelskoia, Mme 129
New Granada (Colombia) 8
New South Wales 1
New York 31, 64
New York Herald 83
New Zealand 3, 6
Nicaragua 5, 63, 86
Nicholas I, Tsar 71, 145
Nicholson, Captain Sir Frederick, Bt 16, 30–1, 40, 42–5, 48–9, 62, 65, 131–4, 184–6
Nikolaevsk, Tartary 56–7, 100, 121–3, 141, 144, 157, 167–8, 180, 185–6
Nikolai (R) 57
Nikolski Hill, Petropavlovsk 37, 44
Ningpo, China 59
Norfolk Island 34
Nova Archangelsk - *see* Sitka
Novo Mikhailovskoi, Tartary 140
Nuku Hiva, Marquesas Islands 33

Obligado (F) 30, 33, 64, 77, 79–82
Obman Bay, Sakhalin 119, 124
O'Callaghan, Captain George 14, 67, 154–6, 159–60, 166–8
Okhotsk, Siberia 17–8, 21, 35, 57–8, 78, 148, 162, 167–8
Okhotsk (R) 119–24, 129, 133, 147
Okhotsk, Sea of 17–8, 21–2, 24, 53, 57, 62, 75, 81–2, 88–90, 95, 99, 104, 113–31, 133, 136, 143, 148–9, 155, 186, 188
Olivutza (R) 51–2, 98–100, 102, 130, 157
Oregon 5–6, 10, 20, 32, 85
Orlov, Russian trader 22
Ottoman Empire 26, 32–3, 51, 52, 170, 188

Pacific Steam Navigation Company 31
Pallas (R) 50–1, 57, 58–60, 100, 104, 130, 141, 151, 158, 166, 181
Palmerston, Viscount, Prime Minister 71, 169–70, 191
Panama 2, 5–6, 9–11, 28, 30, 63, 64
Paris, peace conference of 169, 177
Paulet, Captain Lord George 11
Peking 54–5, 144, 146, 149
Pellew, Rear-Admiral Sir Fleetwood 12–14, 16, 50, 58, 164
Penacros, Captain Le Guillon 66, 76
Penang, Malaya 1
Perry, Commodore Matthew 15, 24, 28, 50–2, 58–61, 63, 148
Persia 170
Peru 8, 28–9, 64–5
Petropavlovsk 18, 21, 35, 52, 57, 72, 89, 99, 104, 109, 113–14, 118, 136, 143, 151, 167; first Allied assault on 35–46, 60–1, 64–5, 70, 74, 138, 142, 143; second Allied assault on 63, 66, 71, 73, 75–83, 117, 130
Petrovskoi, Tartary 57, 121–2, 129
Philippine Islands 52
Pierce, President Franklin 63–4
Pique (RN) 16, 29–30, 33, 40, 45, 64, 66–7, 74, 80–2, 87, 92, 114, 118, 131–4, 148, 175, 180, 184
pirates, piracy 6, 11–12, 24, 50, 60, 90, 165–6, 175, 179
Pitcairn Island 9, 34, 86
Plate, River 6, 7
Plover (RN) 16, 28, 33
Plymouth (US) 14
Point de Galle, Ceylon 14, 16, 58
Poland 169

Polk, President James K. 20
Popov, Midshipman 41, 45
Port Clarence, Alaska 9
Portland (RN) 8, 11
Portsmouth, Britain 51, 157
Powhatan (US) 68
President (RN) 8, 28, 30–1, 33, 35, 38–41, 44–6, 64, 66, 76–80, 82, 84
Prevost, Commander 10
Price, Rear Admiral David 7–8, 14, 15–16, 53, 191; at Petropavlovsk 36–8, 61; burial of 41, 46; first cruise 28–31, 64; suicide of 38–40, 48, 62, 71; voyage to Petropavlovsk 33–5, 60
privateers 31, 33, 175
Pushkin, Lieutenant 125
Putiatin, Vice-Admiral Efim Vasilievich 50–3, 56–0, 68, 70, 72, 87, 100, 122, 131, 143, 144–5, 187

Raiatea, Society Islans 64
Rangoon, Burma 13
Rattler (RN) 150, 164, 165
Rattlesnake (RN) 9, 28, 33, 64, 66
Revue de Deux Mondes 35
Richard, Master J. 91
Rimskii-Korsakov, Captain 157, 183–4
Rio de Janeiro, Brazil 2, 29–30, 33
Rio Sabana, Panama 9
Rodgers, Commodore 125
Romberg, Cape 129
Rosencourt, Lieutenant 77
Round Fort, Petropavlovsk 45
Royal Navy, China Squadron 3, 6, 11, 13–15, 36, 63, 136; Pacific Squadron 1, 2, 6–7, 15, 64, 73
Russia 15; and Japan 50; China trade 19; Far Eastern territories 16–19 – see also Muravev, Siberia

Russian America 9 (*see also* Alaska)
Russian-American Company 16–17, 21, 24, 31–2, 46, 51, 57, 65, 84, 107, 117, 121–2, 133, 167
Ryukyu Islands 52, 58, 94

St Laurence (US) 29
St Petersburg 168–9
Sakhalin 21–5, 52, 56–7, 71, 88, 90–1, 93, 95–7, 99, 105, 114, 119, 129, 133, 141, 155–6, 159, 167–8, 172, 180, 188
Salmon Cove, Sakhalin 96
Samoa 8–9, 15
San Francisco 8–9, 29, 31, 33–4, 47, 69, 81–2, 84, 100
San Miguel Bay, Panama 9–11
Saracen (RN) 91, 148
Sardinia 172, 188
Sarratt, Second Master of *Spartan* 120–4
Schelling, Lieutenant Baron 125
Sea of Japan 94, 151
Sebastopol, Crimea 168, 170, 188
Sergeievskoi, Tartary 140
Seymour, Rear-Admiral Sir Michael 179–81
Shanghai, China 11, 14, 29, 35–6, 51–2, 62, 75, 90–1, 150–1, 165, 175, 179, 183
Shantar Islands, Sea of Okhotsk 21, 118–19, 121, 129
Sharkoff Point, Petropavlovsk 37, 40–2
Sheerness, Britain 8
Shilka River, Siberia 54, 145
Shimoda, Japan 15, 52, 61, 67–8, 87, 95, 109, 144, 172
Shimonoseki, Japan 188
Siberia 16–19, 138, 167
Sibour, Lieutenant 134
Signal Hill, Petropavlovsk 36, 41
Singapore 1, 51, 166, 179
Sitka, Alaska 21, 32, 34–5, 65, 84–5, 118, 133, 161

Sitka (R) 46, 80
Slaves, slavery 66, 86
South America 1–2, 4, 6, 7, 147
South Atlantic Ocean 1
Spain 1, 3, 52, 170
Spartan (RN) 91, 93, 99, 105, 113, 119–21, 126, 128–31, 148
Stehl, E. H. Russian charge d'affaires in Washington 63–4
Stewart, Captain Hon. Keith 164–5
Stirling, Commander F.H. 67, 114–15, 119–21, 124–7, 150–1, 163–5
Stirling, Rear Admiral Sir James 13–16, 24, 36, 50, 53, 58, 115, 120, 144, 162–6, 168, 186, 191; command in China 59–60, 179–80; command against Russia 62, 63, 66–7, 71–5, 82, 87–93, 126–7, 130, 135–6, 147–8, 160, 171, 175–8; negotiations in Japan 60, 87–8, 92, 188; voyage in Gulf of Tartary 105, 110–13, 131, 134–5, 181
Stokes, Lieutenant 122
Strait of Malacca 72, 175
Strait of Sangar 95, 109
Styx (RN) 110–11, 131, 134–5, 148, 164–5, 179
Suez 66, 166
Suffren Bay, Tartary 181
Sunda Strait 72
Surabaya, Java 59
Sweden 168, 170, 172
Sybille (RN) 67, 90, 96, 97, 102–3, 106–7, 113, 119–20, 124, 126–8, 130, 148, 150–4, 175, 180–1
Syria 6

Tahiti 3, 8
Taiping Rebellion 11, 13–14, 67, 144, 146, 150, 171, 183
Tarenski Bay, Kamchatka 41
Tartar (RN) 92, 110–11, 148, 179

Tartary 89
Tartary, Gulf of 21–2, 25, 51, 53, 88, 90–1, 95, 99, 104–5, 120, 149, 177, 187–8; Elliot's voyage in 92–8, 114, 161, 170–1, 175, 180–2
Tavano, Urup 131–4
telegraph 62–3
The Times 35, 77
Thoulou, Captain 125
Tongzhi emperor 189
Treaties: Nanking 3; Aigun 187; Clayton-Bulwer 6; Nerchinsk 20, 23, 25, 139, 159; Paris 169, 179 – see also Japan
Trincomalee (RN) 8, 10–11, 29–30, 33–4, 78, 82, 84, 151
Tronson, J. M. 82, 115, 117, 128

United States of America 4–6, 10, 29, 63, 158, 186, 187, 192; and Alaska 32, 85, 169, 191; and Russian War 63–4, 85–6; Japan expedition 50, 61, 148; Navy 3, 6; whalers from 18–19, 22, 24, 29, 115, 181
Urup, Kurile Islands 89, 93, 131–4, 172, 184
Ust-Strielka, Siberia 54

Valparaiso, Chile 3–4, 6, 8–9, 11, 28–9, 64–5, 69, 75–6
Vancouver, British Columbia 10, 34, 47, 63, 81, 85–6
Vansittart, Commander 96–7, 104, 109
Varanchikov, Lieutenant 122
Victoria Island, British Columbia 10
Vincennes (US) 94
Virago (RN) 8, 10, 28, 33, 36, 38–9, 40–2, 44–6, 77
Virginie (F) 131, 134, 135, 148, 182
Vladivostok, Tartary 135, 177, 187

Index

Vogarov, Colonel 22–3
Volkonskii, Prince 140–1
Vostok (R) 51–2, 56, 57, 122, 130, 157, 161
Walker, William, American filibuster 63
Wars: Burmese 12, 24, 50; First China 3, 11, 23, 50, 55, 148; of 1812 4, 6, 39; Russian ('Crimean') 15–16, 26, 28, 52, 59, 148, 188; Second China 163, 183, 187, 189; Second Pacific 192
Washington DC 31
Washington (state) 5
West Africa 62
Westergaard, Captain 36, 62
Western Australia 14
Whampoa, China 65
Whittingham, Captain P. B. 103, 123, 126–8
William Penn (US) 109–11

Winchester (RN) 13, 91, 105, 111, 113, 131, 134, 148, 163–6, 175
Wood, Sir Charles, First Lord of the Admiralty 73–4, 148–9, 162–5, 168, 170–1, 177–8, 180, 191
Woosung, China 11

Xianfeng emperor 55, 145–7, 148, 183, 189, 191

Yakoutsk, Siberia 127
Ye Minchen, Commissioner 173–4, 177
Yellow River 146

Zavoika, Mme 82–3, 151, 157
Zavoiko, Rear-Admiral Vasili 37, 57, 60, 83, 98, 100–2, 109–10, 122, 123, 141–3, 155, 157